Acclaim for Louis Nizer's *Catspaw:*

"Louis Nizer has written of a real-life murder case that is so bizarre it sounds like fiction."
—Associated Press

"Gripping and unforgettable . . . a spellbinding and haunting narrative."
—Sherman G. Finesilver, Chief Judge
United States District Court for
the District of Colorado

"Entertains and thoroughly absorbs the reader, offering unique glimpses into trial strategy at its finest and the personal qualities of one of America's greatest trial lawyers of all time . . . Mr. Nizer is as gifted a writer as he is a lawyer."—Ronald F. Phillips, Dean, Pepperdine University, School of Law

"Nizer tells the story of Gold's long tribulation engrossingly . . . and he concludes with a 'Lawyer's Prayer' worthy even of atheist attorneys' subscription."—ALA *Booklist*

"The actual case contains more colorful characters and surprising plot twists than any author of fiction would have dared, yet Louis Nizer carries it off with the skill of the talented storyteller and the expertise of the famed trial lawyer he is. A triumph."
—Henry Denker, author of *Outrage* and
A Case of Libel

CATSPAW

**The Famed Trial Attorney's
Heroic Defense of a
Man Unjustly Accused**

LOUIS NIZER

Carroll & Graf Publishers/Richard Gallen
New York

Published by arrangement with Donald I. Fine, Inc.

First Carroll & Graf/Richard Gallen edition 1993

Carroll & Graf Publishers, Inc.
260 Fifth Avenue
New York, NY 10001

Library of Congress Cataloging-in-Publication Data

Nizer, Louis, 1902–
    Catspaw : the famed trial attorney's heroic defense of a man
unjustly accused / Louis Nizer.—1st Carroll & Graf/Richard Gallen
ed.
        p.   cm.
    Originally published: New York : D.I. Fine, c1992.
    ISBN 0-88184-956-1
    1. Gold, Murray—Trials, litigation, etc.   2. Trials (Murder)—
Connecticut—Waterbury.   3. Nizer, Louis 1902–   . I. Title.
KF224.G65N59   1993
345.746′9′02523—dc20
[347.469052523]   93-7968
                                                                  CIP

Manufactured in the United States of America

To Mildred

ACKNOWLEDGMENTS

WITH MANY THANKS to Don Fine and Sam Vaughan for their editing suggestions. With thanks and appreciation to my secretaries, Tatiana Anderson and Patricia Felmar, for their twinkling fingers and organizational skills.

CONTENTS

CATSPAW

PREFACE

THE INNS OF Court in London are built in such a way that one who enters must bow low. In the United States, that gesture of respect is not compelled by structure but it exists implicitly in the exquisite body of rules designed to protect the accused from the power of the government, and the government from sympathy for the defendant who asserts his innocence.

This case involves two murders, and the search for a solution lasting over ten years.

The reader is about to enter the arena of that struggle between the contending forces tested daily in all the courts, including the Supreme Court of the United States. This melodrama exceeds anything I have previously encountered in more than sixty years of trial representation.

In those years, I have seen a trial judge fall asleep in his warm courtroom, and no one daring to wake him for hours, when he suddenly awoke and yelled, "Overruled!", to hide his embarrassment—although there was no objection before him; I have encountered a witness who threatened me with violence during cross-examination; on another occasion, a witness, proudly wearing the croix de guerre, had revealed the adultery of a friend, who rose stiffly to his feet, clicking his heels in salute, and said: "Well done, croix de guerre," falling in a faint as he did so. Yet all these, and more, are exceeded by the twists and turns of the case you are about to read.

The New York *Times*, in reporting this case, said: "The mystery surrounding the murders reads like an Agatha Christie story—with the last page torn out." Before this book is finished, we shall have restored the last page.

The reason that truth is often stranger than fiction is that truth is not restricted by the rules of probability, or plausibility. Events can be established although they defy ordinary experience. In this case they are demonstrated by sworn testimony, physical exhibits, the confirmation of experts, and admissions dragged out of the mouths of witnesses, even by hypnosis, and by revelations from the grave.

You will now come into the Pasternak home, see the murders, and thereafter be present in the many courtrooms in which guilt or innocence will be determined. You may very well find the book itself to be the final courtroom.

It is nine o'clock in the evening of September 26, 1974, the night of the murders, and the place is the home of Irving and Rhoda Pasternak.

Enter.

BOOK
I

1

THE MURDERS

IRVING PASTERNAK, a seventy-one-year-old lawyer in the town of Waterbury, Connecticut, dressed in his blue robe, was reclining in a comfortable chair, reading a brief under a triple-bulbed lamp, which made his eyes feel younger. He was a man whose craggy face, six-foot gaunt stature and unruly gray hair, which curled with vivacity, gave him an air of distinction.

It was deserved. Pasternak had achieved the highest status of a lawyer, that of a trusted, sound adviser.

His wife Rhoda, sixty-eight years old, looked too young and pretty to be his contemporary. Sometimes a rift in marriage is caused by the difference in intellectual growth, or by the disparity of aging. Not so here; hers was a happy life.

Although she had only left her daughter, Myrna, less than an hour earlier, she was sitting in the bedroom at the telephone, "visiting" with her. Myrna lived several blocks away. Theirs was a ritual of chatting about the day, eventful only to them—which proceeded with chuckles and expressions of surprise as if it were their private soap opera. They were planning the religious coming of age, called the bas mitzvah, of Myrna's thirteen-year-old daughter, which involved not only a religious ritual, but an appropriate party.

This quiet, idyllic setting was shattered by a sharp ring at the door. It was 9:00 in the evening. Pasternak expected no one. It was Yom Kippur night. He and Rhoda had spent the day in the synagogue, cleansing themselves spiritually and also physically by fasting.

They had had dinner with Myrna and her family after the service. Who could be visiting at such an hour and on such a night?

With a sigh of displeasure, Pasternak rose slowly and went to the door. He ignored Rhoda's warning to "See who it is first." He did not know that within two minutes, he would be dead.

As he turned the lock, and opened the door, an ominous silhouetted figure confronted him. The man was holding an object covered with a brown paper bag which hid his face. He quickly pushed the top of the bag down and simultaneously squirted liquid from a fire extinguisher into Pasternak's face. Pasternak uttered a scream and staggered backwards. The intruder followed him into the kitchen, off the vestibule, then plunged a Buck knife deep into Pasternak's back. A spurt of blood gushed out of the wound, right at the intruder. Infuriated, the killer brought down the knife again, again and again—and again. Thirty-five times. Pasternak's upper torso, hands and head were viciously mutilated by the repeated knife thrusts.

He collapsed, his hoarse screams ending in a whimper of death.

The sudden motionlessness of death was contradicted by violent movement, streams of blood pouring from the many wounds, turning the white tile floor into a thick carpet of red. It seemed endless, covering much of the killer from the top of his head to his feet.

Rhoda had heard the scuffle and her husband's earlier screaming, "Get away from me, get out of my house!" The assailant was yelling unintelligibly at her husband. She cut off her amiable telephone discourse with her daughter and shouted to her: "Call the police at once, a crazy man is attacking Father."

Her daughter said: "Do you know who it is?"

She said, "I don't recognize the voice," quickly hung up the telephone, then picked it up again and herself called the police at emergency number 911: "53 Fern Street. Please, there's a crazy man up here."

Before she could utter another word, she dropped the telephone. The assailant had bounded up the stairs and was confronting her. He stretched his arm as high as he could, and then brought the knife in his hand down with all his might into her chest as hard as he could. She was probably dead instantly, but in his frenzy he continued to stab her twenty-four more times, creating a macabre explosion of redness, until she lay crumpled at his feet.

If the killer had stayed there a few more moments he might have been caught in the act. Instead, with the sirens of the police cars ringing in his ears, he moved through the red haze and fled the house, even leaving behind the murder knife, the fire extinguisher and the paper bag in which it had been contained, and ran up Fern Street.

Rhoda's blood flowed down the stairs to join her husband's in death.

Two women, Mrs. Dorothy Crocco and Mrs. Annette Walk, were walking down Fern Street in the opposite direction when the assailant rushed through them, almost bowling them over. They would describe him as "running like the devil and his long hair waving in the wind."

There is one prayer in the Yom Kippur services which is extremely personal. It is the plea to God to inscribe one's name in the Book of Life for the coming year, and not in the Book of Death. When I was a choirboy I could tell by the tears in the cantor's eyes that he had reached this prayer in the service. Similarly, the congregation, knowledgeable of the Hebrew text, begged God to inscribe their names for at least one more year in the Book of Life.

How could the Pasternaks, saying this prayer, possibly imagine that within three hours their names were to be inscribed in the Book of Death? When the police arrived, the desolate silence in the bedroom was broken only by the telephone receiver which Rhoda had dropped when the murderer gained on her, and which was swaying from side to side, buzzing its monotonous dirge.

2

The Pasternaks

Waterbury was inundated with grief and dread. These were no ordinary citizens who had been knifed to death. They were highly regarded longtime residents of Waterbury, particularly esteemed in the Jewish community. Their roots were deep. They had lived in the city for more than half a century.

Indeed, their parents had lived their lives in Waterbury too. Irving's father, Ike Pasternak, had owned a home furnishings shop in Waterbury, which later became a hardware store.

Irving was born in 1906. As a boy, he worked in his father's store. He attended Driggs Grammar School and Crosby High School. He was a good student, and his tall slender frame, combined with agility, made him an excellent athlete. This was a road to popularity with his classmates. More important, as it turned out, it brought the admiration of the girls, particularly Rhoda Nierenberg.

Rhoda, three years younger than Irving, knew of his prowess at Driggs and at Crosby, which she also attended. She was beautiful, and if her figure gave promise of diets in the future years, it was the attractive fullness of a figure which would prosper with time. Her father owned a jewelry store nearby the Pasternaks' hardware store.

The Pasternaks: she looked younger than her years; he was a highly-regarded lawyer—with one demented enemy.

Irving, having graduated from New York University, set up a modest law office in downtown Waterbury. His practice was sporadic and at times nonexistent. He could not even afford a secretary. His brother, Sidney, acted as his clerk, and his sister, Tillie, as receptionist.

When Irving and Rhoda decided to marry, the Nierenbergs insisted on financing an opulent marriage ceremony. Both Irving and the Nierenbergs were devoted and devout members of the B'nai Shalom Temple. The event took place on August 10, 1930, and was conducted in traditional orthodox manner by Rabbi Moses Shimkoff.

The parents of the bride and groom met first to sign a marriage contract, a *ketubah*, in the presence of the groom. The contract evidenced a commitment for life, the instructive base if ever the parties, or one of them, later sought a religious divorce from a rabbi. After signing the contract, Irving and the parents entered the Grand Ballroom of the Waverly Inn.

The marriage ceremony was held under a canopy, a *chuppah*, according to Hebrew tradition. Since the ceremony should have been held under the skies the covering of the *chuppah* had been pierced, to conform with the theory that the marriage vows be given under an open sky: "Thus like the stars shall your children be."

The bride, heavily veiled, accompanied by her mother and the groom's mother, circled the groom seven times—to "draw the mystic circle" in a human ring seven times to protect and frustrate any malicious designs of demons reputedly jealous of the happiness of the bride and groom.

Then, after the rabbi had declared the holiness and permanence of the event, he instructed Pasternak to place the ring on the index finger of the bride's right hand, which he did. By tradition the ring had to be smooth and round, and without decoration, to symbolize a smooth and troublefree marriage.

The groom lifted the bride's veil and offered her a goblet of wine to sip. The rabbi placed a glass under the groom's foot and Irving smashed it with his heel, signifying that even in the most joyous moment, tragedy may occur, such as the destruction of the Tem-

The young attorney Irving
Pasternak.

ple in Jerusalem 2,000 years ago when Jews had reached the peak
of their power.

The Nierenbergs had arranged a dinner and dance at the spec-
tacular Waverly Inn, where they presented Irving with a gold-and-
diamond ring as a wedding gift.

Pasternak's law practice began to grow. He prepared his litigation
facts and read his law devotedly, often working throughout the night
preceding a trial. His voice was clear and authoritative, his bearing
elegant, and the litheness of his body impressive as he moved around
the courtroom. Soon, it came to be said in Waterbury that if you had a
litigation and you wanted to win, you had better get Irving Pasternak.
By 1930 he had become successful enough to hire a secretary at the
then going salary of thirteen dollars a week. Still, at the beginning of
his professional growth, he had to pledge his diamond ring in order to
raise money to pay her salary.

As the success of his law practice lifted them, the Pasternaks spread their wings. One day he bought a beautiful house on Fern Street. In his later years, he also acquired a winter home in Hollandale, Florida.

The Pasternaks took great pride in their home, but even more so in the garden which Irving created around the finely mown lawn. No one could look at that garden without being impressed by its carefully nourished beauty. No artist ever had a palette more diverse than the colors nature created; they exceeded the imagination of chemists who prepare the colored paints and acrylics to stimulate the artist's vision. Pasternak belonged to the Chagall school, whose colors dominate, more than the figures Chagall drew stiffly. Pasternak explored the natural advantages by "painting" his garden with contrasting flowers that startled and pleased the eye simultaneously.

In the spring, the crocuses, tinted with many colors, emerged from the snow to the splendid receptivity of the sun.

In the summer, the scene changed to multicolored tulips and contrasting pansies and roses.

53 Fern Street: the scene of the crime—previously known for the beauty of its gardens.

In the fall, the curtain opened on bushy peonies and variegated carnations.

In the winter, white Michaelmas daisies took front stage, with a chorus of chrysanthemums.

The frame, for all seasons, was sweet-smelling lavender and the stately sunflowers.

When the breezes flowed through the garden, it seemed as if the flowers were winking, waving and speaking to each other, all scented by nature's perfume.

The effect was so startlingly beautiful at times that neighbors came from all over town to gaze at the wonders, dazzled as if confronted by breathtaking paintings in a museum. Only this time, the "curator" and "artist" was present and offered to assist visitors to grow similar gardens on their properties. Irving enjoyed spreading his talents, and ultimately Waterbury was grateful to him for beautifying their community.

The Pasternak family grew beautifully too. Three daughters were born to them, Myrna, Ricky Ruth, and Barbara.

In time Myrna married a podiatrist who practiced in Waterbury. They had three children. The Pasternaks were captivated by their grandchildren. Their lives were enriched by a new love, more intense and pure than they had ever experienced before.

Ricky Ruth married and moved to California.

The third daughter, Barbara, was spirited and independent— her nickname "Bubbles" suited her. Irving and Rhoda worried about her, and when she married a young stockbroker named Murray Gold they were delighted. It was good for her to "settle down." Barbara needed a married life.

Pasternak, meanwhile, was an even more impressive presence than when he was young. He retained his athletic physique. Rhoda too had preserved her beauty, but not without dyeing her hair blonde and struggling with a diet to keep her hips from obliterating her waistline. She had even learned the art of adding eye shadow, so faintly that the eyes looked more lovely while the reason was not discernible. "A wonderful couple," everyone agreed.

When Rhoda and Irving Pasternak had reached a joyous climax of their lives, tragedy struck them down. The murderous deed could not be undone. But there was something like a collective sobbing; many felt a personal loss, remembering how good a man was Irving, who had brought such beauty to their homes. Beyond that was a desperate cry for the capture of the culprit and the restoration of peace and safety to the town of Waterbury.

3

THE PROSECUTOR'S TASK

THE DOUBLE PASTERNAK murder was the most shocking of its sort in the history of Connecticut. The shock cut deeper because of the brutality of the crime. A murder by bullet is quick and can be thought of as almost painless. But murder by repeated knife strokes leaves the impression of prolonged agony and torture. I recall the horror of the execution in the early 1950s of Ethel Rosenberg in the electric chair after the espionage trial that found her guilty of releasing secrets of the atom bomb. After three electrical shocks, the physician who must formally announce death staggered back and said: "Her heart is still beating!" Two more shocks had to be administered to fulfill the law's edict.

That is why, in many jurisdictions, a chemical is injected to cause death. The result is swifter and less painful. So, the murder of the Pasternaks was particularly abhorrent because of the sustained stabbings.

The public reaction included a mixture of sadness, intense disgust and, of course, fear. Crimes, particularly when they are violently cruel, evoke such public demands for the apprehension and punishment of the perpetrators that they go beyond a mere search for justice. There is a deep concern that other citizens, perhaps themselves, will become victims if the marauder is on the loose. This fear was heightened by the fact that there had been two other outrageous murders in the Waterbury region in the preceding months. Crimes always have reverberating effects. We are taken out of the torpor of boredom by a horror story. Radio and television multiply and intensify the process. In almost every home in Connecticut the gruesome depiction of the sixty knife thrusts that cut the Pasternaks to pieces was vividly reported. Pictures of the room in which they were found transported the viewer to the scene almost as if he or she were there to witness the event. The images went out not only in Connecticut but across the nation. The murders monopolized concentration. They screamed from nearly every newspaper headline. Soon they were used to emphasize the need for protective police measures. They created a crisis in law-enforcement departments. This crime *had* to be solved and promptly.

The Waterbury Bar Association offered a reward of $3,000 for information leading to the arrest of the murderer. The governor of the state also announced a $3,000 reward. The lurid nature of the crime achieved the distinction of a familiar headline title—the "Yom Kippur Murders." So it joined the St. Valentine's Day Massacre, The Manson Murders, etc., in the pantheon of criminal history.

The state's enforcement authorities responded with intense activity. The public's outcry sounded most loudly in the prosecutor's office. The state prosecutor, Francis McDonald, was vested with the responsibility not only to catch the criminal but to remove the fear that hung like an enormous gray blanket over the city of Waterbury. The whole police apparatus switched into high gear. The F.B.I. joined the police of Connecticut and adjoining states to aid in the identification and apprehension of the killer.

The first task was to make a list of possible suspects. As it turned out, in spite of the Pasternaks' popularity, there were many. Meanwhile, all the forces which could be summoned swooped down on the Pasternak house in a search for clues. Photographs were taken of every inch of the premises. The first major clues, potentially, emerged. The thickened blood that bathed the premises provided impressions of rubber heel prints bearing the trademark "Cat's Paw." A Buck Pathfinder #105 knife, stained with blood, was found at the murder scene.

The fire extinguisher and the paper bag that held it were eagerly taken by the police. On the second day of dedicated search and photography a brown button was found in the master bedroom near the chair Rhoda had been in at the time she was struck.

The prosecutor understood his responsibility for capture and punishment of the Pasternaks' murderer to be the most pressing matter of his career. But the major questions for him were classic: who and why?

4

SUSPECTS

THE WRITERS OF classic murder mysteries contrive to create many suspects, each of whom has a motive to commit the crime. As the spotlight of the novel shifts from one suspect to another, the suspense is, the author hopes, heightened.

Reality often follows the fictional device, and can go it one better. In the Pasternak case the prosecutor's problem was not to find a viable suspect. His difficulty was to select one of them. This required him not just to choose but to eliminate the others. Our criminal trial system does not permit the prosecutor to submit to the jury evidence involving several suspects, if not in league with each other.

So Prosecutor McDonald and his staff eventually had to decide whom to indict. The prosecutor would find it disadvantageous as well as inadmissible to suggest evidence against additional suspects unless there was evidence of a conspiracy among several to commit the crime, and there was none. The police folder entitled "OTHER SUSPECTS" contained reports on some twenty or thirty individuals, of which the following were under special suspicion:

1. James Calca and John Vitale, who were later found guilty of a double murder by stabbing and bludgeoning of two men in Woodbury, Connecticut. Calca was known to carry hunting knives on his person and he had threatened to kill several people.

2. Joseph LeBlanc and Stanley Chenkus, who were at the Woodbury murder scene but plea-bargained, turning state's evidence against Calca and Vitale, and obtained a lesser sentence for robbery.

3. Mark Kahan, the grandson of the Pasternaks, and son of Myrna Kahan, who one week after the slayings was committed to Connecticut Valley Hospital after attacking his uncle with a knife. (Ten years later *he* would commit suicide.)

4. Several ex-spouses of Pasternak's clients, who were disgruntled over their divorce settlements, including one who was a police officer and another who told the police that "Pasternak has ruined my life by giving my wife all my property, money and children."

5. A local eccentric who had a passion for guns; was known to make obscene telephone calls; and had made racial slurs against Jews.

6. The brother of a policeman who was reported as "acting funny" and found to be carrying a Buck sheath knife on his belt.

7. A friend of Pasternak's daughter, Barbara, who was considered dangerous and was wanted by the F.B.I.

8. An unknown man who had attempted to sell a fire extinguisher and a knife to a local storekeeper.

Although the official police folder listed these and other suspects, some received no in-depth investigation.

Instead, they would concentrate on one.

5

A MAN NAMED GOLD

MURRAY GOLD, STOCKBROKER, was the former son-in-law of the Pasternaks. He had been divorced from their daughter Barbara for ten years before the killings. Was it possible that due to his relationship and divorce he might be a suspect? The prosecutor decided to probe his suspicion. He learned more than he had suspected.

Murray Gold had emigrated to the United States with his parents, Meyer and Dina Gold, in 1948. He attended grammar and high schools in New York and graduated from New York University as an engineer. He obtained a position with Grumman Aircraft Corporation, later was employed as a customer's representative at the stockbrokerage house of Bruns Nordeman & Rhea in Cedarhurst, Long Island. He lived in a modest apartment in Forest Hills, Queens. He had dark eyes, which complemented his black hair and dark complexion. His figure was stocky and tended toward overweight. His voice was mellow and low-toned.

In 1962 he met and married Barbara Pasternak, the youngest of the Pasternaks' daughters. The parents, as mentioned, were delighted with the marriage, but almost on the eve of their wedding Barbara announced that she was not going ahead with the marriage. She only gave in because of her parents' earnest entreaties and urgings during a family council. However, before a year of marriage had expired, even Irving and Rhoda agreed that the marriage was a failure. There was no blame involved. It was simply the case of a clash between an extrovert and an introvert. Pasternak, putting on the cloak of wisdom that had made him an excellent adviser in matrimonial disputes, offered generous terms to Murray Gold to arrange a divorce without court conflict. He also arranged to sell their house and gave Gold half of the proceeds. So there seemed no bitterness such as often goes with the dissolution of a marriage.

What nonetheless gave sudden impetus to the police investigation of Gold was the revelation that only seven months before the murders Gold had submitted himself for psychiatric treatments in hospitals in New York and Canada, where he received shock treatments. The shock of this revelation to the police seemed greater than the shock treatments Gold had received.

From that moment on the state's resources were expended almost without limit to trace every step of Gold's movements. Every word he uttered was translated into intention, and soon the police expended their energies in an exhaustive investigation of Gold's past and current activities.

The prosecutor was also spurred on by another revelation. A teenager, Kim Perugini, advised the police that she had seen a "big blue" car bearing license number New York 833-QED parked near the Pasternak home as early as 7:20 A.M.—three days before the murders. A second witness, her brother who claimed a reward later for his revelation, was surprised to see a man sitting in a parked car that early in the morning, and also reported the incident to the police. The license number he had taken note of turned out to be "wrong" by one digit. It was the number of Gold's car, with one numeral presumably taken down incorrectly.

Soon after, the police subjected Gold to intensive interviews. At the first interview a policeman noticed that two fingers of his left hand had cuts on them. Gold explained that he had injured himself scraping carrots. During the interview Gold also

Murray Gold: suspected, convicted, freed, accused, medicated, sentenced . . . more than ten years, four trials . . . (*AP/Wide World Photos*)

volunteered that they might find blood in his car. It had come from his cut finger, he said, but he had scrubbed it away with a tooth brush. Why had he raised the subject of blood in his car? his interrogators asked themselves. Was his explanation a concoction to cover himself and explain the blood?

In a subsequent interrogation Gold told a detective from the New York Police Department that he "remained with his parents having a Yom Kippur meal until 10:30 P.M. on September 26th," the night of the murders. He then went to his own home, where he remained until 11:30 P.M.

The police sniffing increased. They believed they were closing in on the killer.

The Connecticut police requested the authorities in New York City to obtain a warrant for a search of Gold's New York apartment, where they picked up four pairs of his shoes. All of them had "Cat's Paw" heels. They also took a sewing kit from the apartment. They were to look for any jacket which might have a missing brown button. When Gold was confronted with the warrant, he readily gave written consent, which broadened the police's authority.

Gold had twenty-four suits. None had a missing button.

It was learned that Gold had shaved off his moustache the day after the murders. He said he did it because he was going to the Concord, a singles resort, for the weekend. Shaving off his moustache, he said, was not to defeat identification but because he hoped it would make him more attractive for a "perpetual emotion" weekend. The records of the Concord Hotel were produced, including a paid bill and a registration slip proving that Murray Gold had arrived there the weekend of September 27, 1974, and departed on September 29.

The prosecutor's thirst for a solution moved him more and more zealously towards Gold. Having made his choice, the tenacity with which he pursued Gold's movements during the fateful hours, and his prior life, was remarkable. Not only did his investigations leave no stone unturned, they would eventually leave no earth beneath the stone unturned.

True, Gold had no criminal record, no arrests. But the fact that lit the fuse in the police authorities' minds, exploding suspicions into certainties, was Gold's history in psychiatric institutions in Canada and in New York. Such a background, they felt, was provocative enough to pursue him.

Murray Gold had given a voluntary account to the New York police of his movements during the entire day of September 26, 1974. The police report recorded his statements:

8:00 A.M.	Awoke, showered and shaved.
11:00 A.M.	Went to Hess Gas Station on Queens Boulevard to fill his car.
11:30 A.M.	Returned to his apartment.
3:00 P.M.	Walked to his parents' apartment.
4:30 P.M.	Returned to his own apartment.
7:00 P.M.	Returned to his parents' apartment to await their return from Yom Kippur services (he had a key).
7:15 P.M.	Greeted his parents on their return from services (and had a Yom Kippur meal with them).
10:30 P.M.	Arrived back at his apartment.
11:30 P.M.	Went for a drive to Great Neck.
12:30 A.M.	Returned to his apartment.

The murders were committed between 9:30 and 10:00 P.M. at the time when Gold said he was having dinner with his parents.

The police search included a visit to Cantor Earl Rackoff of the Forest Hills Jewish Center to check when the *shofar* (ram's horn) was blown to signify that the religious services had ended. He told them at about 7:30 P.M., which was when Gold said he was at his parents' home to break the fast.

The police then visited the Hess Gas Station in Queens and spoke to the manager, Mr. Swann, to inquire whether he recognized a photograph of Gold and whether he remembered if Gold had a credit card. No, said Mr. Swann.

The New York police joined with the Connecticut police in visiting sporting-goods stores to inquire whether the personnel recognized Gold's photograph and whether he had purchased a Buck Pathfinder #105 hunting knife. The police called on the manager of a Herman's sporting-goods store, Mark Goldberg, at his home. He had no recollection of selling such a knife to Gold, or to anyone else. They also questioned another manager of another branch of Herman's, Pat Garrolin, and he could not help them either.

The police conducted interviews in at least seven other sporting-goods stores in the area. No one could identify Gold via

Sketch of Murray Gold as the author saw him. He fled the Holocaust—but it never left him.

the photograph. They rechecked the same sources to inquire what kind of paper bags were used (in an attempt to find the kind of bag in which the fire extinguisher was hidden). Herman's bags were yellow and had HERMAN'S WORLD OF SPORTING GOODS printed on them. The bag at the murder scene had no logo.

The New York police moved to find out whether Gold had any credit cards. He had none.

The team of four detectives also visited Gold's employer, the stockbrokerage of Bruns Nordeman & Rhea, where they spoke with Mr. Kabat, the manager. In their report they wrote that Mr.

Kabat told them he could not "let us get into Murray Gold's desk, as this was private property . . . and they wanted us to get a court order or a search warrant to get into the desk." Their purpose was "to find a sales slip, a black leather buck-knife sheath, telephone numbers of Irving Pasternak or some other evidence that would tie Murray Gold in with purchasing the buck knife."

They also interviewed George Rodriguez, doorman of Gold's apartment house, who said he had seen Gold with a moustache, and had noticed in early October, 1974, that he had shaved it off. He had remarked that it made Gold look younger.

The detectives then approached Mr. and Mrs. Meyer Gold at their fur piece business on West 29th Street in New York City. The police report of their interview reads, in part, as follows:

> Their attorney told them not to speak to the police about their son, Murray, but in the course of our conversation . . . they [confirmed] that their son had been in Mount Sinai Hospital, New York, and that while there he received treatment for psychiatric disorder, and they also stated he received shock treatment. Meyer Gold also said that Murray had been very withdrawn the last few months, and that even at his apartment he had put double curtains up because he is afraid of people watching him.

Meyer Gold informed the police, their report said, "that he knows that if his son Murray goes to trial the above information would come out and he would not discuss any more about his son because his attorney told him not to speak to the police about Murray."

The detective team visited Murray's one-time employer, checking with the personnel office at Grumman Aircraft about Gold's history with the company. They also went to the security division of the plant and spoke to Harry Voez, who was in charge. They asked for Gold's fingerprints. Voez said that Gold had been fingerprinted to allow him access to "secret records" in the plant. Voez felt the F.B.I., too, might have taken prints for a security clearance.

Gold's statement that he had gone to a singles weekend at the

Concord Hotel in upstate New York the morning after the murders moved the police to go to the Concord Hotel and speak to the manager, Gerald Briggs. They also interviewed the hotel nurse, Beatrice Kolodny, showed her a photograph of Murray, and asked if she had treated him during the time he was at the hotel. She checked her records. She had not treated anyone for a cut finger. They subpoenaed the registration and paid-bill of Murray Gold. The records confirmed that a Scott Brodie had accompanied him to the Concord. Their next step was to contact Brodie.

In tracing Scott Brodie, the Connecticut police needed the help of the Florida police. They went to Fort Lauderdale to interview him and made a detailed background check of Brodie's work history. What they learned was merely that Brodie had been an old friend of Gold and responsible for giving him a large customer account when he was with the brokerage house. He also had accompanied Gold on other occasions to singles resorts.

To build their case, the police turned to another, usually reliable axiom—*cherchez la femme.*

They had information leading them to believe Murray had been seeing a girl named Eileen. Four detectives were assigned to find her. A door-to-door canvass was made. Finally they learned the location of a girl with the rather improbable name of Eileen Kaminski. But they could not find her at home in her apartment near Queens Boulevard. The superintendent of the building said that she was about thirty years old, lived alone, and that the building had been recently sold to one Samuel Wineberg. The police visited Wineberg's office on Queens Boulevard but he was on vacation. Again, exceedingly thorough, the police interviewed the neighbors of "Eileen" and showed them Gold's photograph. No one recognized him. No car was registered in Eileen Kaminski's name.

The police checked with the New York Telephone Company and searched through all the Kaminskis on their records but could not tie anything relevant to "Eileen."

Eventually, though, the police discovered that "Eileen" worked for J.C. Penney. At last they had found her. They showed her Murray Gold's photograph.

She had never seen the man.

The police report ended with an irrefutable statement: "This was not the lady we are looking for."

Scouring Gold's neighborhood, the police interviewed a multitude of shoe-repairmen, showing them Gold's "Catspaw" shoes, and his photograph. Eventually they found the repairman, who confirmed he had put heels on Gold's shoes, and particularly remembered him because he had tipped the shoeshine boy only ten cents.

While it was no doubt admirable of the police to be as thorough as they were, their thoroughness turned out to be tangential—indeed, misleading. It was as if they had blinders on their eyes which prevented lateral views and eliminated serious consideration of other suspects—or at least of adding to that list.

So focused, the prosecutor concluded that the summary of suspicions, from Gold's psychiatric history to his shoes, to his presumed presence in front of the Pasternak house a few days before the murders, through the shaving off of his moustache, and his acknowledgment of blood in his car, were enough to act on.

BOOK
II

6

GRAND JURY

In our judicial system no one may be subjected to even a trial for a felony unless a preliminary jury chosen at random by the prosecutor finds the evidence submitted by the prosecutor alone sufficient not to find innocence or guilt but to subject one to a trial. Unlike a trial, the defendant and his counsel are not permitted into the grand-jury room. Nor is the press. It is a unilateral proceeding.

In effect this procedure is a limitation on a district attorney's power. If he could indict any citizen, exercising only his own judgment, people might be destroyed by the mere announcement that they had been indicted for crimes.

Still, it is so rare for a grand jury to reject the prosecutor's request for an indictment based on the evidence he has offered that when it occurs it is called "a runaway grand jury." This has given rise to the suggestion that grand juries be eliminated, thereby saving much time and expense. Indeed, in England the grand jury is no longer considered "grand" and has disappeared. There, the prosecutor has the sole discretion to decide whether there is enough evidence to require the accused to stand trial.

On October 15, 1974 the grand jury of the State of Connecticut indicted Murray Gold for murder in the first degree for killing the Pasternaks.

After Gold was indicted word went out to the press, television and radio that a suspect in the terrible crime would stand trial. The very title of the indictment was awesome: *The State of Connecticut* v. *Murray Gold.* (If the crime is federal, the title of the proceeding is even more breathtaking: *The United States of America* v. [the defendant].)

Gold's parents seemed more shocked than their son. Meyer and Dina Gold had made many friends. They were respected in their Forest Hills, Queens, community. Now, suddenly, they were disgraced. The most innocent glance became an accusation, as if they had given birth to a monster. Eating became a chore. Tears flowed in unexpected moments, even when they were asleep. Having lost their younger child, Murray's sister, to a Nazi gas chamber, they knew the meaning of a heavy heart, but now this shame was almost more agonizing.

Meyer and Dina Gold, as well as Murray, had been rescued by the European underground from Auschwitz and were taken to England, from where they eventually emigrated to the United States. Here the father built on his experience in a trade, his knowledge of furs. He combined this experience with sewing and decoration skills and eventually joined the ranks of immigrants who had prospered in the new land of opportunity.

Murray Gold, no doubt disturbed by his experiences as a ten year old at the time of his escape, especially his sister's horrific death at the hands of the Nazis, struggled in his young adult life to handle the past and establish himself in a new environment, and was able to achieve a professional status first as an engineer and later as a stockbroker. Then he married into a distinguished family, the Pasternaks. All this presumably added lustre to the immigrant family. Murray's psychological difficulties could not dim his parents' admiration for their only remaining child. Now, the heart-stopping blow of a murder indictment turned their pride into continuous anguish. Their shame was deepened by the disgrace this seemed to bring on them. Their humiliation ran deep, they imagined tongues were wagging and fingers pointing wherever they went.

They had to retain a criminal lawyer to vindicate Murray, prove him innocent, and in the process wipe away the blot on their name. They had heard and read about the well-known lawyer, William Kunstler. When they sought him out he readily agreed to defend Murray.

Apart from reputation, Kunstler's name attracted them psychologically. *Kunstler*, in Yiddish, means a magician or artist, a man of wonderful tricks and abilities. This William Kunstler had long bushy sideburns, and shoulder-length hair, and an authoritative bass voice. He wore his eyeglasses on top of his head, as if to peer above the bustling activities below. He had become known as the defender of unpopular causes. The underprivileged, often blacks, found a ready champion in him. His courage, at times bordering on audacity, depending on one's view, never seemed to fail him. He could be defiant of judicial authority, but some judges admired his dedication to his clients and were tolerant of his unorthodoxy. "I don't know why," Kunstler would say to Judge Robert Wall in Gold's trial, "that you are hostile to me," thereby bringing about an assurance by the judge that he wasn't.

Kunstler and his cocounsel, Victor Ferrante and Timothy Moynahan, both able Connecticut lawyers, prepared themselves tirelessly. They well understood that thorough preparation is, indeed, the be-all and end-all of successful trial representation.

7

THE TRIAL

THE BEGINNING OF a trial, particularly a murder case, is awesome. So it was with the trial of Murray Gold, which began on February 17, 1976.

A court officer dressed in a blue uniform enters the courtroom and raises the venetian blinds of the huge windows, as if eyelids are opening after a sleepy night. The electric lights, switched on almost simultaneously, give the impression of sunlight flooding the room.

The doors are opened and a waiting crowd pours into the empty benches, making scraping noises, waiting for the drama to start. The prosecutor and defense counsel arrive with their staffs. The prosecutor and his assistants take their seats at an oblong table on the left. Defense counsel place their briefcases on the other table. The lawyers empty their folders, putting their notes in order. Counsel greet each other politely with "Good mornings" and even shake hands, but with the formal reserve befitting combatants. There is no sincerity in the gesture. They are duelists who bow before turning, pacing, aiming and firing their pistols.

The court stenographer arrives. He carries the small stenographic machine on the keys of which his fingers will shortly tap dance as he watches the lawyers posing questions to the witness. In some courts there are even more advanced methods of "taking notes." The testimony is recorded on tape and can be played back like a record. The older technique was to have stenographers' notes printed. Under the more modern recording system the appellate court can actually hear the recorded voices of the participants, and not have to read the stenographic record. Trial counsel must adjust himself to the recording technique. At unexpected moments the stenographer, really now a recording technician, signals the judge to halt the proceedings so that he can put a new tape into the machine.

A uniformed bailiff arrives, raps his gavel three times and in sepulchral tones announces the entrance of the judge and asks God to bless the United States of America. From a door alongside the podium the judge enters, gowned in an austere black robe. All in the courtroom rise in respect. It is psychologically necessary to cloak the judge in such a way that he represents the wisdom, if not infallibility, of the judicial process. This motif also accounts for the white wig worn in the English courts—as if massive, flowing gray hair somehow epitomizes wisdom. In the United States the democratic process has whittled down this tradition to merely wearing a black robe. Even so, many judges, desiring to eschew "artificial" devices, appear in a business suit.

The clerk announces in a preacher's voice: "The Honorable Judge Robert A. Wall presiding." The judge mounts the steps to the central podium overlooking the entire courtroom. He bears himself with dignity; no one can doubt that he is extremely powerful and they can only hope that they will not be the subject of his displeasure.

Judge Wall, whose kindly face contrasts with his football player's physique, wears the robe well, which, in addition to his own authority, tends to reflect the majesty of the court.

The first witnesses for the prosecution take their seats behind the prosecutor's table but in front of the rail that separates them from the audience.

The bailiff raps the gavel again while the judge nods to the

Judge Robert A. Wall "wears the robe well," but could not prevent an indecisive jury.

audience and says "Be seated, please." There is a rustle of the spectators sitting down.

The authoritative voice of a judge helps to give him full control of the courtroom. A timid, thin voice is not likely to give the effect of judicial thunder. In the last analysis, however, it is the reputation of the judge that gives him true stature. And that reputation is based not only on his demonstrated knowledge of legal principles but his application of them to a variety of problems so as to maintain a balance of justice even in stormy or novel situations. It is that demonstrated record that earns him stature and admiration, not his gavel.

The judge directs that the defendant be brought in from the lower prison cell. Murray Gold is escorted by two uniformed court officers. He takes his seat next to Kunstler and his co-counsel, Victor Ferrante. Murray Gold is pale and tries to hide his panic. He blinks as the lights of the courtroom hit his eyes, accustomed as he has become to the semidarkness of his cell.

The judge then directs that the jurors from whom a jury is to be selected be ushered in to the jury box, which has fourteen seats (two for alternates). They look uneasy as they are suddenly projected into the limelight.

Filing into their seats, conscious of all eyes on them, they adapt an attitude of exaggerated nonchalance.

The combat begins. One can almost hear the quickening pulses of all who join in the contest for life and death.

The prosecutor seeks to select jurors who appear severe enough to send a man to jail for life without flinching; who will not let sympathy interfere with their critical judgment; and who will not consider the standard of guilt "beyond a reasonable doubt" an insurmountable barrier. Pity is not a desirable ingredient from a prosecutor's viewpoint since it often seems to mitigate the defendant's plight rather than highlight the victim's.

On the other hand the defendant's lawyer seeks jurors who are warmhearted and will be impressed with the defendant's desperate position; who will be horrified by a mistake that can destroy an innocent man; who therefore take the words guilty "beyond a reasonable doubt" very very seriously.

The wild-card factor is the personality of the attorney on each side. Entirely apart from the advantage of skillful cross-examination and the windfall that often accompanies thorough preparation, there is the impact of sincerity. If the jury trusts and likes him or her, the attorney's words reach the inner core of the jurors, which is the ultimate deciding factor.

The selection of the jury is a critical task. In the Gold case it took six weeks to make a choice satisfactory to both lawyers, while the trial itself lasted five weeks.

Once selection is complete, the solemnity of the occasion is heightened by a formal swearing-in of the jury. With hands raised they take their oaths. They sit down. Now they are no longer simply civilians; they are the judges of the facts. The judge is the sole authority on questions of law, but it is the jury, pursuant to guidelines of law as explained by the judge, which will decide the ultimate question of guilt or innocence.

Imponderables such as counsel's sincerity, trustworthiness, emotion and articulation will soon sweep over the jury box. The reaction of a witness to a posed question, his candor in replying or his or her hypocritical gesture are all weighted on the jurors' scales of evaluation about the veracity of the witness.

The judge invites the lawyers on each side to make an opening statement. The purpose is to outline to the jury the substance of what each intends to prove. It is the overture that precedes an opera. It prepares the listener for the journey he is about to take— at times lyrical, at times stormy and dissonant—through the littered paths of evidence.

Such opening statements need to be carefully prepared by counsel. Too much should not be promised. Yet a leaping start to the reasonableness of the advocate's case can be achieved by a persuasive promise of what will be adduced. In addition, there is the strategy of not revealing too much. Indeed, leaves may be placed over the pitfalls in the opponent's case so that he will not be forewarned and can step nicely into the trap.

There is an anecdote about a senior lawyer who entrusts the opening statement to his young, enthusiastic colleague. Suddenly in the limelight, the junior lawyer delivers an emotional tirade. When he has sweatingly concluded, and comes back to his seat, the client leans over and says, "That was an absolutely wonderful opening statement." The senior says, "It sure was—he opened the case so wide I don't know how in hell I'll close it."

After the opening statements in the Gold case, Judge Wall invited the prosecutor to call his witnesses. The first witness for the prosecution took his seat, slightly below the level of the judge's podium and above the stenographer's chair.

Francis McDonald was a brilliant prosecutor, distinguished looking with gray hair, a becoming feature and suitable to his subsequent elevation to the black robe of a judge. His task was formidable. Although he had conducted a substantial investigation, he had no direct evidence that Gold was the culprit, nor could he ascribe a motive for Gold to kill the Pasternaks. He had built his case solely on circumstantial evidence.

A trial is like certain vegetables: layer after layer is peeled off before the edible core can be discerned. So when the prosecutor announced that he had forty-one witnesses, the defense knew that he was referring to many leaves which covered the core.

He called to the stand local and federal experts; a professional engineer and land surveyor who drew illustrations of the first and second floors of the Pasternak home; free-lance photographers who reduced to film the contour of the Pasternak home and series of slides of various rooms and staircases; fingerprint experts who took series of photographs of the crime scene which became the State's exhibits; neighbors of the Pasternaks, who testified to sighting automobiles with New York plates; the designer of the Buttoneer Kit; a chemist whose company supplied the plastic for the Buttoneer Kit; even distributors of buttons for the Buttoneer Kits and merchants who sold them were called by the prosecution; special agents and toxicologists testified as to their findings made in comparing blood types, hair samples and skin scrapings; even Rhoda Pasternak's hairdresser and the Pasternaks' housekeeper were called by the prosecution.

Painfully and slowly he put the more than forty witnesses on the stand to surround Gold with suspicions of guilt. He produced the two witnesses who testified that they had seen Gold's "dark" auto parked near the Pasternak home three days preceding the murders; he produced records that established that less than a year before the murders Gold had required psychiatric treatment in two hospitals in Montreal and New York. In one of these hospitals the record showed that he was given shock treatments. The policemen who searched every inch of the murder home found two small loops of plastic thread coming from a sewing kit. They took a sewing kit from Gold's apartment and attempted to connect the pieces found in the Pasternak home with Gold's kit.

Myrna Kahan, the Pasternaks' oldest daughter, gave emotional testimony of her call to her mother:

> . . . she [her mother] said "someone's yelling at Daddy . . . Daddy is saying get away from my house." Then her voice changed. You can hear it in somebody when they're not talking calmly. She said, "Send Bob over"—Bob's my husband . . . That's the last time I ever

heard from my dearly beloved mother, last words she ever spoke
to me.

She went on to testify that Gold had been married to her sister
and that they were amicably divorced after only ten months of
marriage.

After the prosecutor's witnesses had given this evidence,
McDonald announced: "The State rests." The phrase is a quaint
inheritance from Anglo-Saxon tradition. There is no rest for any
attorney in the courtroom. His antennae are out for the slightest
movement of a juror or a witness. What the phrase signifies, of
course, is that the State has completed the evidence the prosecutor will offer. Time for the defendant's counsel to move to dismiss
the indictment on the ground that the evidence adduced was
insufficient to permit the jury to find Gold guilty beyond a reasonable doubt. This was fervently argued by Kunstler and Ferrante, especially since the evidence was all circumstantial, and
no motive had been presented. Judge Wall denied the motion and
required the defendant to proceed with its proof.

Kunstler and Ferrante rose to the task. Gold had been in the
vicinity of the Pasternaks' home three weeks earlier to visit his
former sister-in-law, Myrna Kahan, to suggest a reconciliation
with his ex-wife. She lived a few blocks away from the Pasternaks. They proved that he was not there three *days* before the
murders, but that his visit was three weeks before the fatal date.

They showed that although Gold had taken psychiatric treatments he had held responsible positions in the Grumman Aircraft Company and in a stockbrokerage firm and had never been
involved or charged with even a misdemeanor.

When the New York police searched Gold's apartment he did
not limit them to the warrant. He invited them to search further
and take whatever they wished.

Gold had explained his cut finger to New York detective Patrick Kelly, who testified that Gold had told him:

... [on the night of the murders] at about 11:00 or thereabouts, he
felt like having a snack, and that he went into the kitchen and

obtained a carrot and a knife, and began scraping a carrot, and in doing so, cut his left index finger.

However, the superintendent of Gold's apartment house, Julio Fernandez, testified:

PROSECUTOR: You didn't see the cut, did you?
A: No, only the bandage.
Q: ... Did he tell you how he received the injury?
A: I said jokingly, 'Where did you put your finger?'
He explained to me he was peeling potatoes and he got hurt.

An expert testified that it would be unlikely that a man slashing a body with his right hand would cut his left-hand forefinger, and if he did it would probably have severed the finger instead of making a minor cut.

Defense counsel must sometimes act not only as lawyers but as detectives to bring out facts that contradict a prosecutor's theory. Kunstler, Moynahan and Ferrante did just that.

8

THE IGNORED SUSPECT

THE DEFENSE DISCOVERED that there was a character who was not mentioned on the police list of suspects. He had been involved in crime in Waterbury all of his life, and more important, he was antagonistic toward Pasternak.

Even a superficial search would have revealed that Bruce Sanford was a Satanist dedicated openly to serving the Devil. He had a beard and down-turned moustache, and a gleaming smooth head he shaved four times a day, to make it look like a missile. He had a number of tattoos, including one on his palm, a prominent Star of David with a swastika in the center. He also had a tattoo between his thumb and forefinger that said, GOD IS DEAD. He was armed with knives of all dimensions. He also belonged to a motorcycle gang, "The Peddlers of Evil," and wore a tire chain around his waist. He was never without so-called straight-edged razors (in England they are called "cutthroat razors"). He wore a violent criminal's favorite rings: brass knuckles. And in his motorcycle boots he carried a large Buck knife.

Bruce Sanford was an admirer of Charles Manson, the man who ordered the killing of actress Sharon Tate with a Buck knife.

Sanford had a long history of imprisonment as well as confine-

Bruce Sanford: "obsessed with graveyards," he dug his own grave. (*Photo by Mitchell Booth*/Journal Inquirer)

ment in psychiatric hospitals. He had been diagnosed at Whiting Forensic Institute as a drug addict and dangerous, with a history of attempting suicide by eating glass. Not only was he suicidal, he also acted out his criminality to the point of being homicidal.

A ward nurse at Whiting, Mrs. Abbey, reported to her superior that Sanford had become very upset when his sleeping medications were canceled. He told her: ". . . that damned doctor doesn't even talk to me, stops my medication anyway. In Salman [another ward] I made a big knife and was going to get the doctor who changed my medication there—if I don't get my sleeping meds about 9:30 there's going to be some trouble tonight. I'll make a knife and get this doctor too." Based on her report, Sanford was put into seclusion, where he attempted to cut his throat with a nail. He refused medical attention until he came out of solitary confinement, and when the nurse, Mrs. Abbey, explained to him the reason why he was in seclusion he told her: "Next time I won't threaten, I'll do something."

Sanford was obsessed with graveyards; at times he spent entire weekends there. On one occasion he dug a grave and tried to commit suicide so that he would fall into his own prepared grave.

His "misconduct" was not sporadic. From the age of eight he had been in reformatories and frequently ran away before his term was served. As early as age ten he was being pulled into juvenile courts. He was a minor, true, but his crimes were major, and they escalated with age.

He became a swallower of pills and proceeded rapidly along the scale of addiction to marijuana, opium, heroin, chemical sniffing, cocaine and all the derivatives that wash away control of the nervous system. He needed eighty bags of heroin a day. He was an alcoholic. Rape was part of his deformed life.

Although his mother, Lillian, attempted to rear him as a Roman Catholic, he had defied her by wearing an inverted cross. He had an obscene tattoo on his leg, then tried to burn it off with matches, which caused severe infection.

Psychiatrists, not unknown for disagreeing about a diagnosis, repeatedly found him to be psychotic and antisocial. He committed crimes that went beyond even criminal sense. In 1970 a sergeant in the Waterbury Police Department on a routine patrol observed three men supposedly repairing a flat tire on a parked vehicle. The sergeant checked his stolen car list; the vehicle was stolen. He got out of his patrol car and approached the driver, requesting identification. The driver was James Calca. One of the other men was Bruce Sanford, who pulled a gun on the sergeant and ordered Calca to disarm the officer and remove the keys from the police cruiser. Calca did. Sanford then ordered the policeman to abandon the car and start walking. He and Calca stole the obviously identifiable police car and drove off in it. Calca later turned himself in to the Waterbury police and identified Sanford, who was arrested. Michael Daley, Sanford's attorney, arranged Sanford's $10,000 bail but it was two years before Sanford was declared competent enough to plead guilty to the charge after spending a year in a mental institution.

Sanford was preoccupied with blood. His ubiquitous razors and knives were continually engaged in causing blood to flow, includ-

ing his own. He repeatedly cut himself to experience the excitement of seeing life-giving fluid seep from his body. The sensations
of seeing streams of blood, even drinking it, were the stuff of his
delusional existence.

He had a special, almost prosaic motive for venting his murderous instincts on Pasternak: Sanford believed that Irving
Pasternak was advising his ex-wife Glorianna to end her relationship with him. She was involved in a custody battle with her
former husband, Eddie LaPointe, for their five children, and was
concerned that her association with Sanford would forfeit her
right to have her children live with her. She had met Sanford in
May of 1974 and married him a month later. He was twenty-nine
years of age, she was forty-three. Her children by her first marriage ranged in age from ten to twenty years. Although Glorianna
had obtained a Haitian divorce from Bruce Sanford on September
10, 1974, after only three months of marriage, he nevertheless
continued to live with her, in her house. But on the eve of her
custody hearing for the children, on September 26, 1974, when he
came back to the house filthy and drunk, she told him she could
not tolerate his conduct any longer and ordered him to "get out of
my house and live with your mother." Psychiatrists had predicted
again and again that if he ever suffered a serious rejection, he
would explode into uncontrollable violence. Glorianna's order
was not only a rejection but an ejection that undoubtedly set off a
fury in him.

That night the Pasternaks were murdered.

Patricia Morrison, a born-again Christian and a friend of Sanford since childhood, was questioned by Kunstler and gave startling evidence of a telephone call she received from Sanford a few
days before the murders in which he threatened to "get Pasternak" because he thought Pasternak was betraying Glorianna.

Patricia Morrison got another call from Sanford on the night of
the murders, when he pleaded for her to help him get out of the
state because he had done a terrible thing. The morning after the
murders Sanford, unable to drive himself, persuaded Glorianna,
still submissive, to help him escape. In spite of their quarrel the
preceding evening, she obeyed him.

Was not this flight a kind of physical confession? Just as significant was the fact that Sanford returned to Connecticut only after
Gold was indicted, which was three months later. He walked and
hitchhiked the entire distance from Florida to Connecticut.

On December 12, 1974, two officers, DeLauri and Velazquez,
had been despatched to 96 Alder Street in Waterbury. Sanford's
mother, Lillian Sanford, had reported that she had found trails of
blood throughout her house. The police broke down her son's
bedroom door and found Bruce Sanford dead on the bed in a pool
of blood, his throat cut. On the mirror was a suicide "note"
written in blood. It read: "CURSE YOU GLORY." Glory for Glorianna . . .

If there is a hell presided over by the Devil, Sanford will have a
prepared seat near him. He had served Satan faithfully. In less
than thirty years of his life he had committed every conceivable
debauchery, all in open loyalty to the Devil. He not only left a
trail of blood, but of victims.

In terms of evil deeds he had lived a long life. In Emerson's
words: "I am the Devil's child. I will live then from the Devil." So
Sanford died by his own hand, still spouting malice.

Another violent death, then, had appeared in Waterbury. Bruce
Sanford, the suicide, ought to have become a suspect in the
Pasternak murders, but the prosecutor apparently considered
him a challenge rather than a solution—or else was simply too
preoccupied with Gold, the suspect he had in hand. The dead
man's criminal record alone, one would think, would have been
enough to find out whether such a horrendous crime as the killing of the Pasternaks with a Buck knife could not be due to his
violent perversity.

Kunstler, Ferrante and Moynahan moved to present evidence that
Sanford had a motive to destroy Pasternak, and that he had acted to
execute it. Working together with investigators, and armed with tape
recorders, they interviewed relatives and friends of Sanford in order
to demonstrate that it was he who had terminated the Pasternaks'
lives. What better defense was there for Gold?

They talked to Glorianna, to Patricia Morrison and to his partners in crimes, Robert Bourassa and Craig Yashenko. The puzzle

yielded quickly to their belief that Gold was innocent. The former shadow of suspicion that Sanford was the murderer took on flesh and blood . . .

At the first intimation of such evidence, the prosecutor jumped to his feet in angry protest. Sanford was dead. Testimony about him was all *hearsay*. It should be barred under established rules of evidence. Indeed, much of it was hearsay, but Judge Wall overruled the loud objections.

Then Kunstler was free to develop direct testimony about Sanford. Prosecutor McDonald and his associates continued a stream of objections based on their contention that such evidence was hearsay and therefore inadmissible but were overruled.

In 1972 Sanford had been seen by Dr. Joel Kovel, at the Waterbury Hospital, who noted that he was under the influence of heroin and had a history of alcoholism. Kunstler asked Dr. Kovel for his opinion:

Q: Now, Doctor, from what you have read in the records of Bruce Sanford, can you, with reasonable medical certainty, give an opinion as to the mental condition of Bruce Sanford for the period covered by these records?

A: In the sense that I define opinion as something short of diagnosis, yes . . . It would appear that psychiatrically in the period of time early 1972 through Sanford's demise . . . he was an individual of rather markedly impulsive, aggressive proclivities prone to abusing the use of various types of psychotropic drugs . . . and that he was a person in somewhat desperate individual straits which accentuated the impulsive, aggressive and various disorganizing qualities of his behavior.

The doctor went on with his diagnosis to say that Sanford suffered from a severe "character disorder" and when asked by Judge Wall to describe the meaning of such a term, answered:

A: . . . the character disorder referred to a pattern of behavior wherein an individual exhibits recurrent difficulties

in adaptation to his external environment ... diagnosis
that seems likely in view of certain evidence in these files
is that of an underlying psychotic condition. This is
based upon the impression of delusional thinking rendered in one of the medical admissions. In addition, you
have to say that there is fairly positive evidence that Mr.
Sanford had significant disturbance in the chronic ingestion of alcohol and various types of psychotropic drugs.

The doctor further testified that Sanford "is the ... type which
could have committed a violent murder. Such a character disorder
is influenced by individual factors such as rejection, drinking,
drugs, etc."

Dr. Kovel spoke of Sanford's record of attempted suicide: In
1972 Sanford was admitted to Waterbury Hospital for attempted
suicide, with stab wounds in the neck. In January, 1974, he was
again admitted to Waterbury Hospital for acute intoxication, and
acknowledged that he was a "pill popper," said that he would kill
himself and was generally violent and unruly in the hospital. He
was admitted again in May, 1974, because he had threatened to
kill Glorianna. At each admission to hospitals he listed his religion as "Satanism."

The doctor ended his testimony with the opinion that Sanford
suffered from a "maladaptation taking the form of frequent acts
of aggression and hostility; failure to conform to ordinary social
code; general lack of regard for ordinary human rules of conduct;
and poor impulse control in general, particularly having to do
with aggressive hostile impulses."

Sanford's underlying disorder, Dr. Kovel said, could be un-
leashed by "psychological blows" spurred on by an organic condition such as the ingestion of alcohol and drugs that could
culminate in a final act of violence on his part.

Kunstler not unreasonably called Glorianna Sanford for the
defense, but since her loyalty to Sanford was overriding she
turned out to be a better prosecution witness.

She testified that on the day of the murders Sanford came to her
house drunk. It was the afternoon, although she would not pin-

point the time beyond it being in daylight hours. Under cross-examination by the prosecutor McDonald she testified:

> A: I didn't want the children to see him . . . I led him right up the stairs to my bedroom, where he passed out on the bed . . . our rooms lock with a key on the outside. I locked it and had the key in my pocket. I went downstairs . . . [Much later] when the house was in order I went up to speak to Bruce . . . I unlocked the door . . .
>
> Q: Is that when you told him he would have to leave if he didn't behave himself?
>
> A: Yes . . . then just within a few minutes he went into the bathroom and he came out and had cut his throat.

Questioned by Kunstler, she said Sanford remained in the house until the police came for him, at 10:37 P.M. that evening.

> A: The only time he left the house that night was when the police came to get him when we called the ambulance.

Sanford had dramatically sliced the skin on his throat, not touching any arteries. This caused a flow of blood, and he was taken to Waterbury Hospital by the police late that evening by ambulance.

All this could very well have been a cover-up for the amount of blood on his body and clothing.

Kunstler continued his questioning of Glorianna:

> Q: You saw him the next morning at some time, is that correct?
>
> A: No. Excuse me . . . I saw he was with . . . Falcone, a policeman, with a white shirt . . . he gave him first aid [the night of the murders], took him in the ambulance, told me it would be better if I didn't go and see him then.
>
> Q: . . . When you saw him that night he was going out with the police?
>
> A: He was in the ambulance.

Q: ... How long was it after he returned home [the next] morning that he left the state with you or without you?

A: Oh no—with me, of course.

Q: Where did you and he go?

A: We got into the car ... believe me, I had no idea I was going to Florida.

She further testified that Sanford did not return to Connecticut until December, after Murray Gold had been indicted.

Glorianna's daughter, Denise LaPointe, was called by Kunstler to testify that none of the bedrooms in Glorianna's house had locks on the outside of any door, "just a little push-button next to the knob ... on the inside of the door," so Glorianna could not have locked the door on the outside.

Robert Bourassa and Craig Yashenko were Sanford's friends in crime and assorted malevolence. They would have no reason to help convict him, as would an enemy of his. This gave special weight to their testimony and the evidence they were about to reveal.

Bourassa testified that on the night of the murders, he and Craig Yashenko went to Glorianna's home, at her request, at approximately 8:00 P.M. (Bourassa was Eddie LaPointe's, her ex-husband's, cousin.) Glorianna was worried about Bruce's absence. Bourassa searched the house for Sanford, who wasn't there.

Kunstler questioned Bourassa:

Q: I call your attention specifically to the day the Pasternaks were murdered ... do you remember the incident, the murders?

A: Right.

Q: And did you see Bruce Sanford that day?

A: No, I didn't.

Q: Did you see Glorianna Sanford that day?

A: In the evening I did.

Q: And how many times did you see her?

A: Twice.

Q: . . . When was the first time?

A: . . . A little after 8:00 . . . that evening.

Q: . . . As a result of a phone call, did you go to her house?

A: . ∴ Yes.

Q: . . . And as a result of [your conversation with Glorianna] what did you do?

A: I looked through the house for Bruce Sanford. Upstairs in the bedrooms and on the first floor . . . and in Gloria's room.

Q: Was he there?

A: No.

Later that evening he again returned to Glorianna's house with Yashenko, at Glorianna's request, and she took them to the basement:

A: . . . I went down to the basement and I was shown a shirt that was there . . . [by] Gloria. . . . It was on a basement landing between two sets of stairs . . . The shirt I was shown was blue, like a blue denim. I remember that it was full of blood . . . The whole front of it was covered and the arms.

Bourassa testified that he had last spoken with Sanford in December, 1974, when Sanford telephoned, saying that he was going to kill himself; that he could not stand living; that he was going to get caught—and that he was sorry that he had killed Rhoda Pasternak.

Craig Yashenko confirmed in his testimony that he had accompanied Bourassa on both visits to Sanford's home on the night of the murders and that during the second visit, late in the evening, Glorianna Sanford also showed him the blue denim shirt soaked in blood. (There was never a challenge to the fact that the shirt was Sanford's.)

Yashenko overheard the telephone conversation of Sanford and Bourassa in December, 1974, on an extension line at Bourassa's home. He heard Sanford say that he was sorry for the trouble he had caused and that he was sorry he had to kill Rhoda Pasternak.

Had these two men been the only witnesses testifying to Sanford's confession, they might be discounted. However, there were others whose reliability was not challenged.

Patricia Morrison gave her evidence of Sanford's confessional telephone call to her.

Her husband, George Morrison, added that late in the evening of a day in December, 1974, shortly before Sanford's suicide, he received a phone call at his home for his wife. Sanford stated to him that he was sorry he had to kill Rhoda Pasternak and that he wanted Mr. Morrison to tell Mrs. Morrison "goodbye."

The courtroom was stunned.

Counsel on both sides were then given the opportunity to sum up their respective positions to the jury.

Causes are won by persuasive marshaling of the evidence. This needs to be done and presented fairly, but with enough earnest sincerity to tilt the inner scales that every person carries with him in deciding right or wrong. Only after such a factual foundation has been established is it desirable to superimpose a righteous emotional peroration.

Both lawyers now struggled with this task.

Kunstler began his summation:

"We cannot permit a gross miscarriage of justice in this case. I have shown ample evidence to indict Bruce Sanford for the crime, much more than any that the prosecution has against Murray Gold, by a long shot.

"We have evidence as to certain physical facts—the fact that Mr. Bourassa went over to 53 Myrtle Avenue sometime after 8:00 o'clock on the night of the murders and went through every room and Bruce Sanford was not present; that he stayed there until approximately 9:00 o'clock—he said an hour; that he went there with Craig Yashenko and went home; that sometime later that night they went back to 53 Myrtle Avenue and at that time neither one of them saw Bruce Sanford, but Glorianna Sanford pointed out a bloody blue denim shirt in the basement.

"We have shown that Bruce Sanford was available, at liberty,

and out of the house during the time these murders were undoubtedly committed.

"You have heard the testimony of Mrs. Morrison, who testified
that she received a call from Sanford two days or so before the
murders, and that in that telephone call he made a threat against
the life of Irving Pasternak; that as Dr. Kovel testified and all
medical records show, he was subject to delusional fits, and that
Mr. Pasternak was someone whose name was known in the Sanford household.

"Sanford made a threat two days before the murders; he called
Mrs. Morrison immediately after the murders and said, "I have
just done something for which there is no turning back. I'm in a
phone booth covered with blood. Would you come and help me?"
She refused to help him and he hung up.

"Glorianna Sanford testified that she took him out of the state
the next morning and drove him to Florida, where there had been
no plans to do so whatsoever. She used the term 'spontaneously,'
and said, 'Believe me, I had no idea I was going to Florida.' She said
she got him out of state, which of course fits in with his statement to Mrs. Morrison: 'You have to get me out of the state.'
Would an innocent man flee?

"Then we heard the declaration by Sanford to Bourassa, overheard by Craig Yashenko, that this man was sorry that he had to
kill Rhoda; that he was going to kill himself.

"Sanford implicated himself in the murder of Rhoda Pasternak,
and it's perfectly consistent with his statement to Mrs. Morrison
that he was going to get Irving Pasternak if his wife [Glorianna]
did not get a fair shake. He never mentioned Rhoda Pasternak—
only Irving. So his sorrow was only not that he killed Irving
Pasternak, but that he had to kill Rhoda as well. There was a
statement of intent that he was going to kill Irving Pasternak if
something happened—something did happen, because Glorianna Sanford said that on the day of the murders she told Bruce
Sanford he would have to leave the house because he was threatening her children and her house. She eventually lost that house
and I believe she lost custody of the children as well. That custody proceeding was pending before Judge Meyers and on the

night of the murders Judge Meyers received a telephone call couched in exactly the language that Mrs. Morrison attributed to Sanford [referring to Jews].

"Despite the fact that there is ample evidence to indict Bruce Sanford for these crimes, you, the jury, are being asked to hold Gold responsible for what Sanford did. You must not allow this to happen."

The judge's charge to the jury instructed them that first the burden of proving Gold guilty was entirely on the prosecutor. Gold had no obligation to prove himself innocent. Therefore, no inference of guilt was permitted to be drawn from his failure to take the stand and testify in his own behalf. The law recognized that a defendant might suffer from cross-examination if he took the risk of exposing himself to it. The judge defined what "proof beyond a reasonable doubt" meant.

Judge Wall concluded his charge by impressing on the jurors' minds that liberty of an individual is too precious to permit any lesser standard.

The jury filed into a large adjoining room for discussion and decision. They took seats around an oblong table, designated a foreman and proceeded to discuss the facts they were to judge.

In the courtroom Gold and his counsel, supported by many of the spectators, felt a certain optimism. The shadow of Bruce Sanford seemed to have blotted out the suspicions against Gold raised by the prosecution.

But hour after hour went by without the knock on the door, which was to announce that a verdict had been reached. Day after day went by and the defense counsels' optimism receded with each delay. What was taking so long? A delay of one day was understandable; two days raised eyebrows; three days was an omen of jury strife; four days' delay might be persuasive signs of a coming deadlock. A famous trial lawyer, Max Steuer, once said that every hour a jury stays out, he loses a year of his life. The media people on hand heightened the tension by emphasizing in their accounts the apparent struggle in the jury room.

Finally, on the sixth day, there was that momentous knock on the door. The bailiff carried a message from the jury to the judge.

It read: "We are deadlocked. We cannot reach a unanimous verdict which you told us was required."

On inquiry by the judge it turned out that the jury stood nine to three for acquittal. In a civil case, this would have been sufficient. But where life and liberty are involved, as in a criminal case, a unanimous verdict is required.

The judge sent the jury back to try again. There was a delay of many hours. Finally the jury sent another message to the judge. The vote still stood divided.

The jury was called back into the courtroom. Higher courts have authorized a judge, faced with a disagreement among jury members, to instruct them for the purpose of encouraging them to reach an agreement by being tolerant of opposing opinions among them. This final effort on the judge's part is called the "Allen Charge." Judge Wall, acting on that authority, urged each juror to keep an open mind to any reasonable argument and to make an earnest effort to reach unanimity "if you can do so without violating your individual conscience and judgment."

So pursuant to this instruction the jury tried again. But the three against acquittal maintained their position. There was no unanimity. They sent the word to Judge Wall once again.

The press announced the hung jury, a quaint phrase really meaning hung in irresolution. Indecision is the enemy of the legal process because it violates two precepts—decisiveness and swiftness. Judge Wall was obliged to declare a mistrial. The case would have to be tried again.

Murray Gold was still under the requirement to post bail of $500,000, which he could not meet. Consequently he had to go back to jail to wait for retrial. However, Kunstler moved to reduce the bail requirement to $100,000 so that Gold might be free until the second trial began. The court denied the motion to reduce bail and Gold was immediately returned to his cell until a second trial.

Another seven months of his life was to be wasted, waiting, until the announcement came that the court was ready to try the case again.

It is said that mysteries beget mysteries. Why did the enormous

prosecutorial efforts concentrate on Gold, while ignoring Sanford? The prosecutor conceded that there was no motive for Gold
to kill the Pasternaks. True, he was their former son-in-law who
had divorced their daughter after a brief ten-month marriage. But
there was no apparent rancor in the events that had occurred ten
years earlier. Could a friendly divorce, ten years old, have incited
the brutal murders?

In sharp contrast, the motive of Bruce Sanford was clear. His
grievance that Pasternak, in advising Glorianna, had ended her
enslavement to him was a further stimulus to his persistent
criminality. Similarly, the life of crime, drugs and alcohol that
Sanford led sharply contrasted with Gold's "good citizenship."
The chief suspicion attached to Gold was his need for psychiatric
treatments to preserve his equilibrium. There were also the accu-
mulated suspicions about his cut finger, which might have been
the result of his wielding the murder knife; his reference to the
blood in his car resulting from the cut; and his statement that he
cleaned the car mat stained with blood with a toothbrush that he
then threw into the incinerator of his apartment building. In the
scales of comparative evidence, did Sanford's flight from the
scene of the crime and his alleged confessions equal or overcome
the incriminating facts against Gold?

To further bedevil the situation, Judge Milton Meyers, who was to
decide the custody battle between Glorianna and her former
husband, had received an anonymous threatening telephone call
on the night of the murders.

Judge Meyers related the details in a filed, sworn statement,
dated November 12, 1974, witnessed by Trooper James Daloisio
of the Connecticut State Police. Although this was never produced at trial, it was sent to the prosecutor for consideration.

In his sworn statement Judge Meyers said that he was the
acting "senior resident judge in the superior court for the judicial
district of Waterbury, Connecticut." Judge Meyers stated that he
was at home with his wife when he received a telephone call at
10:15 P.M. advising him that the Pasternaks had been murdered

that evening at about 9:30 P.M. Judge Meyers then telephoned Chief Inspector John "Jake" Griffin but, not being able to reach him, left a message to have his call returned. At 11:00 P.M. Judge Meyers turned on his television set and watched a broadcast reporting the murders on a local television station. When the broadcast was over, Judge Meyers's telephone rang again. He thought that Inspector Jake Griffin was returning his call. He was mistaken. Judge Meyers described in his affidavit the telephone conversation:

CALLER: Judge, did you hear about the Pasternaks?
JUDGE: I heard about the Pasternaks. Isn't it terrible? Who is this, Jake?
CALLER: Who?
JUDGE: Jake?
CALLER: No. You fucking son of a bitch, you Jewish bastard, you and your wife are next.
JUDGE: Who is this?
CALLER: You fucking Jew son of a bitch, you won't live to enjoy your retirement, you quibbler, you dirty Jew son of a bitch.

When Judge Meyers reported this dialogue to the police and followed with his affidavit describing the threatening call, they placed a wiretap on the judge's telephone and stationed guards to protect his home and courtroom.

Like a volcano that erupts again and again, Sanford's violence seemed to have erupted once more—this time to settle a score with another judge. The malicious anti-Semitic lava that descended on Judge Milton Meyers surely indicated that the source was deadly and very probably the same as that which had destroyed the Pasternaks. It was unlikely that Gold the refugee from Auschwitz would have directed such vitriol against Judge Meyers.

Crimes are like explosions. Some inflict only limited destruction. Others disrupt the reputation of a community. The Pasternak murders had a deep impact not only on the community of

Waterbury. They shocked the State of Connecticut and even the nation. They also created the image of anti-Semitism that spread across the country. The victims were leading Jewish residents of the community; pillars of the local synagogue; admired citizens. They were slaughtered on the holy day of Yom Kippur after returning from their synagogue to break the traditional fast. If Sanford was the murderer, the tone of anti-Semitism was added to the ugly brew. A Satanist, Sanford believed in Hitler. So if he was the killer the authorities were dealing with an anti-Semitic outburst that might give it worldwide attention as a surviving act of Hitlerism in the United States.

On the other hand, if a Jew committed the murders, and particularly one who—as was the case with Gold—had escaped from a Nazi death camp, the crime would be a local event, of no greater significance than any other ugly crime in any other state. The fact that it was committed on Yom Kippur would just be a bizarre coincidence and not a notorious perpetuation of Hitlerism in the United States. At least Waterbury would not be the victim of its extension. It was, one suggests, possible that such considerations helped motivate the pursuit of Gold rather than Sanford.

Is this surmise reaching too far? Some will perhaps think so, but the puzzle of the prosecutor ignoring Sanford is so confounding that it invites such conjecture. Where logic falters, surmise becomes adventuresome.

BOOK
III

9

The Second Trial

The second trial began on October 12, 1976. Judge George Saden presided. Counsel for the state and for the defense were the same as in the first trial, and thus were totally familiar with the prior evidence.

In planning a second effort to convict Gold, McDonald knew now that he faced the necessity of a far stronger presentation to obtain a conviction. He must have been shocked by the close call of a near-acquittal at the first trial. Anticipating that he now had the burden of overcoming the potent evidence of Bruce Sanford's guilt, he undertook to discredit anticipated testimony about Sanford and to strengthen his case against Gold.

So he increased the number of prosecution witnesses from forty-one at the first trial to fifty-five at the second. He was determined at least to offer more suspicions and circumstantial evidence which by its very profusion might challenge the direct evidence of Sanford's guilt.

The prosecutor proceeded to build his case against Gold as if constructing a mosaic, all still based on circumstantial evidence.

And his energies were directed even more intensely to disproving the suspicions against Sanford.

He did not know the surprise that awaited him.

McDonald began his psychological preparation of the jurors by impressing on them the horror of the crime. He called to the stand Dr. Bertrand Bisson, who had performed the autopsies on the Pasternaks on September 27, 1974. Dr. Bisson gave his credentials as an anatomic pathologist, then testified that Rhoda Pasternak suffered twenty-five separate stab wounds, and of those six were in themselves potentially fatal. Irving Pasternak suffered thirty-five wounds, three of which, according to Dr. Bisson, were potentially fatal. He concluded that both died from "traumatic hemorrhagic shock." Dr. Bisson also indicated that he had found "defensive wounds" on both victims. The prosecutor asked him to explain what "defensive wounds" were:

A: . . . defensive wounds are any wounds that are found on the victim when he or she tries to defend himself from an assault of whatever variety it is.

Q: Would you describe those wounds?

A: Those wounds are common cuts of the hands and/or arms of the victim when he is trying to fend off a knife wound. Sometimes they have gunshot wounds through their hands trying to push the gun away. Things of that sort.

The pathologist further concluded that the assailant would be virtually covered with spurting blood from the slashed arteries of the victims. (During summation this testimony would be made vulnerable by the defense: if Gold had been the murderer he would have been soaked in blood from head to foot. Could Gold have traveled from Connecticut to Queens and passed through illuminated toll booths in that condition without being detected?)

Officer Clayton Lavalle, testifying for the prosecution, stated that he was present at the autopsies of the Pasternaks and was entrusted with the scrapings and skin taken from underneath the victims' nails.

Kunstler cross-examined:

Q: Which of these items did you forward to Hartford?
A: Fingernail scrapings, hair samples and skin samples from both Pasternaks.
Q: That wasn't until what date?
A: . . . January 21st, I believe it was.
Q: So they remained in your property room for three . . . months?
A: That's correct.

This delay tended to minimize the effect of this expert's testimony.

The prosecutor again tried to put another piece into the mosaic of damaging testimony. He called police captain Arnold Mark to the stand. Mark was married to a niece of the Pasternaks and lived in the Waterbury area. He had been called to the Pasternak home by daughter Myrna Kahan moments after her mother had told her on the telephone about the struggle going on downstairs. The victims were already dead when Mark arrived. He testified that he recognized the "Cat's Paw" impressions of heel prints on the bloody floor:

Q: What kind of shoes did you have on?
A: I had on . . . bluish-gray loafers, leather sole and heel.
Q: Cat's Paw?
A: No.
Q: Have you ever worn Cat's Paw heels?
A: Not to my recollection, never.

However, on cross-examination he admitted that in the first trial he had testified:

Q: You used the term "Cat's Paw," do you remember?
A: Oh, sure.

Q: Have you seen [Cat's Paw heels] before?

A: Yeah, I have had them. That's why I used the term . . . I know I have had Cat's Paw heels.

Q: You have had them yourself?

A: Oh, sure.

The fact that Mark had worn Cat's Paw heels did not make him a suspect, but his anxiety made him testify that he did not have such heels. Where a clue ends up in multiple forms and with multiple people, there's a dilution in the possible identity of a suspect.

Another witness for the prosecution was F.B.I. agent Thomas Delaney, who testified that the four pairs of Gold's shoes that had been sent to the F.B.I. laboratory for analysis had heels similar to the blood imprints found in the Pasternaks' kitchen tiles:

Q: . . . with reference to the four pairs of shoes that you had examined . . . did you compare the heels of those four pairs of shoes?

A: Yes, I did.

Q: Can you tell us whether or not the general design of those heels is similar to the design of heels on the . . . floor tiles you examined . . .

A: Yes. They are similar.

On cross-examination by Kunstler, however, it was discovered that this witness' initial report stated that they were not entirely similar. Kunstler questioned him about his prior report:

Q: . . . did you say none of the imprints of the [exhibited] pieces of tiles could be identified with any of [Gold's] shoes?

A: That's correct.

Q: You went on to say, "As a matter of information, the general design in the heel prints overlapping the [exhibited] tiles differs from the design in the heels of [Gold's

shoes] which indicate this particular heel print was not
made by any of [Gold's] shoes."

A: That's right . . .

Defense counsel also offered evidence presented by the book-
keeper of a company that was a distributor of "Cat's Paw" products. She said that in 1974 the company purchased 10,000 pairs of
Cat's Paw heels and distributed all of them in the Waterbury area.

The multiplicity of the "Cat's Paw" imprints on the terrain of
the slaughter made it impossible to draw any conclusion about
whose they were. Police, photographers and experts had swarmed
over the premises. Many of them wore Cat's Paw heels, which
prevented specific identification of any one individual who put
his imprint on the bloody floor of the murder scene.

Obviously, a clue so generic was valueless. Otherwise, an ac-
cusing finger would have pointed at any wearer of "Cat's Paw"
heels. Still, the prosecutor, having settled on Gold as his target,
did not follow any other evidentiary trail that might have dis-
proved or modified his thesis.

Detective Patrick Kelly of the Queens Homicide Bureau testified for the prosecution that he interviewed Gold in his apartment on October 11, 1974.

Q: With reference to Mr. Gold's cooperation with you, he
   continued to cooperate in this conversation until sometime after 7:00 A.M., is that correct?

A: That's correct.

Continued cross-examination by Kunstler revealed that by that
time Gold wanted to go to sleep. The long interrogation had also
alerted him to the hostile purpose of the interview. He said that
he wanted to consult an attorney before agreeing to more questioning.

If Gold had been the murderer, would he have been so trusting,
and so cooperative for eight or ten hours of questioning throughout the night? Would not a consciousness of guilt have made him

cautious and alerted him to call a lawyer more quickly? He also had exhibited the same openhandedness when police presented a warrant to search his clothes closet. In short, he had acted at all times without the furtiveness that would have suggested his guilt.

Police authorities pinned many of their hopes on one additional and specific clue. The police photographer found a brown button and two white plastic loops lying nearby in the master bedroom where Rhoda Pasternak had been cut down.

Detective James McDonald, testifying for the state, said that he was searching for a coat in Gold's apartment that might be missing a brown button. Was it a deadly revealing exhibit, torn from the murderer's coat? The witness admitted that a search of Gold's apartment and his clothes turned up no button missing from his coats. There was also confusion about the color of the button, since the button given to this witness by another trooper was black and not brown. The "button" mystery grew as it developed that an artist, drawing the scene of the murder, was directed to draw a button into his murder scene sketch that was used as an exhibit.

During his cross-examination of the detective Kunstler called to his attention his testimony in the first trial that the button was given to him by another trooper and was black, not brown:

Q: Didn't Trooper Luneau tell you something about a black button?
A: He just mentioned a black button.
Q: Do you remember giving that answer to that question?
A: Yes, I do.

Finding a brown button came up again in the testimony of another state's witness, Patrolman Herbert Green of the Waterbury Police Department. He testified that he was at the Pasternaks' home on the night of the murders—and claimed that he had found a button lying near the television set.

On cross-examination, however, Patrolman Green admitted:

Q: [Have you] told your superiors anything about a button that night?

A: They were aware of it . . .

Q: Is that in your report?

A: No.

Q: In doing this report . . . did you use the same pen . . . Do you have any explanation why the word "button" seems written in a different ink? . . . What color is the word "button" written in?

A: . . . The first letter is a lighter blue than the rest of the word "button" . . . I don't believe it was the same night [that he made the report].

Detective James McDonald investigated the crime scene four days after the murders and found two small pieces of plastic on the bedroom rug of the Pasternak house. He subsequently found a third piece of plastic, similar to the plastic pieces found in Gold's Buttoneer Kit taken from his apartment. He conducted tests and concluded that they were part of the stubs left on the base of the Buttoneer tie of Gold's sewing kit.

The evidence was not pointed enough to overcome coincidence. Several million similar kits were sold in the United States. But suppose, reasoned an expert, that it could be demonstrated that these particular plastic loops which were found on the scene of the crime came from Gold's kit and no other!

A forensic expert, Dr. John Reffner, director of the Institute of Material Science at the University of Connecticut, was retained by the prosecutor to make such an identification. Since the end of the plastic "thread" on Gold's kit was irregular, it might be demonstrated that the loop found at the murder scene fit the irregularity of the infinitesimal plastic "thread" of Gold's kit.

Dr. Reffner testified that he prepared six mounted photographs on a twenty-five-by-twenty-inch cardboard, enlarging the ends of the strands one hundred forty times. It was a daring device. By analogy, if one tore a cotton thread several times, and then attempted to demonstrate which of the torn pieces matched the first, second and third tear, the problem would be the same. Could such an extremely tiny area of a torn piece of "cotton" have such a consistent pattern of irregularity as to match the connection with other strands? The prosecutor attempted to prove that this could be done:

Q: How many areas of correlation have you marked out?
A: I have marked out eighteen areas.
Q: ... can you give your opinion based upon reasonable professional and scientific ... certainty as to the mating of these two pieces prior to the fracture?
A: It is my opinion these were mated prior to the fracture ... [and that] these two came from the same piece.

When cross-examined, Dr. Reffner admitted that he did not make any experiments with polyurethane polymers, a soft material compared to glass or plastic, and that he had not taken any notes on his experiments.

Professor Herbert MacDonell, an authority on criminalistics and director of the Laboratory of Forensic Sciences, testified for the defense that he was not able to match the threads because of the elasticity of the plastic, which, when shorn or torn apart, distorts. Using a modern scanning electron microscope, he conducted one hundred experiments. He took a shank and a fastener and sheared the two or tore them apart. Then he compared the two parts under a comparison or electron microscope and gave his conclusion:

A: Even though I had two that came from the same source, I was unable to get [a] sufficient degree of identification ... [and] I could not state they were one and the same ... the nature of the material did not allow that match.

In a sense, Gold's life literally hung by a thread.

Dr. Milton Schwartz testified for the state that he had treated Gold for his cut finger on September 27, 1974, and that Gold had told him the wound was from a broken glass.

When cross-examined about the extent of the injury, the physician stated:

A: [The wound] didn't need sewing up . . . I cleaned [it] and put on a dry sterile dressing.

The prosecutor went on pursuing his suspicions of Gold—near-fanatically. In the meticulous search for a single damning clue, a thorough examination had been made of Gold's automobile. A hair was found. The prosecutor's hope was that it could be identified as one that belonged to Rhoda Pasternak. Since Gold had been divorced from her daughter for ten years, and had not visited the Pasternaks during that period, it would indicate a recent contact. On such a structure of assumption, an inference could be drawn that the murderer's struggle with Mrs. Pasternak resulted in the tearing of her hair and therefore was a potent clue.

F.B.I. hair expert, Frederick Wallace, testified for the state:

Q: Did you compare . . . the hair taken from the floor mat [of Gold's car with] the hairs taken from the nightgown and dressing gown [of Rhoda Pasternak]?
A: Yes . . . I would have to say that the possibility of the hair originating from anybody else . . . would be extremely remote.

On cross-examination the expert was asked:

Q: It is true . . . that hair comparisons do not constitute a basis for positive personal identification?
A: That's correct [he conceded].
Q: Didn't you . . . receive vacuum sweepings taken from the Pasternak house . . . ?
A: Yes.
Q: . . . there were no hairs there similar to that of Murray Gold?
A: There were none that exhibited the same individual characteristics as his [Gold's] hair.

The defense presented its forensic expert on hair, Dr. David Spain, a professor of clinical pathology at New York University. He was also chief medical examiner for Westchester County and had personally performed several thousand autopsies. He testified that it was impossible to determine from which person a hair came, or whether from a male or female, and that it was impossible to distinguish between hair cut with a scissor, a razor or a knife, but if hair had chemicals such as dye one "couldn't tell what kind of dye or whether it matched any other dye." His conclusion was:

> A: One cannot specifically state that . . . hair unquestionably comes from a particular individual . . . [and] being able to distinguish how a hair has been removed from a body would be very rough . . . I don't think any techniques are sufficiently developed for examination which will distinguish between scissor cut and knife cut.

In short, the proof had been presented that a lone hair was a totally inconclusive clue, and no inference could be drawn from it in modern science that would aid identification.

Myrna Kahan, Gold's former sister-in-law, testified for the state. She had also testified in the first trial and had then described Gold as "soft-spoken, quiet and easygoing." Her testimony in the second trial, however, described him as "peculiar, strange and weird." Her description had turned from compliment to invective in a rather short period of time. Was her concern that her son Mark (who had attacked his uncle and shortly after the murders was taken to Whiting Institute) might himself be a possible suspect the reason for her extraordinary reversal? In fact, he was on the police list of possible suspects.

Barbara Pasternak, Gold's former wife, also testified for the state. She said that when she was interviewed by detectives and was asked who, in her opinion, might have killed her parents, she did not mention Gold. She listed one suspect, Onie Kilpatrick, a former boyfriend of hers, who was on the F.B.I.'s "most wanted" list. He had been arrested for possession of a sawn-off shotgun, and counterfeit money.

The F.B.I. issued a warrant for unlawful flight to avoid prosecution, stating that Kilpatrick was considered dangerous. Kunstler believed it significant that when Barbara Pasternak was questioned by the detectives the only name she gave them as being a possible perpetrator was Kilpatrick—she never mentioned Gold.

Judge Saden excused the jury and the witness, Barbara Pasternak, while Kunstler argued for the right to question her regarding Kilpatrick:

KUNSTLER: . . . the only member of the [Pasternak] family that lived with Murray Gold, when asked who could have done this, pointed to an entirely different person, and gave them a name . . . she gave the name, we didn't give it. This is a man considered dangerous who is now a fugitive from justice. I think the jury is entitled to know . . . when she was asked the question, that the only person she mentioned she thought could have done this was not Murray Gold but Onie Kilpatrick.

Despite Kunstler's valiant effort to question Barbara Pasternak in the presence of the jury about Kilpatrick, the judge did not permit him to do so.

Nonetheless, when Kunstler's cross-examination resumed, he still attempted to question Barbara Pasternak:

KUNSTLER: . . . Ms. Pasternak, back on September 30th, 1974, when you were asked who could have done this to your parents, you did not name Murray Gold, did you?

COURT: . . . Mr. Kunstler, if you ask that question again, I'll find you in contempt.

And that was that.

After all the prosecution witnesses had given evidence, the state once again "rested."

The defense began presenting its witnesses on November 3, 1976, and ended on November 13, 1976. It was ready to inundate the

Attorney William Kunstler
and his co-counsel "rose to
the task"—but Murray
Gold fell at the second
trial. (*Photo by Richard
Gwin*)

state's "suspicions of guilt" with substantial evidence, including
the testimony that another man, Bruce Sanford, was the killer.

Both defense counsel and Murray Gold must have been in a
cheerful state at this point. For in spite of the attempt to bolster
the evidence, the state's "proofs" still consisted of inferences.
Again, not a single piece of evidence involved Gold directly or
offered a motive of his to commit such a terrible crime. The
state's case, consisting of suspicions and inferences, had failed
with a previous jury.

But soon the first warning to the defense that it might be in
trouble was sounded. The jury was not permitted to hear the
testimony of Sanford's friend, Patricia Morrison. While Kunstler
was grateful that Judge Saden was taking the precaution of hear-

ing the testimony, though not in the presence of the jury so that if it was excluded the upper court would know precisely what had been offered and rejected, it was nevertheless a sign of some doubt in the judge's mind. This was the surprise development and the good fortune that came to the prosecutor that he had not anticipated. Indeed, it changed the whole complexion of the trial.

Kunstler pushed ahead, even when the jury sat restlessly in another room. He desperately attempted to remove the judge's doubt concerning the admissibility of evidence against Sanford. The judge's hesitancy was like an unexpected black cloud about to burst on the scene . . .

Kunstler offered the evidence of Patricia Morrison, which vividly involved Sanford in the murders. Mrs. Morrison had known Bruce Sanford for twenty years:

Q: . . . how long before the murders was your last conversation with him?
A: Two nights before . . .
Q: . . . tell . . . what he said to you and what you said to him.
A: . . . He was very mad and upset . . . he started the conversation by swearing. I asked him what was wrong. He said he was angry. He kept on swearing. He told me he was upset about Mr. Pasternak. When I asked him why, he said that it had something to do with Pasternak representing his wife . . . He said, "I feel like he's selling her out." I asked him what he meant. He said that "if she didn't get what she had coming to her from this hearing" that he would get the no-good Jew bastard one way or the other. He just went on and on . . . until I could get him calmed down about it . . .
Q: Did there come a time after this conversation that you had another conversation with Bruce Sanford?
A: Yes, I did.
Q: And when was the next one?
A: The night of the murders.
Q: Can you indicate to the court, as best you can recall, what time this conversation took place?

A: It was late at night . . . possibly after one in the morning
   . . . When I picked up the phone he said, "I need your
   help" . . . He said he had just done something that he
   wasn't gonna be able to get out of and would I help him get
   out of the state. I asked him what was wrong. He said, "I
   can't talk now." I said, "Where are you?" He said, "I'm in a
   phone booth. I'm covered with blood." I said, "Bruce, what
   happened?" He said, "Are you gonna help me get out of
   state?" I said, "Not until you tell me what's wrong. What
   happened?" He said, "Will you come and get me out of the
   city?" I said, "You know I won't. Will you please tell me
   what happened?" He said, "I have to go." And he hung up.
Q: Did you ever talk to him after that time?
A: Yes, oh, yes.
Q: Do you know where he went?
A: He went to Florida . . . he called me about it.

Kunstler then addressed the court:

KUNSTLER: Judge, may the witness, Mrs. Morrison, be instructed to remain under subpoena, because this is testimony we hope to put before the jury.
COURT: You may be recalled to testify, Mrs. Morrison. So
   you're still under subpoena subject to call.

The prosecutor anticipated, correctly, that if the judge permitted the jury to hear this testimony it might be considered a
confession by Sanford to the murders, thereby clearing the defendant.

There was another extraordinary development during the second
trial. Was there ever a murderer who, in effect, left his calling
card?

An anonymous tip came to Kunstler. It advised him that a
business card of a lawyer had been found near the body of Irving
Pasternak.

It appeared that the police who flooded the murder scene,

equipped with scientific instruments and cameras to detect clues, found this card, which read:

Michael J. Daly, III
Attorney-At-Law
50 Holmes Avenue
Waterbury, Connecticut 06702

The significance of such a card was plain. Daly was a public defender, and Bruce Sanford was his client. In view of Sanford's drug habits, and criminal activities, he had kept his lawyer very busy for many years. At the very time of the Pasternak murders, Daly was trying to extricate Sanford from the serious charge of aiding James Calca in the holdup of a police cruiser.

What other inference could be drawn but that in the grappling death struggle between Pasternak and his assailant, the Daly card fell out of the assailant's—Sanford's—clothes? It lay there as mute evidence under Pasternak's body, as an almost irresistible revelation. The police also established that Pasternak had never represented Sanford and did not know him.

During the second trial defense counsel Kunstler made earnest inquiry of the prosecutor's office about whether such a card had been found at the scene of the murder. He got an emphatic denial.

Kunstler then launched a legal campaign to dismiss the case, on the principle that a prosecutor owes a duty under law to present to the defense any evidence that comes into his possession that would exculpate the defendant—a principle well-established as a means of protecting innocent defendants. If the prosecutor hides or fails to disclose any fact that would help establish the defendant's innocence he becomes the *per*secutor, not the prosecutor. His duty is to see that justice is done, and in theory, at least, he must be as solicitous about the defendant's innocence as he is determined to convict him if guilty.

So, the law supported Kunstler's application to dismiss the indictment. But did the facts?

Kunstler's affidavit stated that he had received "reliable information" that Mr. Daly's card was found at the murder scene and was in fact turned over to Francis McDonald, the state's attorney. Presumably this suggested that one of the police or detectives who searched the house for clues had found such a card and given it to his superiors. But the claimed "reliable information" was not set forth.

The solution of a crime by means of an unexpected clue can be as mysterious as aspects of the crime itself. An historic example is the Leopold-Loeb case. With no other purpose except the elation of committing the perfect undetectable crime, the two young men lured a third, a young neighbor, into a car, coolly crushed his skull and rode a long distance to hide the corpse in a culvert. It was likely that the body would never be found. Even if it was, who could possibly trace the deed to Leopold and Loeb? They were wealthy, educated and had no apparent motive for such a crime. For the rest of their lives they intended to harbor the perverse "joy" of a perfect crime, never to be solved. However, hiding the body in the culvert, Loeb's eyeglass case in his jacket's outer pocket fell out. After that, no crime could have been more easily solved. The police traced the prescription glasses to Loeb. They visited him and asked to see his glasses. He looked frantically throughout the house and reported they were missing. Soon thereafter Loeb and Leopold were both talking their heads off, blaming the other for the vicious crime. Loeb denounced Leopold's stupid brutality and Leopold denounced Loeb's brutal stupidity. Many years later, while serving a life sentence, Loeb was slashed to death by a fellow prisoner because of a homosexual quarrel.

So, even the most carefully devised scheme or assembly of confounding evidence can yield to a pair of eyeglasses, or a calling card.

Kunstler's motion to dismiss also claimed that McDonald had telephoned Mr. Daly to inquire whether he could explain how his office card had been found at the murder scene. Mr. Daly had no explanation. Kunstler then said that he had called Daly himself. Both McDonald and Daly denied that Kunstler had called them to inquire about the card.

Mysteries beget mysteries, disputes beget disputes. Under

these circumstances Kunstler demanded that McDonald be put on the stand to be cross-examined, and McDonald sought a reciprocal privilege against Kunstler.

The combination of a denial by McDonald, an official of impeccable reputation, and Daly, who had no motive to be partisan and who stated under oath that he had no conversation at all about the card with either McDonald or Kunstler, predestined the result. Judge George Saden, in a memorandum opinion steeped in acerbic comment, found in favor of the prosecution and refused to dismiss the case.

One of the anomalies of war is the rule of civilized behavior in the course of killing your adversary. Once he is captured he must not be shot but rather protected by minimum rules of decency preserving his welfare. Even during battle, weapons such as chemicals and gas are deemed beyond the pale. When President Truman was berated by religious organizations for destroying noncombatant Japanese populations with the atomic bomb he replied: "I am still waiting for an apology for Pearl Harbor." So while we may try to be civilized in the midst of slaughter, passions survive even if principles don't.

Since trials are legal warfare, similar inconsistencies occur. The Gold case exploded into a relentless battle between the attorneys. Kunstler suggested at the top of his voice that Judge Saden had been "imported" to preside at the second trial. The judge intimated that Kunstler had misrepresented being retained in another matter and therefore obtained an adjournment on false representation. He threatened a Bar Association inquiry. Kunstler charged the judge with being hostile to him. The prosecutor, McDonald, accused Kunstler of giving distorted stories to the press. Kunstler called McDonald an "animal."

As heat inflated insult, the two lawyers ceased to be only representatives and became combatants themselves. The fever that accompanies such a contest rarely aids the client. Although the jury was not present during this inner trial between the attorneys, their antennae must have picked up the waves of a contest witnessed by so many in the crowded courtroom, seen from the emanations coming through the television tube and read from the newspaper headlines. In any event, they sensed a struggle, and the faces of the combatant lawyers revealed who was triumphant. Perhaps this created a prejudice against Gold that the rules were intended to eliminate.

Then came the unexpected blow to the defense. Judge Saden ruled that he would not permit testimony about Sanford to be admitted into evidence, or heard by the jury, because it was defective.

In his ruling about testimony, including Patricia Morrison's recital of Sanford's confession and flight, Judge Saden said:

> The court's ruling is that the evidence ... with respect to the admissibility of the proffered hearsay confessions [by Sanford] ... does not measure up to the requirements of [Connecticut or] Federal law, which reads ... "A statement tending to expose the declarant to criminal liability and offered to exculpate the accused is not admissible unless corroborating circumstances clearly indicate the trustworthiness of the statement." I don't think that this additional evidence adds anything to the corroborating circumstances ...

Gold's defense team was stunned. It meant that all of the testimony involving Sanford would be excluded. Gold's lawyers would not be permitted to show Sanford's threat "to get" Pasternak; his telephone call to Morrison immediately after the murders; Sanford's flight to Florida and his return only after Gold had been indicted; his suicide and more and more—all excluded from the jury's consideration.

The defense's sword had been taken from it. It was left with a limp sheath.

The attorneys summed up their positions to the jury. Now McDonald had a clear road. He could list the suspicions, tinting them with credible colors to sound like proven facts: Gold's psychiatric frailties and previous shock treatments; his car being sighted three days before the murders near the Pasternak home;

his inconsistent explanations regarding his cut finger; the linkage of the pieces of plastic found at the murder scene with Gold's kit; the blood in Gold's car; the woman's hair found in Gold's car supposedly belonging to Rhoda Pasternak; and Gold's general eccentric demeanor.

Kunstler, deprived of his most effective argument—that Sanford was the real killer—did what he could to deny the suspicions against Gold and stressed that Gold had no motive to kill the Pasternaks.

The time came when the jury was ready to announce its verdict. It was the breathless moment when the clerk of the court addressed the jury and asked what its verdict was. The foreman arose and said: "We find the defendant, Murray Gold, guilty of the murder in the first degree of Irving and Rhoda Pasternak."

There was the usual gasp of all in the courtroom. Only one voice rose above all others. It must have been the scream of Gold's mother. The judge's gavel silenced the room. He dismissed the jury with thanks for their service. He announced that sentence would be imposed a month later. Gold was led out in handcuffs by two attendants to his cell beneath the courthouse, flushed, but silent, head low and eyes almost closed.

But there was a new and even more horrific suspense. What would the punishment be? A month later Gold was brought from his cell to stand alongside his attorneys, Kunstler and Ferrante, and the sentencing commenced.

The judge briefly analyzed the history of the case. He stated that, as was customary, the probation department had prepared a full history of Gold, which the judge said he had considered in imposing sentence. Then came the ominous words: "For the murder of Irving and Rhoda Pasternak I sentence you to imprisonment for twenty-five years in the Connecticut Correctional Institution in Somers."

As Gold was led away handcuffed for fingerprinting and then to the darkness of his cell, the only sound that accompanied him was the wailing of his parents.

The court, in a lengthy opinion, denied Kunstler's motion to set aside the verdict.

It was at this point that I entered the case.

10

The Parents' Plea—and a Reverie

Gold's parents now sought a new lawyer. Meyer Gold turned to Rabbi Blech of his synagogue. He wanted an appointment with me. The rabbi wrote asking me to meet with his congregant.

Since I was committed at the time to other legal engagements in other states, my partner, Angelo Cometa, replied, urging him to seek different counsel, preferably in Connecticut. The rabbi persisted. Meanwhile, Gold's parents had learned that their friends Mr. and Mrs. Sam Blum were also friends of Mrs. Nizer and myself. Meyer Gold appealed to them to arrange a meeting with me, and they did so.

When Meyer and Dina Gold were shown into my office their faces were etched with the agony of their ordeal—the deep lines evidence of their sleeplessness.

When they tried to speak, tears coursed down their cheeks and onto my desk. I tried to talk lightly to them until they could recover, which only increased their weeping.

Finally they broke through their tears to speak.

"Please, please, save our son. He is innocent. He is a good man."

It did no good to tell them that even if I accepted the responsibility of an appeal there could be no assurance of victory. Understandably, they were beyond reason. Desperate, they clung to the assumption that my undertaking the appeal would free their son. They assured me over and over that he was a good person, caught in a trap of misunderstanding and lies. They were unabashed beggars, ennobled by their mission. No one could have resisted their suffering.

I finally said that I would read the record of the two trials Murray had already endured. They accepted this halfway step as agreement to undertake the appeal and I didn't have the heart to contradict them as they rushed around my wide "partner" Lincoln desk and covered me with wet embraces.

Before leaving, Meyer Gold also assured me that he was successful in his fur business and that he would pay the necessary fees. He did not listen to my reply that it was the reading of the record and not a fee that would determine whether I took on the case. Indeed, although unnecessary in the Gold case, there are times when our law firm, like many others, undertakes pro-bono cases and gives full time and effort without fee.

When Gold's parents were gone I sat back for a few moments and thought of my own parents. After arriving in London from Poland my parents met and married. I was born in London. My father was a tailor, and working hours were so long in those days that he complained he never saw me awake; I was asleep when he left home and when he returned. He decided to emigrate to the United States, but since he didn't have enough money for steamship travel for all of us he sent my mother and me ahead to the "new land of opportunity" until he could earn enough to join us.

The scene when we finally met at Ellis Island was no less emotional than my encounter with Gold's parents. When happiness turns into ecstasy, laughter, it seems, is replaced by tears. The three of us cried, hugged and embraced, and during this happy scene—I never forgot it—I inadvertently brushed my father's bowler off his head. Seventy-five years later I would be asked by Lee Iacocca, chairman of the Committee for the Reconstruction of Ellis Island and the Statue of Liberty, to accompany Bob Hope and James "Scotty" Reston of the New York *Times* to have our photographs taken at Ellis Island, which we had all passed through.

As my parents grew older, they began to resemble Meyer and Dina Gold, it now occurred to me. Perhaps that was why, in part at least, I found myself so moved by their ordeal.

My father had worked fanatically—yes, that word applies—to establish a better life for our family, and particularly for me. He saved enough to open a cleaning and pressing store, which the window clarioned as the "California Cleaning and Pressing Establishment." (Geography had its linkage; many years later I would become general counsel to the Motion Picture Producers and Distributors Association, whose films were produced chiefly in California.)

My parents insisted that I enter Columbia College and then its law school because they wanted the "best education" for me. My father was profoundly grateful to the United States and his patriotism was fervent. Although as he aged the doctors ordered him not to exert himself because of his heart condition, they couldn't stop him from climbing a ladder to fly a heavy large American flag in front of our home in Bethlehem, New Hampshire, which he would lovingly remove at dusk. I could never forget my parents' pride in me and love for me . . .

As I emerged from these reflections I almost prayed that I would find some fatal error in the trial record that might make it possible to reverse Murray Gold's conviction.

I had no doubt that as I studied the record of the trial I would find errors; discover evidence admitted that should have been excluded, or vice-versa. After all, it is almost impossible to try a long case that is errorproof.

However, ordinary errors would not reverse the decision. The error had to be so profound that it required nothing less than a new trial. To throw out a case that has been tried for weeks, with many witnesses, required not just the finding of an error but one so profound that it enervated the entire trial. That kind of error, I knew, would be extremely difficult to find.

One night as I was rereading the trial record, sitting elevated in my bed with heated blanket and a spotlight on the writing stand across my knees, I found it!

I suppose the exultation I felt must be similar to a scientist's whose test tube confirms his theory, or the composer who achieves a rhythm between lyrics and music, or the computer technologist who discovers that the chips can perform still one more miracle. We did need a miracle, and one did seem to be at hand.

BOOK
IV

11

THE ERROR

THE ERROR THAT I believed was so profound as to require a reversal of the whole second trial, the verdict of guilty, and the ordering of a new trial involved the "hearsay rule."

The law does not permit a witness to testify to what someone
else has told him or her. That "other person" must appear on the
witness stand to testify so that he or she can be cross-examined
under the watchful eyes of the jury. Cross-examination is presumed a basic test for truth. The rule barring a witness from
quoting someone else instead of producing that person on the
stand is the hearsay rule, which states that a witness may not
quote someone else's version of a story because it deprives the
cross-examiner of the opportunity to challenge the creditability
of the original statement. "I hear say," or "Mr. X told me," is not
valid testimony. Which is how such testimony gets its name.

Still, like all legal rules, there are exceptions. Life is expansive,
it can't be compressed into a permanent mold. Developments of
science, change in customs, evolution of knowledge all require
a tolerant approach to the principles that otherwise guide us.
So there are exceptions to the hearsay rule: A deathbed statement may be testified to, though it is hearsay. So may a doctor's

conversation with his patient, because it is deemed to be based on a unique relationship of trust that is likely to assure accuracy.

The exception that struck me as critical was one I believed could be applied to the Gold case. It is called a *statement against one's own penal interest*.

What does it mean? A declaration by a person that subjects him to punishment for a crime is admissible because one assumes that a person would not so involve himself against his own interest unless his statement were true. Common experience teaches that people do not place their reputations and safety in jeopardy by lying against themselves. So the law gives credence to such "confessions" even though they are hearsay statements. This rule of law, I believed, was violated by the judge in the trial that found Gold guilty. The exclusion of statements made by Sanford, even though hearsay, was gross error: His confession, which clearly was against his own "penal interest," *should* have been heard by the jury.

Furthermore it's elementary that one accused of a crime has the right to prove that someone else committed it. "Rules of evidence," wrote Justice Holmes, "are devised to get to the truth. The exclusion of testimony which might establish the truth, but results instead in a terrible error and injustice, is the greatest concern."

Is there danger of perjury in such a rule? Suppose a gangster is ready to lie to save his superior. He makes false statements to a friend to the effect that he and not his boss had committed the crime. Then he disappears. The friend testifies to the "confession." Even though the gangster has acted against his own penal interest, the whole setup may be a ruse to absolve the real killer.

The law protects against such a contingency. It provides that *the statement against penal interest must be trustworthy* or it is not admissible.

So the law moves, even if glacierlike, to correct technical rules that become too constricted and result in injustice. Equity and the broad principles of justice have prevailed over the ancient hearsay rule. No longer is the objection on the ground of hearsay granted as a matter of course. A lawyer faced with this problem

needs carefully to research the growing number of exceptions
that qualify or overcome the hearsay rule. A lawyer's frustration
at having important testimony blocked by "a technicality" is
yielding to an ever-growing list of exceptions—inclusion rather
than exclusion is the tendency of the law. It is encouraging that
more exceptions will be granted, even though these will require
the resourceful demonstration not only of their service to a just
result but also the creation of safeguards, such as the trustworthiness test.

In the Gold case, the trustworthy elements were easy to make
out. Recall: Sanford had threatened to kill "the bastard" Pasternak for, he thought, advising his wife to break up their involved relationship. He called Mrs. Morrison, saying he was in a
telephone booth, his clothes full of blood, and that he wanted
her to help him get out of the state because he "had done
something terrible," which this time he "could not get out of."
Also showing that his statement against his own penal interest
was genuine was his flight the next day. He drove away to
Florida with Glorianna. The possibility that Sanford's statements were fraudulent was clearly overcome by the inherently
trustworthy nature of the statements and actions themselves,
not of the man.

Sometimes there are ways of checking logical concepts like a
column of figures. There was no doubt in my mind that the error
of the judge in ruling out as evidence the hearsay statements of
Sanford was not a minor error. It excluded critical defense evidence so profound that it undermined the entire proceeding. In
my opinion it did require a complete reversal and new trial.
Otherwise, it was nothing less than preventing a man charged
with murder from proving that someone else had committed the
crime.

I decided to undertake the task of demonstrating on appeal that
the exclusion of testimony about Sanford constituted reversible
error and that Gold was entitled to a new trial.

I asked Gold's parents to return to my office. Even though they
had previously assumed that my reading of the record was tantamount to a decision to represent Gold, and indeed, more, that my

representation of him at a new trial would inevitably be successful—a confidence that was touching as well as questionable—when I advised them that I would undertake the argument on appeal they sat down on a couch and, again, cried quietly.

12

THE APPEAL

THE PREPARATION OF an argument before an appellate court requires unusual effort. Of course I had the benefit of a legal brief and reply brief researched by Tim Moynahan, independent Connecticut counsel for Gold, as well as the assistance of my partners, Alan Mansfield, Sheila Riesel, Angelo Cometa, Martin Wasser and a host of associates. Briefs should not to be read by counsel out loud to the court; they are to be read by the judges and their clerks in the quiet privacy of chambers. In spite of the judges' repeated warning to counsel that their briefs were already read, and that the court would prefer counsel's views on the significance of the facts, and the interpretation of a few controlling legal rules, in making their oral statements lawyers still sometimes just read passages from their briefs.

Justices of the U.S. Supreme Court overcome this persistent problem by confronting counsel at the outset with troublesome questions, thereby forcing him to involve himself in the principles and facts that will decide the issues rather than parroting the printed brief.

I have never made a speech from a script. A speech or argument in a court is made for the ear, not the eye. It demands instan-

taneous comprehension. Unlike a written work, it does not provide the opportunity for digestive deliberation. A reader sets his
own pace and can call a recess at his own pleasure. For the most
part a listener is at the mercy of the speaker's pace. As a speaker
once said to his audience: "It is my duty to speak and yours to
listen. If you quit before I do, please let me know."

The rule is reversed when one writes a book or an essay. I believe
it should not be dictated to a stenographer; the rhythm tends to be
wrong, it will too much resemble conversation in which the sentence may not end and the eyes punctuate. The grace and balance
of well-written sentences can't be achieved as well orally. So an
argument before an appellate court ought not be read from either
the brief or any document. Counsel should be prepared to look
into the eyes of the judges and make his argument, holding their
attention by a rhythm that is slower and natural for oral delivery
and comprehension rather than the speed, which automatically
takes over when one reads from a script.

I readied myself for the argument in the Gold appeal by walking
up and down in my library and organizing my thoughts and
talking to myself. No notes. The only exception would be to read
an admission from the opponent's brief so as to give authenticity
to the quoted statement. In all other respects the appeal should be
a preparation in logical sequences, presented in conversational
tone and at a slow speed to accommodate instant comprehension.

As I approached the argument before the five Supreme Court
justices of the highest court in Connecticut I felt prepared for any
question about the hearsay rule, which I had made the essence of
our contentions. Of course, it was advisable to quote all admissions made in the prosecutor's presentations, and there were two
such passages that I wove into my argument. The first was a
quotation from McDonald's summation. I argued:

The Prosecutor conceded and still concedes that there was no
motive they knew of for Gold to have committed this deed. At
[page] four thousand and two [of the record] the able Prosecutor

said, "But why did Murray Gold kill these people? . . . I think we would all like to know that, myself included. However, most candidly, I admit I don't think I know."

Such candor reflected McDonald's integrity. He would not even by silence omit his concern that he could not present any motive that would involve Gold in the murders.

The second admission by McDonald when he addressed the jury followed directly on its heels. I went on with my argument:

The Prosecutor also conceded that there was no direct evidence in the case; that it was a case solely of circumstantial evidence. At [page] thirty-nine eighty-one I quote him, "Now, ladies and gentlemen [of the jury], in this case the State has no direct evidence [that Gold committed] the murders."

I emphasized his admissions:

No motive could possibly be found for Gold. His relationship with the Pasternaks was that he had married their daughter . . . eleven years before. They had no children. They were married one year . . . There was an amicable divorce, an attorney so testified. And the murders were committed ten years after that amicable divorce. Indeed, Gold had reason to be grateful to Mr. Pasternak, who had presented him and his daughter with a house which was divided in title equally between them and they divided the proceeds on the divorce. There was no alimony. There was no reason for recrimination. That was the sole relationship.

I concluded the syllogism by pointing out to the judges that even all the circumstantial evidence failed to meet the needed test in a criminal case—proof of guilt beyond a reasonable doubt. Indeed, I contended that the circumstantial evidence pointed to *Sanford* rather than to Gold.

The rest of the argument focused chiefly on the rule of law that an admission by Sanford that he had committed the murders should have been heard by the jury even though it was hearsay and had to be—Sanford had, after all, confessed his crime and committed suicide before the trial began.

His confession to his friends constituted admissions against his penal interest. They were an exception to the hearsay rule. True, they had to be "trustworthy." And they were—for a number of reasons. He made a confession to Mrs. Morrison, which was not challenged. She was not a friend or even an acquaintance of Murray Gold. There could be no suspicion that she was trying to help extricate Gold. That fact went to the trustworthiness of Sanford's confession.

There is one way of sensing even during the argument that it is, or is not, making an impression on the judges. As I quoted passages from the trial briefs and record I stated the number of the page in the stenographic record where they appeared. Soon the judges, sometimes all of them, were leaning forward to write down the page of the record where the admission I was stressing could be found. As I went on it was necessary only to cite the page number of the record after my statement. When the judges moved forward to make a note I could tell that they considered the admission I alluded to important enough to mark down for consideration in conference.

After I finished my argument Francis McDonald replied. He praised the diligence and expertise of law enforcement and expert personnel who testified on behalf of the State of Connecticut. The prosecutor's chief argument was that, after conceding that the state found it difficult to find a direct motive for Gold to have committed the murders, nonetheless there was such strong circumstantial evidence against Gold that the jury had made the correct decision in their verdict of guilty. He then turned to the issue of a third-party confession. He called Bruce Sanford a "crackpot" whose confessions were not trustworthy. He tore down the credibility of Sanford's friends who testified to those confessions. He cited case law and pressed his point that "confessions of crackpots, unreliable people, not being uncommon in the case of murders or other crimes of wide notoriety, did not have the requisite hallmark of trustworthiness to render them admissible before the jury." He stressed that it was for this very reason that the courts' policy was to "exclude these third-party confessions," and concluded:

> These murders were dreadful, shocking ... We do submit, most
> respectfully, that there was strong evidence that linked Mr. Gold to
> these murders; that no injustice has been done here ... The evidence of Sanford's involvement simply does not exist. It's all ...
> woven by ... individuals with criminal records who came from
> psychiatric wards to testify with respect to this man's statements ... And we submit that this [Gold's] conviction should be
> affirmed.

The Court now granted me an opportunity to reply. I had
anticipated the prosecutor's answering argument that pursuant
to law, the judge properly excluded testimony about Sanford since
it was hearsay. I was prepared for immediate refutation. The
physician, Sir William Osler, once described the secret of preparation:

> There is an old folklore legend that there is some mystic word
> which will open barred gates. There is, in fact, such a mystic word.
> It is the open sesame of every portal: the true philosopher's stone,
> which transmutes all the baser metal of humanity into gold. It will
> make the stupid man bright, the bright man brilliant and the
> brilliant steady. With the mystic word all things are possible. And
> the mystic word is "WORK."

In rebuttal, I corrected a number of mistaken statements
which I said were "inadvertently made by Mr. McDonald."

First, I reminded the Court that McDonald stated that the
Court did allow Mrs. Crocco to identify Sanford as the man
fleeing on the night of the murder. I said that it did not, citing
from the record, which even eliminated Mrs. Crocco from having
been put on the stand to identify Sanford.

Second, I emphasized that McDonald stated that there was no
print found on the paper bag. I quoted testimony that proved a
palm print was found (even though it was unidentifiable).

Third, as to the prosecution's claim that the hair found on the mat of Gold's car "most probably" belonged to Rhoda Pasternak, I pointed out that a defense expert clearly testified that it was even "impossible to make an analysis [whether] that hair came from anybody's head, either male or female."

I then turned to the prosecutor's argument that Sanford's confession was not trustworthy since he was a "crackpot":

> Mental condition is one of the indicia of trustworthiness. That is true . . . [But] the aberrational action of Sanford all his life was entitled to be judged by the jury as to whether he was capable of such a murder . . .

I listed the several occasions of his confessions, the number of people he confessed to. "These must be evaluated together with what [Mr. McDonald] calls the crackpot condition of Sanford."

I then turned to the main legal point:

> There are three states, Your Honors, New York, California, and Hawaii, which require not even a test of trustworthiness. As long as the jury is considering many other conflicts they may consider, in a murder case, whether the declaration was true. Did it come from a close friend of the defendant who is a gangster? That's one thing. [If, however, it came] from four people who were the friends of [Sanford]—that's another [matter].
>
> Consequently, the policy ought to be not merely that we require no test of trustworthiness. We do not make such an argument here. We do insist that the trustworthiness test has been met in this case. Certainly, it is far more significant that a man makes a declaration [as Sanford did] which may land him in jail or the death house than if he makes a declaration merely about money.
>
> Fundamentally here we are dealing with a philosophical question. We trust juries on the theory of democracy; that as you multiply judgments you reduce the incidence of error. There is the basic theory that two heads are better than one and [thus] we would rather trust two hundred million Americans on a question of right or wrong—not on a mathematical question or scientific question, then you want a mathematician or a scientist—but on [a question of] right and wrong; we go on the theory that we trust the multiplicity of judgments.

How can we philosophically say that testimony demonstrating that another man [had committed the murders should be excluded] who had a record of knives; had been caught knifing people [a man who had] in this very case a motive to kill Pasternak—and threatened to do him in; [a man who had] confessed on the night of the murders to his close friend of twenty years, Mrs. Morrison; [a man who had] fled from the jurisdiction; [and] before he did so was found with bloody clothes from shirt to shoes, and doctors testified to that[?] And then [he] only returns after the other man is indicted and, finally, whatever little [conscience] he has—I think because [he said he was sorry that] he killed Mrs. Pasternak—he had no regret for having killed Mr. Pasternak . . . he said, "I regret I had to . . . kill Mrs. Pasternak." And the reason for that was [that] she was on the phone. She heard the skirmish; she told her daughter; and then she confronted the man. She said to her daughter—it's recorded at the police station on nine-eleven and there's a recording of it—"There's a crazy man [here]." Her own former son-in-law? A crazy man fits in my mind with a mad dog.

The Judges of the Supreme Court of Connecticut—to whom the author's deeply felt appeal was addressed.

And when that record is made so clear and all of it is removed from the jury so that they are blind to the proof of another man's guilt, how can that be due process of justice . . . ?

I respectfully request not only that this case warrants a reversal, but even if Your Honors examine the circumstantial evidence perhaps a dismissal of the indictment as inadequate proof in any event.

Seated in the second row of the crowded courtroom were Gold's parents. Our specific arguments might as well have been spoken in Latin so far as they were concerned, but the occasion was awesome to them. They knew very well from the first tense moment when the five judges emerged from a velvet drape in back of the judicial bench that the whole occasion was to review their son's conviction for murder; that the very apparatus for justice contrasted with their knowledge of crude, cruel condemnations in tyrannies, where political considerations determined the result. There may have flashed back in their minds the Nazi salute that substituted military power for justice—a military power that they knew intimately sent innocents, of all ages, to die in its gas chambers.

And if they did not understand the special rules of law debated by counsel, they nevertheless were attuned to the atmosphere of an attentive hearing of their designated champion by the judges, and that it might vindicate their son.

So when the presiding judge, Justice Speziale, announced that the hearing had ended and all stood again as the judges departed, the Golds were taut. I approached. They embraced me once more with tears, again acting not as if we had merely made progress but had already won. "Murray will be freed," they told me, usurping the judges' right to decide.

Murray Gold's fate was now in the minds of the five supreme court justices of Connecticut.

I had not yet met Murray Gold and so I wrote to him on December 28, 1979, at his prison cell in Somers:

My dear Murray Gold:

I had intended to visit you before the argument in the highest court of Connecticut. However, as I was retained by your dear parents a very short time before the argument, I was unable to make the trip. In the two weeks I had to prepare for the appeal, it was necessary to spend every available moment to absorb some 6,000 pages of the trial record, voluminous briefs and conferences with Mr. [Timothy] Moynahan. I assigned special research tasks to four associates in my office, who worked with me into the early hours of the morning time and again. I set this forth to indicate that no effort was spared to reverse the guilty verdict. I accepted this task because I believed in your innocence, and that a terrible injustice had occurred.

. . . What tipped the balance in favor of undertaking your appeal was your parents. I could not resist their anguish and their implored entreaties.

I have postponed writing to you so that I could send you the Court's stenographic minutes of the argument. The transcript was received today and I enclose a copy. Now you will be able to evaluate the effort realistically. It should give you hope. All who attended the argument were optimistic, and I share that feeling.

Nonetheless, as I know you must realize, the problem to overcome is not merely factual. There is a profound legal rule which prevails in Connecticut and in many other states. We are attempting to change this rule. It provides that third party hearsay admission will not be admitted into evidence. That is why the evidence about Bruce Sanford, his confession of the murders for which you were convicted, and his suicide were never heard by the jury.

It is an archaic rule, but in certain circumstances it makes sense. If, for example, a Mafia criminal was tried for murder and he produced his cronies to testify that they had heard someone else confess to the crime, such hearsay confession would make it difficult to prove any defendant guilty beyond a reasonable doubt. The prosecutor could not cross-examine the person who had supposedly confessed because he was dead or missing.

In your case, the people who heard Sanford confess were his friends, not yours. They did not know you. They had no motive to lie in order to save you. Indeed, they were condemning their own friend. I leave the rest of the contentions to the briefs and to the transcript of my argument.

I referred to this legal matter here briefly in order to indicate that the highest court may have to change a rule of law existing in the State of Connecticut since the 19th century. Unless the Court decides in your favor on other grounds, a reversal of your conviction will have wide-spread impact on the law in Connecticut, and there may be a long delay before we receive a decision from the five appellate judges.

I hope to visit you and give you added encouragement, but in the immediate future my engagements will take me to Washington and California, and I do not know whether I will be able to see you. So for the present I depend on this letter, the enclosed copy of the minutes of the argument and your loving parents' ministrations to carry you through the ordeal.

Recently, I was invited to light the largest Menorah in the world at 59th Street, opposite the Plaza Hotel in New York City. I was lifted by a huge derrick to light the Chanukkah candle. It commemorates the heroic fight for freedom. As I lit the Menorah I thought of the fifty American hostages in Iran. I also thought of you.

I hope 1980 will be a Happy New Year for you because it will mark your freedom too.

Sincerely yours,
Louis Nizer

13

THE DECISION

WE ALL SETTLED down impatiently to wait for the Supreme Court's decision. We knew that it would take weeks before they would resolve the matter and reduce their opinion to writing, but after a few weeks we called the clerk of the court almost daily to inquire whether a decision had been filed. There was none. Then, exactly six months later, my managing attorney called me breathlessly:

"There's a decision in the Gold case!"

"Just look at the last page," I told him. "Is it favorable?"

He answered immediately: "Mr. Nizer, you've won! The conviction is reversed. A new trial has been ordered . . . It is a long opinion."

Our managing attorney was no longer on the phone. The young man had already learned the ropes. He announced, "You have won!" If the case went the other way he would probably have announced, "Gold has lost."

My associates had already arranged to obtain a copy of the thirty-two-page opinion.

The news of victory traveled faster than telephones could carry it. Within minutes the decision became public and then a new momentum set in, fed by television, radio and newspapers. Many who heard it joined the ranks of communicators. Magically, the news acquired ten-league boots as it spread everywhere.

But I realized the decision might not have penetrated prison walls and so I sent the following telegram to Somers, Connecticut, and congratulated Murray Gold:

> THE HIGHEST COURT HAS JUST REVERSED YOUR CONVICTION. IT HAS ORDERED A NEW TRIAL, BUT I HOPE THERE WILL BE NONE. CONGRATULATIONS!
> LOUIS NIZER

I sent a second telegram to Warden Robinson of Somers prison to convey the news to Gold.

The parents were ecstatic, as if they knew it all along. Kunstler called to express his delight.

Oddly, there was not a word from Murray Gold.

Restraints on judicial power are embodied in a valuable tradition: Judges do not merely render a decision, they cite their reasons for it. This, in turn, requires a full statement of the facts. Then, on the foundation of the facts, there is an analysis of the principles of law that apply to them, which gives an opportunity for higher courts and scholars to find any flaw in the facts or in the principles of law that may vary as the facts do.

In the process we arrive at one of the highest functions of the law: a keen examination of the facts that may change an applicable rule. That is why all the new miraculous data machines, Lexis, Westlaw, which spit forth guiding rules of law without taking into consideration the differences in the factual base, cannot be relied on. The analytic process that weighs a difference of facts may require a change in the applicable rules. The lawyer needs to be a legal philosopher who fashions or reshapes the rule to create equity. If he fails to do so, the process may bring him out at the wrong end of the conclusion.

The five Supreme Court Justices of Connecticut—Cotter,

Loiselle, Bogdanski, Speziale and Peters—lived up to these rather lofty precepts in their written opinion.

First, they ruled out robbery: "In a pair of blue trousers hanging over a chair in the Pasternak master bedroom $1,174 was found. There was no evidence of robbery or theft. All moneys and valuables were intact and the house was not ransacked."

Then they reviewed the evidence, or lack of it, of fingerprints; the testimony of Patricia Morrison, a friend of Sanford for twenty years, of his intentions and confession, which was not heard by the jury; the testimonies of Bourassa and Yashenko; and the testimony of Dorothy Crocco, one of the two witnesses who had seen a man running from the murder scene, "his long hair flowing in the wind," and who, when shown a photograph of Gold, confirmed that it was not Gold.

The opinion then foretold its vehement conclusion:

> The trial court ruled inadmissible the testimony in connection with the alleged confessions . . . of one Bruce Sanford, and thus excluded in toto the evidence set forth above.

Finally there was a judicial trumpet-sound—"Thus none of the testimony specifically relating to Sanford was heard by the jury." The five judges concluded that Gold had been deprived of due process of law to defend himself.

And then came the magical words of freedom and exculpation:

> This Court now rules that a statement against penal interest is one which at the time it is made so far tends to subject the declarant to criminal liability that a reasonable person in the declarant's position would not have made the statement unless he or she believed it to be true. . . . We conclude that the trial Court abused its discretion. We find error and order a new trial.

The chief judge usually designates one of the judges to write the opinion of the court. In their conferences they learn of dissenting views and if there is disagreement the minority has the privilege of stating its view after the majority opinion has been set forth. So, as is shown in hundreds of cases, the law is not a scientific inevitability. The best trained minds may differ.

I believe the reason we have so many dissents in complex philosophical precepts is that our backgrounds fashion different views of governing principles. Every object looks different, depending on the view from which it is seen. It even happens that a unanimous decision will in later years be reversed by the same court. Experience sometimes teaches us things we did not want to know.

Dissenting opinions are not always collegial. In spirit, judges tend to have strong views and when they are in the minority they often criticize their brethren mercilessly.

In the Gold case, though, the court was unanimous.

So after six years of struggle, throughout two lengthy trials and an appeal, Gold's conviction had been unanimously erased. It was doubtful, we felt, that the prosecutor would try him again. Under the circumstances it was in McDonald's discretion whether to drop the matter, but while waiting for him to decide I wanted Murray Gold out of jail. He had already been confined for five years awaiting the trials and appeal.

Of course I had invited Gold's parents to come to my office to receive a full report of their victory. They expressed their elation with yet more tears. When they recovered they asked when Murray would be free. I told them that I would make a motion to reduce bail so that they might be able to raise the money and free him. If this could be done I intended to obtain an order for his immediate release and go to the prison and be there for the great event.

14

GOING HOME

MURRAY GOLD WAS still under a heavy bail of $100,000. I made an application before Judge Roman Lexton to reduce the bail to an amount within the capacity of his father, Meyer Gold, to pay. Once more the Golds attended the hearing. The judge listened to my recital of the history of the case, the trials, the resolution and the Sanford story. He observed the suffering of Gold's parents, white with anxiety, faces registering painful expectancy. The judge was a sensitive man and apparently felt that there had been enough anguish and no real establishment of guilt. The prosecutor argued against any bail reduction. When the arguments were over, Judge Lexton did more than reduce the bail—he eliminated it. More than that, he gave his reaction to the case:

> . . . it seems more relevant on the motion to dismiss the case rather than to reduce the bond, based on the fact that you had a hung jury, conviction that was set aside by the supreme court by reason of the fact that evidence which was introduced in the first trial was not introduced in the second, thereby resulting in a conviction; that the presumption of possible conviction on a third trial is very weak. We have a man incarcerated now for five years when the

probability of conviction is certainly doubtful at this point. The bond serves primarily to insure the appearance of the defendant in court. It would seem to me Mr. Gold has every bit of motivation not to run, but to stay because his chances of prevailing at this point appear to be in his favor.

So not only had we reversed a conviction of murder in the first degree and eliminated bail so that Gold could be released immediately, now we had the comment of a distinguished judge that it was unlikely there would be another trial, and that Gold had no reason to flee the jurisdiction. What could be a better omen?

At this point the case began to take another turn—one which carried us beyond the ordinary realm of the account of a crime committed and into the realm of the mind of a man, and thereby into the unfathomable.

My eagerness to see this man freed, to see justice done, impelled me into the next phase. As soon as the order could be prepared and signed by Judge Lexton we could take Gold out of jail. I was determined not to let any time go by so I drafted the authority for release by hand and persuaded the clerk to accept the informal documents in order that not one hour of freedom for Gold would be lost. I was ushered into a prison cell at the holding area of Hartford jail, where Gold had been brought from Somers. The guards who had come with him from Somers were standing outside of the cell, and by special permission I was admitted to this section.

I was surprised by my first view of Murray Gold. He was somewhat older than I had thought, well-dressed in a tan suit and a nice collar and tie, having shed his institutional clothes on learning that he was to be a free man. The saying that "clothes make a man" is particularly true if the contrast is between prison garb and a civilian suit. A change of style from lateral to pin stripes can be the greatest sartorial improvement known to man. Gold now looked like the graduate engineer he once was and the stockbroker he later became. His hair was gray on the sides, he was

Murray Gold. (*Sketch by the author*)

slightly balding, he had a pleasant face and a gracious smile. He was wearing eyeglasses and was rotund rather than gaunt from his five years in jail. He appeared to be somewhat withdrawn; certainly not effusive. I congratulated him warmly, and in a subdued voice he said, "Thank you." I asked if he had received my telegram advising him of the favorable decision in the Supreme Court of Connecticut.

In a quiet flat tone he replied slowly: "It's nice to get a telegram."

I said: "We're going home."

He looked surprised and said, "When?"

"Now. Your mother and father are outside in my car. You will join them and we'll drive to New York. Pack whatever things you want to take with you."

As he gathered a few personal articles, slowly, as if unsure about what was happening, I looked around at the dismal scene. Everything was cramped, a cot, a toilet and a chair. The darkness seemed to get the better of the electric bulb that hung from the peeling ceiling. How could anyone be confined in a place like this for five years without wishing at times he was dead?

I tried to draw him out slowly.

"How were conditions in the jail?"

"Very small, uncomfortable cells."

"How was the food?"

"Breakfast was good, enjoyed it. The rest of the food is only edible".

Did he have a radio and television? "Yes," and it gave him great comfort. I asked him if he liked to watch sports on television. "I used to like baseball, but now they slide to second base when they're only halfway to the base and slide right into the bag."

I shifted again and praised his mother and father, leading up to the question . . . "Did you get along with them well?"

He thought for a long while and then said in that same soft voice, head hanging a little low, "There are divergencies. They come from a different world, and there is a gap when you are brought up and graduate from college as an engineer and later you are a broker and they still live in an atmosphere . . ."

It was an awkward, surprising but candid admission that his relationship with his parents was strained.

Then, slowly, we walked out into the corridors and finally past the guard's office into the sunlit street. He blinked and walked to my parked car. His parents had gotten out, and when they saw him they uttered an exultant cry of welcome. He stood motionless. They covered him with kisses and hugs that he stiffly received. He squinted at the sun, as if it were an unfriendly intruder.

I put Murray in the middle of the back seat, and his mother and father on either side of him. I sat next to the driver. My purpose was to give Murray and his parents a chance to chat, to get reacquainted after years of separation.

I doubt that Murray spoke fifty words during the two-and-one-half-hour trip from Waterbury to my office. On the other hand his father and mother were so ecstatic throughout the entire trip they couldn't contain themselves. Every time I looked back his mother would put her two palms together in a prayerful motion of gratitude, and his father talked perhaps too much about his appreciation of my effort. His mother, I was sure, must have been wondering why Murray was silent. Why no exuberance—not even a smile? The weather was glorious, but inside that car it was somber and cloudy. The mood was as if we were driving to jail rather than from it, to freedom.

I kept an ear open for what I hoped would be some bit of affectionate exchange between son and parents. Not a word from Murray.

I made another attempt at conversation. "Murray," I said, "everything around you celebrates your freedom. Doesn't it feel glorious?"

No answer. It was easier to free a man from the government's prison than to free him from himself.

A whimsical thought crossed my mind and I had to suppress a smile. It was an anecdote of the husband and wife quarreling while driving, and then stubbornly being silent for the next fifty miles. The husband sees a mule. He breaks his silence.

"A relative of yours?" he asks his wife.

"Yes, by marriage," she replies.

Once out, Gold needed his own home after five years of churning about in a locked cell with no privacy. Instead of doors there had been locked gates through which anyone could peer, no matter how personal the inmate's activities. Gold's parents understood his yearning for real freedom. They did not suggest that he live with them. They helped him to lease his own apartment on Union Street, in Flushing, New York, and paid his rent.

Murray now proceeded to furnish his apartment. He had the walls painted such a heavy gray that they looked black. He bought French-style furniture of the lightest pink. The startling contrast of the dark walls and almost white furniture must somehow have symbolized, or crystallized, the tragedy of his past and his hope for the future. At least now he could feel his freedom was real.

He immediately had letterheads printed with his name, address and telephone number to give further impact to the new-found normalcy of his life . . . He was no longer a number among criminals—he was a name and number in a community.

We soon learned, though, that normalcy in Murray Gold's case would not come so easily. The scars began to show in seemingly small but revealing ways. When the furniture arrived he claimed that it was different from what he had ordered. He instituted a suit *pro se*, which meant that he was acting as his own lawyer. He apparently enjoyed representing himself, until he realized that ignorance of legal procedure was not helpful to his purpose and he came to me for help. One of my partners took over, and managed to resolve the dispute to Gold's satisfaction.

It was only the calm before the storm.

15

THE WIG

THE OPINION AND victory in the Connecticut Supreme Court gave us high hopes that the prosecutor would drop the case, which he had the power to do. True, the reversal was accompanied by the granting of a new trial, but it was in his discretion to abandon the matter. This has often been done where the prospect of a successful prosecution is dim. Here, the prosecutor had suffered a hung jury in the first trial. Now the brilliant analysis of the supreme court indicated that the testimony about Sanford had to be admitted into evidence. How could a jury with such evidence before it find beyond a reasonable doubt that Gold was the killer? Since Sanford, by suicide, had imposed a death sentence on himself, there was no need to pursue the matter further and, in addition, Judge Lexton had eliminated bail, stating flatly that he saw almost no probability of a successful prosecution. So a continued attempt against Gold by the prosecutor did not appear likely. Under less compelling circumstances, prosecutors had exercised their discretion to abandon further attempts where two trials have failed to convict.

We had underestimated McDonald. These developments in Gold's favor did not turn the prosecutor away from Gold but rather had induced him to try a new attack.

On June 6, 1980, shortly *after midnight* we received notice that in the morning, at 9:00 A.M., Sanford's grave would be opened.

An inspection was to be made of his feet. The purpose was to establish that Sanford's feet and heels were too small to have made the Cat's Paw imprints on the bloody floor. We were advised that a podiatric expert and an anthropologist would be present for the state to support this claim.

We protested the inadequate notice given.

I wrote a letter to McDonald:

My dear Frank McDonald:

A short while ago your office informed Mr. Moynahan that you intended to exhume the body of Bruce Sanford . . . Although we inquired, no indication of the purpose of such an investigatory exhumation was given.

Then, suddenly after midnight . . . on June 5th, County Detective James Foley telephoned Mr. Moynahan to tell him that Sanford's body would be exhumed at 9:00 A.M. that very morning. For the first time Mr. Moynahan was told that the examination involved the measurement of Sanford's feet, and that we would need a podiatrist as our expert.

Mr. Moynahan protested that we had no opportunity to engage a doctor or photographer between midnight and 9:00 A.M. that morning, but to no avail. While a Dr. Gunn and Dr. Robbins were there on behalf of the State . . . we had no expert or opportunity to test the procedures.

Furthermore, the occasion was publicized, obviously by your office. Two television stations were represented; reporters were there. . . . Also, your representatives spoke to reporters about Mr. Gold's background . . . Although irrelevant and inadmissible, such spreading of "stories" is highly prejudicial, particularly if there is to be a third trial.

We protest all of these happenings. . . . You have been fair enough to concede that Gold (in contrast to Sanford) had no motive to commit this crime, and that only circumstantial evidence could be offered against Gold . . .

In this context, I'm sure you recognize your duty to protect the innocent as well as to convict the guilty . . .

You may be endangering the State's interest by prosecutorial fanaticism . . .

An able prosecutor can only achieve the high standards of his duty if he is not blinded by prosecutorial zeal, and acts to right a wrong, particularly as grievous as this.

I hope you will give this earnest thought . . .

Our protest was to no avail. Photographers and newspaper representatives would be on hand. We were told that we could bring our own podiatrist. We arranged for Tim Moynahan to appear for us and give us a report so that we could try to meet this surprise attack. The theory of one of the state's experts, Louise Robbins, was that since Sanford had small feet, his heels therefore were also small and presumably could not have registered the Cat's Paw marks on the floor. So clearly, the prosecutor had decided to absolve Sanford.

Even before the investigation proceeded this theory seemed to us to be forced and false. So many policemen and cameramen had trampled over the ground that even if Sanford's imprint was not the same size, it would not eliminate his guilt. His confession and flight could not be ignored. The prosecutor's other expert, a Dr. Gunn, a podiatrist, was seeking to establish that X-rays taken of Sanford's feet during the exhumation would prove that he suffered from Moreton's syndrome, a condition in which spurs form on the heels of the foot and cause the sufferer to walk with feet pointed outward. However, we knew that the examination of his heels five years after burial could not yield any meaningful result.

In the early light of the morning, the entire scene of Sanford's body being exhumed was as macabre as Sanford's life.

The earth was shoveled away and the casket that had rested underneath it was slowly hoisted to the surface and opened.

What came to view were the ghastly remains of a decayed face. Red pools of fluid substituted for eyes, nose and mouth, forming a hideous mask. But that was not the real revelation. Nor were his feet.

The horror was heightened by a long-haired, brown woman's wig covering Sanford's head and falling down his shoulders.

Photographs taken of the horror scene depicted not only the deterioration of the human flesh but the preservation of the wig, which covered the rotting scalp. The prosecutor and his experts had come to examine Sanford's feet, but instead, what they found was this wig on Sanford's head—evidence supporting Gold's innocence. For the scene brought back the testimony of the women who were walking on Fern Street on the night of the murders and reported a man running from the direction of the murder scene, his long hair waving in the wind, who had almost bowled them over. Their testimony had appeared to eliminate the bald Sanford as the killer. Now, with the macabre evidence raised from the grave, the description fit Sanford perfectly.

Sanford's criminal friends had reported that he often wore a

The hasty exhumation of Sanford. (*Photo by Tom Kabelka*)

wig during his criminal acts. It was an effective disguise that concealed his glistening scalp.

When Bourassa was asked by Kunstler in the first trial to describe Sanford's physical appearance, Bourassa answered:

Q: . . . Can you describe [Bruce Sanford] to the jury?
A: Yes. He was about six foot, six one, muscular, a little dark skinned, like he had a tan all the time. He was bald but he used to wear a wig frequently so, you know, it wouldn't show he was really bald . . .
Q: What kind of wig was it?
A: It was a woman's wig, a dark color. I believe it was a dark color brown, but I'm not one hundred percent sure.

His mother, Lillian Sanford, considered the wig he wore at times as a disguise to deceive the Devil, and therefore a return to virtue. So it was she who had placed the wig on his head at burial, to soften his face and make him less attractive to the Devil he had served in life.

The irony of the whole incident was that the testimony of the two women who had actually identified Sanford fleeing from the murder scene was discounted because it described his long hair "waving in the wind," which seemed to contradict Sanford's shiny, bald scalp. But Sanford's exhumation, five years after his burial—which was to provide evidence of Sanford's innocence by examining his feet—only confirmed his guilt. It was, of course, the wig that was flowing in the wind, and tied him to his flight from the murder scene. To make the incident even more bizarre, was the fact that Sanford's heels were so eroded that they provided no meaningful evidence. But his long-haired wig had resisted the corruption of time and constituted preserved evidence against him. Sanford, the Satanist, might well have smiled at the deviltry of it all.

Sanford, an avowed devil worshipper, no doubt believed that the Devil in his cunning would betray those most loyal to him. Such was his devilishly perverse standard. So had Sanford been alive he might well have enjoyed the shock to the prosecutor, who

The satanist—as rarely seen: with hair. Or was it a wig?

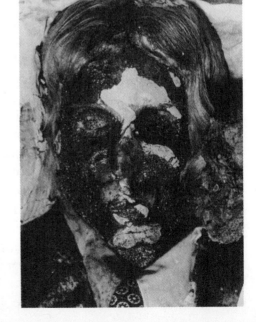

Unexpected evidence from the grave: "The ghastly remains of a decayed face"— wearing a wig.

in searching for evidence of Sanford's innocence by examining his feet only confirmed his guilt by exposing his head.

Still, it was necessary to advise our clients immediately that our hope to avoid a third trial was gone. It was obvious that the prosecutor was preparing for a new campaign. So, on July 23, 1980, I wrote to Gold's father:

My dear Meyer Gold:

First, let me review the background of your present plea that I continue to represent Murray in the pending proceedings.

1. As I originally set forth very explicitly in our retainer letter, my representation was limited to arguing the appeal. Whatever the outcome of that appeal, my duties ended.

2. When the conviction of Murray was reversed, I could have under our retainer simply congratulated you and him, and accepted your warm expression of gratitude, which I have received in abundance, and considered my representation ended. I felt, however, that if the prosecutor did not know that my duties ended, it might be helpful in persuading him not to proceed with the third trial. Therefore, I did not announce that my representation had ended, since it was confidential between us. I also felt that my presence might assist in reducing Murray's bail and get him out of jail, while we awaited the possibility that the prosecutor would not press the matter to a third trial. I, therefore, made the motion before Judge Roman Lexton, and argued for Murray's complete freedom. Here, too, the result was perfect . . .

3. Our hopes that the prosecutor would decide not to try the case a third time received a shock when the prosecutor gave notice to us that he was exhuming the body of Sanford and that an X-ray specialist and an anthropologist would be present at the grave to make certain examinations. I wrote a strong letter of protest to Mr. McDonald concerning that matter, a copy of which you have. So it became clear that the prosecutor was preparing what he hoped would be new evidence for a third trial.

Later his determination not to drop the matter was evidenced by an application to the U.S. Supreme Court to review the decision of the highest court of Connecticut which had reversed Murray's conviction. This application for permission to appeal is still pend ing. My judgment is that the Supreme Court of the United States will deny it. Nevertheless, Mr. McDonald appears determined to proceed to a third trial.

4. In the meantime, I have gathered some data from Mr. Moynahan of other murders in the vicinity and have met with James Conway, an investigator, at his request. I am meeting with Mr. Moynahan tomorrow. All this is for the purpose of making a motion in the Connecticut Court to obtain the reports of experts who examined Sanford's body and for other relief.

Sincerely yours,
LOUIS NIZER

BOOK
V

16

A Supreme Appeal

No adversary is more dangerous than one who won't quit.

So we had received another shock. We were served with a twenty-eight-page printed brief addressed to the Supreme Court of the United States to accept jurisdiction and decide the legal question involved in the "hearsay rule." Such an application is called a "Petition for Certiorari." The word *certiorari* derives from the Latin, "to inform" or "to be informed of," and was applied under early English common law to an order of a superior court to call up the records of an inferior court in order to determine whether there were any errors or irregularities in them. Unless there is a profound federal rule involved or conflict among federal district courts, the Supreme Court will not accept jurisdiction. Which means that the thousands of litigants who would like to take their losing cases to the United States Supreme Court must first apply to the court for permission to do so, and that application is the petition for certiorari.

Why this closed door, with few exceptions, to the highest court? The reason is that otherwise the nine Supreme Court justices would be inundated by tens of thousands of cases, and the Court would collapse under a burden that nine judges and their

Judge Roman Lexton, who
did more than reduce
Gold's bail.

clerks could not bear. As it is, the Court is flooded with Petitions for Certiorari. If four of the nine judges approve the petition the case is put on the calendar for oral argument and briefing. In 1988, for example, only 1.4% of the petitions were granted.

Prosecutor McDonald's printed petition set forth a conflict of law concerning the exception to the hearsay rule. It argued that the exception we had depended upon to get the admission of Sanford before the jury was wrong. There were conflicting state rules even about the interpretation of trustworthiness, and this created a conflict of law that the Supreme Court should settle. The petition was scholarly and written with considerable eloquence and force.

We had only thirty days to file a brief in opposition. In that short period we analyzed and answered the cases cited in the petition. We demonstrated in our seventeen-page answering argument that there was no federal question involved. Nor was there any constitutional question presented. We were dealing with the law of the State of Connecticut. Therefore, we contended, the Supreme Court should not accept jurisdiction.

To keep Gold informed, I wrote him on September 16, 1980:

My dear Murray:

We recently sent you the brief and petition for certiorari filed by the State of Connecticut with the Supreme Court of the United States. This is the procedure by which the State asks the highest court of the land to review the determination of the Connecticut Supreme Court in your favor. Unless permission is given, the matter may not be brought to the U.S. Supreme Court.

I now send you our brief which we filed on September 12, 1980, on your behalf in opposition to the request made by the State of Connecticut. I will, of course, advise you as soon as the Court renders its decision on the petition for certiorari. We are still confident that the highest court will not grant the State of Connecticut's request for review.

Even if the Supreme Court permitted a review, this would not constitute a decision on the merits. It would merely mean that counsel for the State of Connecticut and I, representing you, would argue the case orally and file briefs in the Supreme Court of the United States to determine whether the State of Connecticut was right in reversing the verdict against you.

On the other hand, even though the petition may be denied, it will not preclude the Connecticut prosecutor from proceeding to a third trial. That is something we will still make efforts to prevent.

I hope to see you soon to learn how you are getting on. We all send you warm regards.

Sincerely yours,
LOUIS NIZER

On October 20, 1980, the Supreme Court of the United States denied certiorari. We had beaten off another attack, and I so informed Gold and his parents.

Murray responded on October 25, 1980 (the misspellings are in the original):

Dear Mr. Neizer:

I want to take this opportunity to thank you for the work which you have doune in my behalf. I thank you specifically for the document which you filed at the United States Supreme Court. It was adequate for them to rule in my favor. I am very pleased that the United States Supreme Court has ruled that the Connecticut's Supreme Court ruling which overturned the illegal conviction is valid.

I am in the process of getting reestablished. I recently moved into an apartment in Flushing, New York which I am currently furnishing. I hope to develop new friendships and become established in either engineering related work or stock market research work. Thereafter I hope to get married.

But, he added:

I am disappointed that after the favorable United States Supreme Court decision you did not speak to me personally, though four days after I received the news your secretary caled me on the telephone and read to me the letter which you wrote to me.

MacDonald though nasty and unfair should drop the charge voluntarily. If he does not, he may be persuaded because after all these years and two lengthy trials the result from the court is that I am not guilty.

Sincerely,
MURRAY R. GOLD

17

"FIRED"

MURRAY GOLD, HAVING been relieved of bail, was, it developed, not exactly basking in the favorable decision of the highest court of Connecticut and the Supreme Court of the United States.

It was about this time that he visited my office. The happy news of the decision by the U.S. Supreme Court had recently come down, like an exclamation point at the end of a paragraph of favorable developments. They all spelled freedom.

So when Murray entered my office I rose to greet him, expecting him to be in a cheerful mood. Not so. He was solemn, actually sullen. I pretended not to notice. I talked about the denial of certiorari and its significance. His face darkened.

"Why didn't you show me the paper you filed?" he asked.

"Murray," I answered, "I did send you our answer, a couple of days after it was filed, and you responded very graciously after we had received the favorable decision. In any event the answer to a petition for certiorari is exclusively a legal analysis of the cases cited by the prosecutor and a demonstration that no federal or constitutional question is involved. A layman can't contribute to such a pure legal analysis."

Now his complexion grew even darker and seemed to make his eyes glow angrily.

"You had no right to file a paper without my reading and approving it," he said.

I tried to deflect his belligerence.

"I don't know what we are arguing about. The petition was denied, as we requested. You won. How could your reading of our brief [which had to be prepared and printed within thirty days] have made the decision more perfect?"

In slow, emphatic cadence, his eyes ablaze, he said, "You had no right to file anything until I approved. I don't want you as my lawyer. You're fired!"

He stormed out of my office.

My secretaries, alarmed, rushed into my office to ask what had happened. I said, "Calm down, ladies. Gold is innocent of any violence in the past or today. He is a victim of it. However, I must admit that if ingratitude were a crime he'd be guilty in the first degree. *But* let's remember . . . Murray Gold has been confined for five years in jail for a crime someone else committed. It's surely understandable that he would be unreasonable and cantankerous."

Gold's parents now came to see me, saying they were devastated by their son's dismissing me. Almost all of their prayerful hopes for their son's vindication and freedom had been realized. If Murray was left to his own devices, they feared real disaster. They had tried to make light of Murray's instability which had taken him to the psychiatric institutions on two occasions almost a year before the trials. But his discharging me was pretty clearly continued evidence of his neurotic behavior. They asked me "to understand" the strain he was under and "forgive him."

I tried to assure them on both those counts, but told them in view of his frame of mind I just could not impose myself on Murray. They had better retain another attorney. I also assured them that I would cooperate with my successor, give him my notes, briefs and personal review of the facts and law. But to impose me on Murray, even at their request, would only upset him more and turn him more angrily against them.

They left disconsolately. What a contrast it was between Murray's perversely angry exit and his parents' weeping departure. I confess that at the moment all the understanding in the world couldn't offset my feeling of being a little put out.

18

THE THIRD VICTIM

IN BITTER LITIGATIONS it is difficult to settle. Any overture to end a dispute may encourage the opponent to accelerate the attack in the hope of total victory over a disheartened adversary.

So lawyers engaged in vigorous litigation find it difficult to extricate themselves by suggesting settlement. No matter how disguised, any overture to "talk it over and stop hostilities" may be misunderstood as weakness, and the opponent encouraged to press harder. Settlement hints must be diplomatically surrounded with assurances that the client is ready to fight to the end but that the attorney would be willing to explore a peaceful resolution if it were not misinterpreted as weakness.

In a criminal case, "settlement" is far more difficult and under certain circumstances actually forbidden by law. So, for example, the withdrawal of a criminal complaint in consideration of a payment, even if made in a pending civil action, is a crime called "compounding a felony." The public has a basic interest in the pursuit of a criminal violation that may not be bought off by paying money to the complainant to withdraw his criminal charge.

Yet everything unexpected happened in the Gold case. The

prosecutor did face reality. The vigorous clear reversal by the state's supreme court and the cumulative growing testimony of Sanford's guilt dimmed the probability of a conviction. Under these circumstances the prosecutor made an offer to "settle." He would exercise his discretion not to begin a third trial, provided certain terms were met to protect the public interest. He suggested that if Gold would submit himself to treatment by a psychiatrist for one year, agree not to enter the State of Connecticut, and plead guilty to a lesser charge, he would be freed immediately on the basis of the time he had already served—more than five years.

It was not difficult to interpret the background of this offer.

But how could Gold plead to a lesser degree of a murder charge while contending that he was entirely innocent? The law provides a remedy for such a dilemma. It permits a defendant to enter the Alford plea, which allows him to assert his innocence while pleading guilty for the sake of resolving the problem. Murray Gold could assert his innocence but, for the sake of disposing of the matter, plead guilty under the Alford rule.

Here was the best outcome of all for Gold. He was free, without bail. Now he could be guaranteed to remain free without being subjected to another trial, and not have to engage another lawyer.

I gave the good news to Gold.

The resolution never happened. Gold would not agree to psychiatric treatment for a year. The very word "psychiatry" infuriated him. To him it was equivalent to a charge of insanity.

He wrote on January 22, 1981:

Dear Mr. Nizer:

Yesterday during our telephone conversation when I asked what is the positive development that you have for me, you stated that I should get psychiatric treatments for about a year, then the psychiatrist's statement to McDonald will cause him not to prosecute me. I consider such a statement incoherent and absurd. As I told you on the phone I will get another attorney.

I hereby no longer give you any authority to represent me. Good Buy.

MURRAY R. GOLD

Gold was a graduate of New York University, an engineer who later became a stockbroker. Was there an explanation for his peculiar spelling, here and earlier? Yes. Those who suffer from paranoia lose their "cognitive" ability, which includes spelling. This thought disorder has been described by the noted psychiatrist Von Doramus in *Language and Thought in Schizophrenia* and has been given his name.

I responded on January 26, 1981:

My dear Murray:

I have received your letter of January 22, 1981, advising me that you do not wish us to represent you any longer. I accept your right to make such a decision. What I say from here on does not alter this conclusion. However, a few comments.

1. I am sending you copies of my letters to you dated September 4, 16, October 22 and November 20, which deal with our brief in the Supreme Court.

I never, in all these months, during those letters, heard from you orally or in writing protesting that you should have an input into this brief to the United States Supreme Court. Only in the last few days did you contend that you were deprived of a right to contribute to that brief. . . . You won in the Supreme Court. Would you have liked to resubmit it so that you could have an input? These matters, in the United States Supreme Court particularly, are extremely legalistic and are always prepared by counsel and then briefs are sent to the client, as it was in this case. Perhaps you will understand the matter better if we put it in medical terms. A doctor has performed surgery on you successfully. Then you accuse him of breaking his word because you wanted to give him advice as to how the surgery should be done. When you told me that you had read an article of law in an encyclopedia, as if this has qualified you in effect to become co-counsel, I was patient, but had to say to you, "I wish you would stop practicing law."

2. Far more important than all this is the question of a third trial. In order to understand the situation, you must first appreciate the problem. I am not sure you do, despite all our talks. Let me analyze it again.

The Supreme Court of Connecticut reversed your conviction on the ground that you had not received a fair trial. It did not dismiss the indictment. Therefore, the Prosecutor has the right, indeed he may consider it his duty, to try the case a third time, complying with the rules which the Supreme Court set down. His task in obtaining another conviction of you is far greater than it was before. The Sanford testimony must now be admitted. The Prosecutor's determination, however, to counteract, to whatever extent he can, the Sanford testimony was indicated by his exhumation of the body of Sanford, and having an anthropologist and another expert ready to overcome Sanford's guilt. He and his experts will claim that these studies will show that the footprints in the blood did not come from Sanford, and still claim, falsely, that they are yours, according to measurements of your shoes, etc. I do not for a moment think he can succeed, but it did reveal a firm intention on the part of the Prosecutor to proceed to a third trial. This would mean an ordeal of maybe two or three months of trial, since now there would be additional testimony on both sides concerning Sanford, as well as experts on both sides concerning the exhumation—all at enormous expense. Need I tell you the personal ordeal for you and your dearest which would be involved? Therefore, the objective, as I wrote you in the enclosed letters, at all times, was to find some way to persuade the Prosecutor to give up the third trial, and close the matter with honor to your reputation.

3. Only a short while before you called, and insisted on knowing what the "progress" was, which I had indicated to you in this connection, we learned that there was *a possibility*, that is all it was, that the Prosecutor might put his own conscience and duty to rest if we could work out a year of psychiatrist's consultations with you. I was delighted with this possibility, and was determined to visit Connecticut to see if I could advance the idea. Why was I delighted? Because it constituted a solution of the problem, namely, avoiding a third trial and clearing your reputation at the same time, because the indictment would be dropped. This I hoped would be achieved upon a condition of psychiatric consultation, which I felt would be no burden to you. Millions of people in all walks of life, executives, lawyers, doctors, consult psychiatrists and take treatments to relieve their emotional distress. I recommended this to you initially when you first got out of jail, because I

thought it would help you to adjust yourself to the stream of life after you were so unconscionably in jail for five years, and facing a much longer term. Even if it had nothing to do with avoiding a third trial, I would have recommended, and I believe I did, such visits with a psychiatrist. For you to call this solution, if we could reach it, "incoherent and absurd" shows a lack of comprehension of the magnitude of the problem and the magnificence of the solution, which would be to your benefit in any event. If we could succeed in such a resolution, you would avoid not only what I have outlined above, but another factor, which must not be ignored, namely, the risk, no matter how slight, of another unjust conviction. After all, have you not gone through such an experience? The Prosecutor admitted you had no motive, that you had a perfect record previously, and that there was only circumstantial evidence—and yet a jury of twelve unanimously and unjustly found you guilty.

I would consider the solution of a psychiatrist's treatment for a year, if it could be worked out, a very small premium for the insurance against such a risk—yet you call it "absurd and incoherent."

4. Finally, knowing the anguish and ordeal you have gone through, I do not want anything I have said above to offend your sensitivity. I stand, as I said in the first sentence of this letter, by your decision to terminate our representation. I wish you luck with your new counsel. I think a great injustice has been done you. That is what induced me to undertake your case in the first place, when the odds against a reversal were overwhelming. . . .

My warm regards,

Sincerely

LOUIS NIZER

So an opportunity to avoid a third trial; to walk out a free man and without the official mark of Cain on his brow, was forfeited. I reported to Gold's father:

My dear Meyer Gold:

I enclose copy of a letter I received today from Murray Gold. He is wrong about his facts, and besides, he does not understand. I have full sympathy for his confusion, but I must abide by his decision. I regret particularly that Mr. McDonald will get the comfort of knowing I am no longer on the scene, and that Murray will now be subjected to risks which I was trying desperately to avoid.

Murray's misunderstanding of events is a special injustice to himself, when one considers that the brief to the United States Supreme Court which he "wanted to contribute to" was successful, and he won.

As I told him on the telephone, we do not have clients participate in the preparation of legal briefs, particularly where they are as legalistic as this one, namely an objection to jurisdiction. This is a rule for all clients.

I enclose a copy of a letter I have sent to Murray.

I wish you and him well.

My warm regards,

Sincerely yours,
LOUIS NIZER

Murray Gold remained adamant. He was like a man parched and dying of thirst rejecting a cool glass of water. He wrote again, repeating his grievances, and ending his letter:

I now have to search for another attorney who will represent me more comprehensively. One who will defend my reputation and ease the attitude against me by speaking out about my innocence to the press, encourage me to speak to the press, and sue for lies printed about me in newspapers and magazines and stated on airways. One who will take issue with a Judge who did not allow my attorney to present the defense witnesses and statements fully before the court, resulting in an unfair trial. I hope that the new attorney will be successful in obtaining freedom for me permanently.

I responded on February 4th:

My dear Murray:

I have just received your letter dated January 31st. It is heartbreaking that we, who know that you are innocent, and have succeeded in freeing you from two unjust 25-year concurrent terms in jail and brought you into the sunlight where you belong, should be engaged in controversy with you instead of using our talents against the prosecutor. It is particularly tragic because what you write indicates a *misunderstanding.* Without attempting in the slightest to change your mind as to who shall represent you in the future, but simply to correct any misconceptions you have so as to persuade you not to injure your noble cause, I write the following. Please keep your mind and heart open.

First, concerning the possibility of preventing a third trial and clearing your name without that ordeal; it is too bad that the information you received on this came on the telephone and therefore might have innocently been misunderstood. Let me make it clear. My purpose was to have a psychiatrist of your choice and mine, and not one of the prosecutor's choosing, whom you would visit on and off over a period of about a year. I had in mind a friendly psychiatrist of high reputation who, I was sure, you would like. My hope was that if such an arrangement were made, and only with your approval, the prosecutor would agree *now* to drop the third trial, dismiss the indictment and clear your reputation. While I cannot say that I was sure he would do so, I had indications that such a negotiation would be successful. As I wrote to you before, important men and women who have suffered much less than you, have voluntarily sought assistance from a psychiatrist to give them comfort and calm. If I could reveal confidences, I would mention distinguished men in all walks of life who aided themselves by such visits. As I told you before, and as early as when you first came out from that gruesome imprisonment, such psychiatric assistance, if you consented to it, was well indicated. After all, you had suffered a terrible injustice—a five-year incarceration, although innocent, and that injustice alone was enough to be a burden which might warrant psychiatric help. When I combined this thought with the fact that it might induce the prosecutor to give up a third trial, it appealed to me even more. Had I had the chance to explain this to you in person in more detail, as I intended to, I would have emphasized the fact that only if you agreed to this plan, and we chose either a psychiatrist you recommended or agreed to one I introduced you to, would we proceed with the plan. On the other hand, while it was my duty to offer this possibility to you, if you had said "no" we would have dropped the whole psychiatrist idea and made other efforts to avoid a third trial. However, all of this was subject to your veto. I repeat—you would have the choice of acceptance or rejection.

Second, as to your statements about the brief which we filed in the U.S. Supreme Court, and your desire to have assertions of your innocence in it . . . we *did* assert fully your innocence in the brief despite the fact that the brief was based on jurisdictional grounds, which means that the Supreme Court had no authority to review the case decided by the state court. You have a copy of our brief and I quote from the following pages which show how carefully we set forth the facts of your innocence:

Page 2:
". . . The respondent, who has asserted his innocence throughout, has nonetheless served more than five years of this sentence."

Page 3:
". . . Respondent, a New York City stockbroker with an *unblemished prior record* . . .

. . . The prosecution conceded that it had no direct evidence of guilt and that its case was based exclusively on circumstantial evidence (T.3981). Thus, no eye-witness testimony placed respondent at the scene on the night of the crime; and no fingerprints, of the more than thirty prints found in the murder home, were those of respondent (T.1802). Moreover, the prosecution announced to the jury that it knew of no motive for Respondent Gold to have committed the crime (T.4002)."

Page 4:
"The defense sought to establish that another person, one Bruce Sanford, a man with a criminal record, and with the motive and opportunity to commit the crime, had in fact killed the Pasternaks. . . ."

Finally, let's not forget you won.

I now have been informed by Mr. [Tim] Moynahan that you have discharged him, too. Solely because of our heartfelt interest in your welfare, I cannot understand why you are denuding yourself of your successful legal army. Also, I am told that you are giving statements to the press and I can only advise you out of friendship and loyalty that this may be counterproductive with the prosecutor. If he learns that your legal defense team is no longer at your side, it can only encourage him in what is clearly now a vindictive effort on his part.

So, dear Murray, I hope you will weigh these facts carefully and in your own interest. I shall continue to hope fervently for your vindication and happy future.

Sincerely yours,
LOUIS NIZER

I wrote to his father, Meyer Gold, on the same day:

My dear Mr. Gold:

I enclose copy of a letter I received from Murray and a copy of my answer. I have also spoken with Mr. Moynahan. We agree, as I believe you do, that Murray's present conduct is contrary to his own best interests. We are doing everything we can to have him come to his senses so that he will not be victimized by his own rashness. I assure you that my heart goes out to both you and Mrs. Gold as much as it does to Murray.

I shall advise you of further developments. Please let me know if you hear anything.

My warm regards,

Sincerely yours,
LOUIS NIZER

It is said that it is the destiny of some men to live tragic lives. Meyer Gold had outraced the flames of Auschwitz that were about to devour his wife, and only son, and himself, having lost their daughter to those fires.

Meyer's odyssey to the United States, and the establishment of a home, and the education of Murray, though familiar in our times, were genuinely herculean achievements. True, a unique opportunity was open to Meyer Gold in our wonderful country and he had seized it, at the cost of interminable work but with rewards. Above all, there were the achievements of his son, Murray. To be sure, there were upsetting incidents. Murray's behavior was at times neurotic but he was treated psychiatrically, which is hardly a crime. He had regained his balance and married into the distinguished Pasternak family.

Then the devastating blow. Murder! From the first moment of accusation Meyer was tormented and tense. Thereafter, he devoted his life to proving his son innocent. When finally the courts freed Murray, there still was no letup of the pressure within his father.

Now Murray's arbitrary discharge of his attorneys had proved even to his father that there was something wrong with him mentally. Meyer grieved at the revelation.

Meyer Gold had suffered familiar humiliation long before the murder charge. It was the common experience of immigrant parents, who had expended their energy and resources educating their children, to discover that in the process they were alienated from them. The educated children were ashamed to submit their friends to parents with a foreign accent and background. The Yiddish Theatre was full of plays that used this theme. The experience was common to all immigrant groups; Italian, Polish, Russian and many others who strove hard to give their children a good education, children who then found themselves ashamed of their "ignorant" parents who spoke bad English.

Murray's moody silence on the ride home from jail to freedom was just one illustration of his inability to communicate with the "old world." So the parents' public embarrassment was enormously increased in private by what seemed an unappreciative son who gave them pain without apparent gratitude or affection.

Meyer's distress built as he became convinced that there was something vitally wrong with his son's judgment. He cried through many nights. On January 3, 1985, his heart gave out. He died suddenly, five days before his son would stand trial for the third time.

Meyer's trials were over, but he was, in more than one sense, the third victim of the Pasternak murders.

BOOK VI

19

THE THIRD TRIAL

A NEW DEVELOPMENT encouraged the prosecutor to try for a third time to convict Gold.

Bourassa, who had testified that he heard Sanford confess that he had killed the Pasternaks, reversed himself and told McDonald that he had lied.

(Although never presented at trial, he would claim in a letter to Victor Ferrante that he had been pressured into withdrawing his testimony while in jail for his own crimes. He charged that the prosecutor's office took advantage of his vulnerability by threatening him with dire consequences if he did not recant. Undoubtedly Ferrante and Kunstler felt that Bourassa's changing his mind would present a danger to the defense. They decided to let well enough alone. Bourassa's reversal had forfeited his credibility and would have made him too hazardous a witness.)

For his defense in the third trial, Murray had now engaged John Williams, a prominent and able Connecticut criminal attorney and a teacher at Yale Law School. He had a clear, strong voice, which together with his keen knowledge of law made him a formidable advocate.

Before the third trial began, Williams filed a series of charges

John A. Williams, prominent
and able criminal attorney,
with a clear, strong voice—and
an impossible client. (*Photo by
Gary Lewis*)

against the prosecutor, requesting a dismissal of the claims
against Gold. Some of the accusations were so daring that only
their responsible source, Williams, gave them credibility.

Williams pointed out that during the second trial of Gold, the
jury, in an unprecedented ruling in Connecticut's history, was
sequestered (locked up overnight in a hotel), and alleged that
"members of the jury were drinking alcoholic beverages, purchased by the bottle . . . [and that] such drinking was in direct
violation of an order of the trial court . . ." This is hardly the spirit
of justice one seeks to inculcate in jury deliberations.

Williams's motion further stated that "since the second trial
significant additional information has been discovered which
strongly supports Mr. Gold's innocence . . ." For example, George
Morrison, the husband of Patricia Morrison, testified in a bail-
reduction hearing that Sanford had also confessed to him that he
had killed the Pasternaks; that testimony was presented that "the
Sanford family" owned a car very similar to the one seen on the
scene of the crime, implying that Sanford ran to his car while

escaping after the murders. Even more startling was the accusation that the sewing kit taken from Gold's home by the police had been taken from the prosecutor's office by Peggy Gowlis, who bragged to Glorianna, "Look what I took." Although Gowlis later denied her statement, it appears very likely that the kit which was used by the prosecution to identify Gold with the pieces of plastic allegedly found at the murder scene was fraudulent since it was not the kit taken from Gold's home.

Williams also charged that instructions were given to a trooper to alter his sketch of the Pasternak premises and draw in a button that the trooper did not see when he first examined the murder scene; nor did the housemaid who testified.

Finally, Williams referred to the inflammatory summation by the prosecution in the second trial which prejudiced Gold and violated the rules of responsible argument. The rule is that incendiary language in a summation warrants reversal. It is based on the theory that emotions may be stirred but should not be demagogically inflammatory. So, for example, setting feelings ablaze by reference to race prejudice or homosexuality goes far beyond legitimate argument on the merits. The law requires a normal reading on the summation thermometer. When, instead, it is increased by prejudicial, hateful rhetoric, the appellate court will recognize and prohibit the feverish language and reverse.

Williams quoted the prosecutor's summation, which said that if the jury finds Gold not guilty ". . . you'll wake up screaming if you return a verdict of not guilty . . . because to do good to the bad . . . is to do evil to the good and makes you responsible, you, yes, you, for all the acts this man may subsequently commit, because you let him go free . . ."

The motion concludes with this plea:

"The prosecution's case against Mr. Gold has not improved with age, and the state has no new evidence . . . against Mr. Gold. As noted . . . Mr. Gold does have substantial additional evidence of his innocence . . . To further burden the defendant, the Judicial Department and the taxpayers with yet another trial . . . would constitute an abuse of discretion . . . This court has inherent authority to dismiss the case under such circumstances and the facts hereof cry out for such relief . . ."

On November 8, 1984, Judge Gill denied Williams's motion to dismiss without a hearing.

It was not long before Murray Gold was in conflict with John Williams. It began at the first step in the trial, when each lawyer is given the right to "challenge" a juror and excuse him from serving. If the juror reveals a prejudice, or knows any of the participants in the trial, such "challenges for cause" are a matter of right and unlimited in number. Each lawyer also has the right to a number of so-called peremptory challenges; these are based largely on his instincts rather than on any demonstrated partiality. He just doesn't believe the juror will be fair because of his background or his answers. He has a limited number of such challenges as granted by the judge.

A number of jurors were accepted by the defense who were highly questionable from a defendant's viewpoint. From an analysis of Williams's files I saw that he had wished to challenge certain jurors but Gold had interfered and insisted on having them sit. Time and again Williams's judgment concerning the selection or rejection of a juror was overruled by Gold. It was his emotional problem that was operating, his paranoia. He was suspicious of his own lawyer being in league with the prosecution! Gold "advised with his lawyer"—but what tragically self-destructive advice.

The question does arise whether the test of a defendant's competency is met when he continually clashes with his lawyer, who is, after all, trained to detect hidden prejudices. Surely that kind of advice and conduct, in which the client believes his lawyer is conspiring against him, is not the "cooperation" that the law requires.

Beyond all this, selecting a jury is an art as well as a legal exercise. Our views are conditioned by personal predilections. We are all the products of our environment. In a landlord and tenant controversy, counsel for the tenant obviously does not want any landlords on the jury—not because he believes all landlords are unfair but because their daily experience may make them automatically lean against a complaining tenant. A liberal Democrat is more likely to approve the Supreme Court decision permitting the burning of an American flag than a conservative Republican. People who work in police enforcement may very likely have an affinity with the prosecutor rather than with the accused. The lawyer's duty and expertise is to detect the probability of such a "prejudice," and the rule is: "If in doubt—reject." The stakes are too high to gamble on the impartiality of a juror whose background may condition him or her against the lawyer's client.

Judge Charles Gill presided over the trial with courtesy but did not lose his touch of firmness. Generously, at Williams's urging, he allowed forty peremptory challenges. Gold conferred with Williams concerning every selection.

Williams made notes of his quarrels with Gold concerning jury selection: "An excellent black woman whose husband was falsely arrested—defendant insists we remove her!" Conversely, when advised by Williams not to select certain jurors, Gold insisted they be taken. Williams's notes continue: "Picked because defendant strongly wants her!; Picked because defendant likes him!; Defendant insists!; Defendant insists over strong [JW[illiams] protests, etc."

Despite Williams's advice, Murray was adamant in his contradictory instructions to his lawyer, although at other times he appeared to be nodding off or asleep.

These challenges by Murray were of a piece with his discharge of the lawyers who had saved him and thereby inviting the prosecutor to try again.

After a week of this painful jury selection extraordinary measures were taken for security purposes. Five plainclothes detectives guarded the courtroom, and all spectators who entered the room were searched by a deputy sheriff with a hand-held metal detector. This tended to be prejudicial to the calm and confidence that should have prevailed in a courtroom, and certainly might have been prejudicial to the defendant, suddenly cast in the lurid light of gangsterism, despite the fact that we depend on the presiding judge when he instructs the jury to stress that atmospheric impressions from extreme precautions must not affect their judgment.

A further influence was at work.

Television had also arrived in the courtroom. A debate has raged as to whether it is a helpful extension of the public's interest or an interference with the judicial process. Naturally, the issue arose in this third high-voltage Gold trial. A large television camera was wheeled into the courtroom to record the testimonial excitement, but the whole trial was not to be televised. Television is a selective technique, the choice of pictures favoring the dramatic snippet rather than a comprehensive presentation. The danger of presenting an admission here and there, or omitting the confession or confusion of a witness, may distort the record and the course of the events.

Williams protested the presence of the television camera. He argued:

> . . . As your Honor knows, I feel very strongly that the news media have the right to cover this trial, but I feel even more strongly that we have a right not to have anything done or omitted in the course of that which might lead the jury to think that some things are more important than others and particularly in a television-dominated era in which people think nothing is real if it's not on TV.

After a lengthy argument by Williams, Judge Gill made his decision:

> COURT: . . . It should be stated that it was agreed that however technically the television cameras were set up that they should not be turned on and off; that the red light should not go on when a certain witness is testifying and turned off when another witness is testifying so as to indicate to the jurors which testimony is more important in the eyes of the news media. . . . I would charge the

jury both before the trial and after the trial on the significance of the cameras, vis-à-vis its presence or absence. . . . The court's ruling is that television cameras can be here whenever they see fit to bring it in here under the conditions previously imposed by the court, with the caveat that it should not be indicated one way or the other whether it's on or off for the jurors' observation.

Williams immediately took an exception to this ruling as constituting a denial of Gold's rights by allowing the trial to be subtly dominated by the television camera.

My own view is that the television camera should be barred from trials, but should be permitted when appeals are argued. The reason is that witnesses on the stand are disturbed enough by their surroundings not to have to bear the fear of a television camera sending their words, mistakes and grimaces to millions of people. A witness on the stand may for the first time in his life be facing an audience. Through the corner of his eye he sees his opponent's lawyer looking up, ready to pounce. His opponent may merely be sharpening his pencil, but the witness imagines he is preparing to knife and destroy him on cross-examination. To his left sit twelve jurors watching every movement of his face, the tight clasping of his hands. In front sits a stenographer recording any misstatement he may make, and on his left sits a judge in a black robe. The blood is rushing to his head, and it is a wonder he can state his name and address correctly. Must we add a television camera to make him conscious of the fact that any mistake or stutter will be seen and heard by an audience infinitely larger than the one in the courtroom? In short, the trial process is injured by adding the high-blood-pressure impact of the invader, television, otherwise welcomed in millions of homes.

On the other hand, in appellate argument there are no witnesses. The printed record of the trial minutes substitute for the live witness. This is the reason that appellate courts rarely overrule the jury's finding of the facts. The jury has had the opportunity to evaluate the witness' credibility by seeing him and his reactions to questions. The appellate court sees only the cold type of the record made when the witness testified.

Furthermore, lawyers arguing appeals are accustomed to their surroundings and are likely to be relatively unaffected by the impact of a television camera. While judges, too, may act up a little for the benefit of the camera, they are also accustomed to their task and are not likely to be unduly affected by its presence.

Gold had been free and living quietly in his apartment in Queens since I had brought him back after the appeal. His third trial began on January 8, 1985. Some three months earlier, Judge Gill, apparently anticipating the difficulties to come, if not the specific form they would take, had asked Murray to agree to an examination by a New Haven psychiatrist. Not surprisingly in view of his feelings about seeing a therapist, he did not keep his appointment.

The prosecutor now put Ms. Perugini (Now Mrs. Kim Perugini Kelly) on the stand to make the claim once more that Gold and his car were in the neighborhood of the Pasternak home three days before the murders at an early morning hour. John Williams's skill in diminishing the impact of Perugini's testimony was obvious. Gold had conceded to the police that he had visited his ex-sister-in-law, who lived near the Pasternak home, three weeks before the murders to explore the possibility of a reconciliation with his divorced wife. Its purpose was innocent and peaceful.

Ms. Perugini could have observed his car on that occasion rather than precisely three days before the murders occurred. In any event, what inference could be drawn even if she were correct? That Gold was "casing" the Pasternak home? But that made no sense. As the one-time son-in-law of the Pasternaks, he knew the house, its entrance, exits, as well as the neighborhood. To found a charge of murder on the possibility of Gold's car simply being in the vicinity was to stretch reason unreasonably. (A more likely inference was that Gold might have hoped to plead with Pasternak for a reconciliation with his daughter when the lawyer left his home to go to his office.)

During this third trial Gold continued to interfere with his lawyer's efforts as he had in the selection of the jury. At one time Williams told him "too many cooks spoil the broth," but he was dealing with a client with an irresistible impulse to push the broth off the stove. Sooner or later, a spill was sure to come.

At one point Williams had almost completed his deft cross-examination of Mrs. Kim Perugini Kelly and had wrung from her a series of admissions about identification.

Q: Mrs. Kelly, as you look at the gentleman [Gold] that you identified here in court today, he, of course, doesn't look anything like the person that was behind the wheel of that car back in the fall of '74, does he?

A: He looks very, very different.

Q: And the person that you saw that day, was his hair as thin as the hair of the gentleman who is sitting here?

A: No, there was more hair.

Q: Okay, quite a bit more hair?

A: Yeah.

Q: And the person you saw that day had a different kind of haircut, too, didn't he?

A: He had a receding hairline, I really don't remember what kind of haircut he had.

Q: You recall whether the person you observed had sideburns?

A: No, I don't remember.

Q: Okay. Whether he did or didn't, you just don't know?

A: Right.

Q: And as you sit there in the witness box today and as you try to picture the scene in your mind, that part of the face you really can't recollect, isn't that so?

A: Right.

Q: Okay. And actually the description that you gave to the police when you first talked to them was simply that the man had dark features, dark hair, a mustache and a receding hairline, is that right?

A: Yes.

Q: And those were the only features that really were, that really sort of stuck with you at that point, isn't that so?

A: Yes.

Q: Beyond the things that I just listed, that I was reading to you from this statement you gave, any other aspects of the person's face, his complexion, for example—

A: No.

Q: You don't recollect that?

A: No.

Q: But whether he had dark skin or fair skin you don't recollect?

A: No.

Q: You didn't notice whether he was really freshly shaven or perhaps needed a shave?

A: No, I didn't.

Williams referred to the previous trial. Kunstler had asked the witness to close her eyes and, after a while, to estimate what time has passed, which he checked with a stopwatch:

Q: And as you sat here in the courtroom in 1976 and the lawyer had the watch on you, it did seem to you, did it not, that the amount of time that was involved was the amount of time that you actually spent watching that person?

A: Yes.

Q: And wouldn't you agree that it might have been roughly that, thirty-seven seconds?

A: It could have been.

Q: Can you tell us, was the weather that day pretty much the way it had been the day before?

A: I can't remember that.

Q: You don't remember what the weather was like the day before?

A: The day before, no.

Q: Do you remember what classes you were taking that day?

A: I could remember classes that I took but—

Q: What were those classes?

A: In order?

Q: Yes.

A: Chemistry, let's see, U.S. History, Algebra II, steno, typing, bookkeeping, a little bit of College A, a little bit of business.

Q: Was it in that order you just gave me?

A: No, no.

Q: In fact you don't remember the order?

A: No, the order, no.

Q: And you surely knew whether by reading a newspaper or just by people talking about it, you certainly were aware that they had made an arrest, they had a suspect?

A: I can't, I really cannot remember if I read that, you know.

Q: In other words, it's your testimony you might have read it, you might not, you just don't remember whether you did?

A: Right.

Q: And as a matter of fact, they brought in another man, Lieutenant Solimita, who took your oath, do you remember that?

A: No, I don't.

Q: But you remember that there was a police officer in a white shirt who took your oath?

A: No, I don't remember that.

Q: Now, by that time, of course, you certainly knew that somebody had been arrested and charged in this case, isn't that so?

A: I can't remember, I really can't.

Q: You simply don't remember one way or the other?

A: Yes.

Q: Now, as you looked at this collection of ten photographs, obviously one of the things you noticed was that there was only one of them that had a mustache that had been drawn in over the top of the photograph, isn't that so?

A: Yes.

Q: And as a matter of fact, you have known for some time now that this was coming up and you were going to have to go through this thing again, didn't you?

A: Uh-huh.

Q: And you have in the last few months, you have seen further pictures of Murray Gold in the newspapers as we have been getting ready for this new case?

A: Uh-huh . . . I saw one picture in the paper.

Q: A picture of him walking into the courthouse?

A: That's probably it.

Q: This picture right here as a matter of fact, wasn't it?

A: Yes, I believe that was the one.

Q: And you would agree, would you not, that Mr. Gold here does not look at all like the Murray Gold whose photograph you picked out on that board on the 17th of October—

THE WITNESS: He looks very different.

Williams's cross-examination of this witness was deft and effective—he had torn down the "identification" attempt of Gold by the prosecution. There was no reason for any comment by Murray Gold, except perhaps a "well done." Instead he got out of his chair and, addressing his lawyer in the presence of the judge and jury, said:

John, I'll have to get myself another attorney. I'm going to dismiss you from representing me and I'm going to ask the judge to give me time to find an attorney to represent me.

The jury gasped. Suddenly they saw Gold in a different light and it was not helpful to him.

Judge Gill caught his breath and bridged the embarrassment by declaring a brief recess.

Gold told Judge Gill that Williams "is endangering my life!" He set forth other frankly preposterous grievances, such as Williams's motion to change venue, to transfer the trial to another county in Connecticut that would not be as prejudiced by the proximity of the crime and, therefore, more dispassionate. Another complaint was that Williams had walked ahead of him on the way to lunch. It did not occur to Gold that Williams might have been conferring with an associate or a witness. Gold apparently considered it a silent expression of Williams' contempt for him.

Gold told the judge that he considered his right to select his lawyer, even if it meant to include the privilege of changing lawyers in the midst of a trial. To do so would grant to every defendant the power to prevent a conclusion of the trial in process. The defendant would simply discharge his lawyer and plead for time to select a substitute. The court could not hold the jury indefinitely. Still, in an effort to give Gold an opportunity to substitute another lawyer to represent him, the judge declared an adjournment for four days.

On January 29, 1985, Gold asked Judge Gill to permit him to state for the record his objections to Williams's continued representation of him. He told the judge that he had approached eight lawyers in the interim. When Gold told the judge in open court that he wanted to state his objections to Williams on the record, Williams replied that if Gold did so he would also have to set forth his own position on the record.

The judicial system, like any other constitutional arrangement, requires basic compliance with certain disciplines. Gold's defiance of these rules tended to create an imbalance. The judge had to improvise procedures to meet the, frankly, aberrational crises Gold was creating. When previously had a defendant in a murder trial challenged his lawyer in open court, particularly one like Williams, who had an outstanding reputation? What was Judge Gill to do with such a unique development?

The State of Connecticut had been making unusual sacrifices because of the unorthodox circumstances of Gold's trials. For example, during the second trial the judge had taken the precaution of sequestering the jury during the length of the trial—which meant that the jury members could not even go to their homes at the end of the day. They had been set up in hotels so as not to be subjected to outside influences in what was being covered as a sensational case. This special precaution cost the State of Connecticut hundreds of thousands of dollars. The rule that jurors are not acceptable if they have been conditioned by information in the press and television has often been criticized—even ridiculed—as setting a standard of ignorance. The risk to be avoided is the insidious impact of being misinformed by commentators who sometimes seek sensationalism more than sense or who rely on rumor or unchecked stories from prosecutors or defense lawyers. Admittedly this procedure makes for an anomaly. The jury is "jailed" while the defendant's fate is being weighed.

When Lincoln was a trial lawyer he once sought to assure himself of the impartiality of the jurors by asking them whether they knew his adversary. The case was being tried in a small town. The judge interrupted Lincoln to caution that everybody in that town knew his opponent.

Lincoln replied, "I am not worried about those who know him. I am worried that there may be some who don't know him."

Lincoln and the little town are gone, but the need for an unbiased jury remains. The judicial process is adulterated if strong measures aren't taken to keep prejudices to a minimum.

In his response to Gold's request for even more time to find a lawyer, Judge Gill said:

> I think because this request is really so unusual it behooves the court to make a full record of your request and of my reaction and ruling on it. I will note, first, for the record, this case is nearly ten and one half years old; it's the oldest case in the State of Connecticut; it has been tried twice before, in 1976 by William Kunstler, counsel of New York, and Victor Ferrante of Connecticut. There was an appeal handled by Mr. Louis Nizer of New York and Timothy Moynahan of Connecticut and that appeal was successful in 1980.
>
> Attorney John Williams has been in this case nearly four years . . . The trial commenced on or about January 8, 1985; at this point in time the state has produced some fifteen witnesses, fourteen of whom have testified completely, and some 75 exhibits . . . Any new attorney, Mr. Gold, would be unlikely to be able to put

himself in a trial posture within any reasonable time . . . the right to have counsel of one's choice stops at the gate when the issue is met by the public interest and the prompt and efficient adminis-tration of justice . . .

. . . Mr. Gold, the possibilities for you are as follows: you can retain Mr. Williams as counsel and proceed on trial, or you can have other counsel present and try the case with Mr. Williams's cooperation and assistance or . . . you are entitled under our law to represent yourself.

So, I'm going to do the following in regard to your request . . . I have indicated to you that two or three weeks would probably be impossible for a . . . competent attorney to do this, but I'm going to give you an opportunity to see if you can obtain other coun-sel . . .

GOLD: May I ask a question?

COURT: Yes, sir.

GOLD: You have in mind to continue with the trial and with the same jury?

COURT: Oh, yes.

GOLD: I see. Well, I don't object to it; as of now, I have until next Tuesday to find a new counsel. Thank you for giving me the same, however, I don't know if he will be ready to proceed—in such short time.

COURT: You can indicate to him that I'm not allowing Mr. Williams out of the case so that if you have new counsel here, he may sit next to you but Mr. Williams will be sitting next to him, so that what is in Mr. Williams's mind can be quickly conveyed to—

GOLD: . . . I don't know how Mr. Williams will fit into this situation.

COURT: Well, that's something for you to discuss with any new counsel and he can discuss that, I am sure, with Mr. Williams. All right?

GOLD: I see.

Judge Gill then asked if the state wished to be heard, and the assistant prosecutor, Mr. John Connelly, responded:

CONNELLY: . . . First of all, we take exception to the ruling. As your Honor knows, the state is ready to proceed. There is a great deal of inconvenience by this delay put on the state and its witnesses. . . . We have already made arrangements . . . to fly here, they have to travel great distances to get here, so we would be prepared and the state wouldn't delay in any way the trial of this matter . . . The state's position is that this delay, this request for delay is only dilatory and there is no basis for it whatsoever. I would ask that when the jury is called down here they are told in no uncertain terms that this delay of almost a week is at the request of the defendant and not at the request of the state. . . . So I take exception to your ruling and I ask you to instruct the jury as requested.

Judge Gill had the jury brought back into the courtroom and gave an explanation for the delays:

COURT: . . . It's a situation that has arisen where I have decided that it's in the best interest of this trial that we [postpone] the trial from now until Tuesday morning at 10:00 A.M. . . .

The jury was excused and left the courtroom, and State's Attorney Connelly asked to be heard:

CONNELLY: The state is going to take an exception to your instruction. . . . At this point in time in this trial we are into the state's evidence. I think the jury could easily presume that a delay of a week was at the request of the state and I think it should be clarified.
GOLD: I'd like to comment.
COURT: You don't have to. Exception is noted.
GOLD: I know, I—I wish to comment. It's important for me to comment. I resent this man's saying that I made an irrational request because I'm making a request to save

my life and my future. I wish to be represented by new
counsel, I have this right.

COURT: Mr. Gold—

GOLD: And I resent—

COURT: Mr. Gold, sir.

GOLD: This nasty and abusive wrong comment.

COURT: Mr. Gold, sir, I have ruled in your favor and I have
indicated that there is no fault on either side, certainly
not on the state and as far as I am concerned not on the
defendant's because it's the ruling of the court that has
caused the delay. I didn't have to grant the request and
that's just the way it is.

Gold's loud denunciation of his attorney and his discharge of
Williams in the presence of the judge and jury created an unprecedented crisis, but Judge Gill acted with caution and a sensitivity
to Murray's predicament, even if self-imposed.

Gold's insistence that he put on the record his reasons for firing
Williams could create another storm, because, as Williams said,
he would then have the right to answer an attack on his reputation. This would have involved a recital of Gold's conduct toward
his counsel, and it was not too difficult to divine that such a
recital would not do Gold any good. So Judge Gill made every
effort to protect Gold against his persistence.

When Murray returned to the courtroom four days later with the
frustrating news that he had contacted eight different lawyers but
none would agree to enter in the middle of a murder trial, he asked
Judge Gill to grant him another month to search for a lawyer.

The judge denied Gold's request for another month and briefly
repeated the reasons for his decision.

When Gold interrupted to say that with new counsel he would
not have "the same problem" again that he had with Williams,
Judge Gill dropped his protective approach for a moment.

COURT: One of the problems is, sir, that if you were to obtain
other counsel there is no guarantee that you wouldn't
have the same problem with the next counsel.

A judge named Charles Gill,
whose patience, despite the smile,
was severely tested.

GOLD: Well, I will not have the same problem.

COURT: Obviously you did make the same objection with the last three sets of counsel that you had.

GOLD: He is the first man who has represented me in this case. I have had no one else represent me in this trial.

COURT: Now I'm referring to Mr. Kunstler and Mr. Nizer.

GOLD: Those were other trials at other times.

COURT: I understand.

GOLD: There has been no one else representing me at this trial and he has been dismissed last Tuesday.

Judge Gill continued to explain to Murray why he wanted the trial to go forward.

COURT: ... The scales of justice just tip slightly now in favor of continuing the case. I think that the pendulum has swung to the public side, the public-interest side of the case, so I'm going to have you at two o'clock let me know how you wish to proceed with this.

GOLD: Yes. I just want to say, you have given me about a week to find another attorney, in order to make my mind up to represent myself. I'll come back and as I said I need additional time and you don't know whether you are going to give me more time because you don't think I'll find an attorney and I feel that I will. I would like to state on the record what my reasons are for dismissing Mr. Williams.

COURT: Yes, well, your reasons as summarized by myself are in the record, but I don't think there is any reason to put them in the record of the court right now. So I decline your request and we'll recess.

GOLD: If I may plead with you . . .

COURT: Recess.

GOLD: To state the reasons now . . .

COURT: Recess.

When the recess ended, Murray made another request:

GOLD: Yes. Firstly I'd like to say that I'm not the one who has interrupted these proceedings, it's the actions of Mr. John Williams that has interrupted the court proceedings.

COURT: Thank you. Is there anything else you'd like to bring to my attention?

GOLD: Well, yes. I'd like to say that I'll follow your suggestion with regret. I'll represent myself, and at the same time I'll try to find a new counsel.

COURT: All right.

GOLD: And if I may, I would also like to state the reasons that I have dismissed Mr. Williams.

COURT: Well, Mr. Gold, as you know, you have indicated those reasons to me. I have reduced them to writing, they are in the court's possession, they will be part of the record of the case and I'm quite confident that protects you to the extent you have to be protected and on that particular issue. If there is anything else that you think has to be put in the court's record, I'll allow you that opportunity, but I don't see any advantage or benefit to anyone to go into those reasons on the record.

GOLD: Well, in that case, I will not state the reasons. I would simply like to state that it's my constitutional right to be represented by an attorney of my choice and I chose that John Williams does not represent me, I do not wish him to be my counsel.

To invoke an old saw: Knowledge knows no restraints, ignorance knows no bounds. Gold, deeply, tragically disturbed and trying to represent himself, continued to tax the judge's patience.

GOLD: ... I would like to make a request of you. I'm not pleased with the way the jury has been selected. I feel that their impartiality has not been established; as such I feel that they should be requestioned to establish their impartiality and if some of them are not adequately impartial or not qualified to be jurors, they should be dismissed and the size of the jury should be reduced.

COURT: The motion is denied based upon the following: the court points out the defense in this case had forty challenges to it and that two challenges had not been used, twelve jurors were chosen. Further, the court listened to the entire questioning of each prospective juror and finds that the standards of competency in this regard is clearly exceeded by Mr. Williams. It should be noted the court also observed Mr. Williams and Mr. Gold discuss each prospective juror at great length before making a decision and such discussions were never terminated by any action of this court regardless of their length. The court then finds that this claim is not only totally without merit but in addition, this claim was brought after nearly three months that jury selection was initiated ... and is tardy.

The sad irony of Gold's request was that it was he who had overruled Williams time after time in the selection of the jury. Now he was displeased with his own judgment.

It had become evident that Gold could not represent himself without injuring his case. The antithesis of the saying that a lawyer who represents himself has a fool for a client may well be that a layman who represents himself has a fool for a lawyer.

An example: the judge had to decide a motion made by Williams to exclude Mrs. Perugini Kelly's testimony on the ground that her identification of Gold sitting in the car near the Pasternak home three mornings before the murders were committed was faulty evidence since it was obtained by "suggestible" photographs. The judge agreed on this point but said that the rest of her evidence would be admissible.

To protect Gold's right to appeal, he added, "I grant the defendant an exception."

Gold cried out: "No, no. I don't have any exceptions." The very testimony that had caused him to explode and fire Williams on the spot, he now said just as vehemently, was acceptable to him. He did not want to reserve his right to appeal, which the word "exception" preserved for him.

Williams could not stand the silence Gold had imposed on him. He finally forced on Murray the realization that he had unwittingly accepted Perugini's testimony that had so inflamed him when she was on the stand. For a moment Gold dropped his attitude towards Williams and permitted him to correct the error. Williams then made a comprehensive legal argument that stressed that the Supreme Court of Connecticut, with the appeal from the trials before it, had the same "totality" of facts and yet had ruled out the Perugini testimony.

The judge said that he would reconsider his decision. All this did not convince Murray that he needed Williams, and his hostility toward him resumed.

Finally the prosecutor Scanlon, apparently mindful of his duty to see justice done even to a defendant in a criminal case—and along the way winning points for high-mindedness—made a motion to have the judge order a competency hearing.

Williams, showing his loyalty, opposed the proposal, which would humiliate his client. He insisted that Gold could proceed without the intervention of a competency hearing.

So the customary procedure was turned topsy-turvy; the defense lawyer, who usually argues that his client should not be subjected to a trial because he is incompetent to defend himself, insisted that the trial should go forward. Williams could not have done otherwise or his position would not be viable in view of Gold's suspicions. On the other hand, the prosecutor, who usually asserts that the defendant is competent to stand trial and should not escape that burden, was urging that Gold's conduct might indicate his incompetence to stand trial and requested a psychiatric determination.

This reversal of the contestants was another instance in which the trials of Murray Gold look like trains running on trackless roadbeds. Judge Gill ordered Dr. James Merikangas to give his opinion about Gold's ability to advise with and aid his attorney.

The doctor conducted two court-ordered psychiatric examinations. In his first report to Judge Gill of December 2, 1984, Dr. Merikangas said:

I examined Murray Gold at the courthouse in Waterbury on November 27, 1984, ... in the presence of his attorney, John Williams....

My examination of Mr. Gold was limited to the criteria in Section 54–56 (D)(c) of the General Statues, namely, is the defendant "able to understand the proceedings against him and assist in his own defense?" We discussed his previous history in general terms ... He adamantly states that he is not the man who committed the crime ... He would not discuss anything that had to do with the charges against him. As he is not claiming to be insane, he was not willing to discuss those issues which might be appropriate for a person claiming insanity nor was he very open about reviewing any psychopathology whatsoever.

I will simply state that in my opinion to a reasonable degree of medical certainty, he is competent to stand trial at present.

Dr. Merikangas's second report to Judge Gill of February 4, 1985, reflected a new, dramatic change:

At the second examination, I interviewed Mr. Gold alone after he had dismissed his attorney. The circumstances of this dismissal and the motivation for this act are relevant to the question of competence. . . .

My discussion with Mr. Gold indicated that he had been convinced that there was a conspiracy against him and that his attorney was part of the conspiracy. This is consistent with his long history of paranoia.

During the trial Gold was lodged at a motel, and Dr. Merikangas referred to reports from there:

We have, in addition, statements made by employees of the Holiday Inn in Waterbury describing his behavior . . . which refer to daily occurrence of the previous month of yelling and making animal noises. Mr. Gold is quoted as saying he was not causing the disturbance but that someone was causing one from other areas of the hotel. Mr. Gold stated that, although he could not hear specifics, the perpetrator was usually yelling or arguing about an innocent party accused of a certain crime. Mr. Gold made other statements to me which were not in accord with the facts which were also of a paranoid nature. . . . Mr. Gold also indicated that he had special knowledge of a witness but would not reveal the source of it. . . . It is apparent that this knowledge is of a delusional nature and could have no basis in reality.

Dr. Merikangas referred again to the criteria for competency of the Connecticut Statute, and said that in his opinion:

[Gold] has admitted on interview that he believes he is the victim of a plot and that his attorney is part of the conspiracy to convict him of a crime which he claims he did not commit. Clearly one cannot consult intelligently with counsel if it is believed that the counsel is part of the conspiracy involving the court and other unnamed forces to convict an innocent man. It is clear that such an accused person does not comprehend his position and we have in the case of Mr. Gold exactly such a circumstance. I had examined Mr. Gold previously . . . and Mr. Gold was quite aware that I had found him competent to stand trial at that time. Despite this fact, on the second examination he continued to withhold information from me and when I alluded to certain facts that I know of his background he became agitated and defensive. He suggested to me that Mr. Williams had misrepresented his [own] religion in order to gain favor with him and that was additional evidence of the conspiracy. Mr. Gold is, therefore, unable to provide his counsel with the relevant and necessary data for structure of his defense. . . .

In conclusion, it is my medical opinion that Mr. Gold suffers from paranoia which renders him presently incompetent to stand trial.

Dr. Merikangas's report was analytically chilly. It might even have given some the impression that Gold was an evil person— which he distinctly was not. However, Dr. Merikangas was not hopeless about Gold's future. Paranoia was curable. It could yield to treatment. So he concluded:

. . . I am of the opinion that there is a substantial probability that Mr. Gold, if provided with a course of treatment, will regain competency within a period of twelve to eighteen months.

20

THE AFTERMATH OF AUSCHWITZ

IT SEEMS TIME in this narrative to leave the chaos of this court-room for a moment to consider the improbable, irreconcilable, almost incoherent conduct of Murray Gold to see if it's possible to come closer to an understanding of such a man, such a mind. Was he, is he, just a disturbed fellow breaking glass in order to attract attention? Or was he in some deeper, darker sense pursuing his own oblivion, actually seeking injustice as we had sought so hard to find justice for him?

Gold's early childhood was marred with the fearful storm cloud of World War II that spread over millions of people. He was born in 1933 in Frankfurt an der Oder, until recently East Germany. In 1939 his parents found themselves in Poland, running from the terror of Nazi domination. At nine, he saw men in Auschwitz reduced by starvation to living skeletons, every rib showing, their heads shrunken to fleshless skulls. What nightmares could be more frightening than his, as he huddled next to his fleeing parents, who were saved by sympathetic local families, who risked death themselves by putting the Golds up for the night? Surely this terror must have left its cruel distortions later in his life.

The Gold family was able to escape from Auschwitz just before the Nazi horror inexorably closed the gates on its doomed victims in this place of abysmal infamy.

They had literally passed through the shadow of death in Nazi Germany. The father, Meyer, his wife, Dina, their daughter and Murray had been slated for extermination in one of the death factories the Nazis built according to modern "scientific" specifications to achieve the inhuman purpose of killing Jews, Catholics, gypsies and dissenters as brutally and savagely as prehistoric cannibals killed their victims. Fortunately Meyer was able to shepherd his wife and son through a then relatively inefficient camp that had not yet closed all means of escape. But it claimed one near and very dear victim. Gold's younger sister was separated from her family during the flight, when it was too dangerous even to look back for a second. While clinging to her brother and parents, the little girl was lost in the trampling of the desperate mass of people, was captured by the Nazis, and destroyed.

Gold's conquest—I use the term advisedly—over such beginnings deserved enormous respect and admiration. At the very least it warranted tolerance for his eccentricities. When he arrived in the United States at the age of fifteen he had not only suffered the anguish of his flight and deep fears, he was burdened with other heavy handicaps. He knew no English. He had been reared in the language and customs of his parents. He was a child, but like many immigrants he carried the sorrows and anguish of the adults. He had been deprived of the joys and lightheartedness of childhood.

Yet Murray seemed to overcome all, graduating from Roosevelt and Rhodes High Schools in New York and then, as mentioned earlier, receiving a degree from New York University. On graduation he held a responsible position at Grumman Aircraft, obtaining security clearance, and later qualified as a stockbroker. He had courted and married the spirited Barbara Pasternak.

But Murray Gold paid a heavy toll for the journey of pain, horror and loss in fleeing from Nazi Germany. Wherever there is persecution there is a terrible selectivity. Thousands escape, individuals perish. Unreasonable fate selects those who die and those who survive. This perverse phenomenon became so prevalent after the Nazi persecutions that it resulted in a pervasive illness of the psyche; the symptoms are guilt feelings, which in the annals of medical/psychiatric history are identified as "survivor guilt." The germs of this new psychological disease had been spread by the Nazi regime through its carriers of genocide and willful murder. Noted psychiatrists, such as Doctors Niederland, Friedman and Modell have written extensively about this modern emotional illness and have presented proof of the resulting survivor-guilt syndrome.

Dr. Friedman, summarizing the writings of Dr. Niederland, stresses that the survivors of the Holocaust suffer from a severe and persevering guilt complex. They may, after a blessed interval of relief, be again thrown into the abyss of their illness, carrying with them "the ever present feeling of guilt, accompanied by conscious or unconscious dread of punishment for having survived the very calamity to which their loved ones succumbed."

According to Dr. Niederland, the most serious aftereffects of such persecution trauma can be observed among those who at a very early age became victims of life under Nazi rule and who have lost loved ones. He lists several components of this psychopathological personality disintegration, such as paranoid features, querulousness, suspiciousness and fantasies. He points out that the clinical consequences are "a state of chronic depression . . . tormenting feelings of being persecuted . . . endangered, or on the verge of renewed persecution." A major complaint of these victims is "I sit and brood all day long."

After the Golds arrived in the United States, Murray might well have seen the photographs or newsreels showing General Eisenhower looking at the mile-long ditch filled with skeletons, tears streaming down the general's cheeks. Gold may have also seen the gruesome scenes of Nazis hurling hundreds of skeletons into long narrow trenches near Auschwitz, imagining that every small skeleton flung into one of these ready-made graves might have been his younger sister. Had he only held on tighter to her she might now be radiant and living in the United States. Such

thoughts can give nightmares twenty-four hours a day. With such
moody thoughts, symptoms of the survivor guilt, added to those
other personality traits of Murray, with a ubiquitous suspicion of
others plotting to punish him, and, suffering the agony of guilt
("why my sister, why not me?"), he apparently came to the distorted view that he somehow *deserved* punishment, losing his
ability to discriminate and believing only that everyone was there
to betray him, his lawyers included.

Gold sounded to me like a prime example of the survivor-guilt
complex, an awful burden destined to become, over time, a full-
blown paranoia. It would seem his illusion of his counsels' disloyalty was translated by him into his responsibility for his sister's
death while *he* survived. Such illusions not surprisingly ultimately turned into schizophrenia. They also made him a forbid-
ding personality—silent, introspective, distant and vulnerable.
And since he had submitted to medical treatment and even shock
treatments, this record, plus his relationship as a son-in-law of
the slain Pasternaks, all tended to magnetize the police's attention, diverting them from other suspects, including Bruce Sanford.

Paranoia may likely be the extension of fear and insecurity, not
an incitement to imitate one's tormentors. Yet the conclusions
drawn by the prosecutor McDonald and perhaps some members
of the jury was that someone who has suffered psychiatric damage in his youth might very likely be capable of injuring others
rather than, in fact, be unduly fearful of violence.

Kunstler was able to obtain a hung jury in the first trial; but
from the very first, the defense should have, I believe, included an
expert in psychiatry who could point out to the jury that psychiatric treatment does not necessarily equate with a violent dispo-
sition to commit violent acts; indeed, it might well be consistent
on the part of the afflicted person to *avoid* aggression and not do
damage to others.

In measuring the strain Gold was subjected to by his tragic past
and present imprisonment, one can't overlook the torment of the
murder trials to which he had been subjected. In addition, to be
held up in the press and television as a vicious murderer could

have been enough to unsettle a more stable mind than Murray Gold's.

Add to Gold's paranoia the reasonable assumption that to others the disordered mind may be consistent with uncontrolled criminal behavior and one has the factors that may have driven Gold to his bizarre action in the courtroom. Not least was his knowing that he had not committed the crime. Imagine the excruciating, almost unbearable ordeal of complicated trial procedures that attempted to prove what he knew was untrue? How painful and frustrating it must have been for Gold to hear "evidence" that would "prove" he was the monster who had cut the Pasternaks to pieces.

But now Murray seemed bent on cutting his own defense to pieces—to seeking, unconsciously, the death for himself that he had escaped while his sister was destroyed.

21

SELF-DEFENSE

THE PROCEEDINGS CONTINUED on February 5, 1985. Murray Gold had not obtained other counsel—and was to conduct the trial himself. Dr. Merikangas took the stand and gave his qualifications. Both John Williams and Walter Scanlon had been given copies of his report and the judge directed that Gold be given a copy too. After Gold had read it he requested that he, rather than Williams, be permitted to cross-examine Dr. Merikangas. This request was granted.

Gold, obviously untrained in the art of cross-examination, faced the doctor. Instead of using the scalpel of cross-examination in an attempt to expose the frailty of the doctor's conclusion, Gold engaged in praise of himself, as if giving direct testimony.

GOLD: Well, you have known me briefly, you haven't known me a long time and when we first talked briefly you decided that I was competent to stand trial. Now, I am most certainly not a crazy man, I'm not an irrational man, I'm not a man who imagines things. I assure you completely that I'm realistic. I'm a kind man, I'm a human man, and because there has been some negative publicity about me and because there have been false charges brought against me, certain types of irresponsible people have been lying about me. Now, as I read this most certainly most of what is in here which is absurd and ridiculous didn't come from our conversation, did it?

DR. MERIKANGAS: As I stated in the beginning, my sources for the examination came from the records and from other people with whom I had discussion.

GOLD: Well, I would like to say without hesitation, and I swear before you that I tell the truth, that just about all of this, just about all of it is a complete lie, a ridiculous lie, and an absurd lie. I never contemplated suicide. I like life, I like people and I have never stated that there is any kind of a conspiracy against me. Now, have I stated that to you?

DR. MERIKANGAS: My understanding of our conversation is that you stated the same.

GOLD: That I used those words?

DR. MERIKANGAS: You may not have used the word "conspiracy," you may have used the word "plot."

GOLD: No, I did not use the word "plot." I had simply complained that it was unfair and it was a smear to have me see you at that time. I did not use the word plot. Do you recall that?

DR. MERIKANGAS: My recollection is different, Mr. Gold.

GOLD: Well, I didn't use that word. Now, I have no hallucinations and I completely disagree and deny just about all that is in here and I also assure you that the judge had asked me if I would like to represent myself, and I think he has shown basically an opinion that he thinks I could represent myself. Now, this is a court of law and since he feels that I'm generally competent to do this I don't think he was mistaken. In addition to this, I really don't know if you wish this letter [to Judge Gill, of February 4, 1985] to remain intact as such. Would you like to modify it?

DR. MERIKANGAS: How would you suggest modifying it?

GOLD: Well, I suggest as follows: In the third paragraph . . .

where there have been some irresponsible complaints from some employees, you say at the inn? . . . I have been staying at the inn for approximately two months. I wasn't there just a few days and no one has complained to me, no one has had any complaints about my staying at the inn, there hasn't been a single employee who has complained to me. The manager has not complained to me, no one has asked me to leave. Now, I'm not a man who generates noises. What has been transpiring is that occasionally there are some very loud, extremely loud yelling voices from some other part in the inn but most certainly they do not come from me and I assure you that this complaint here is unfounded, misleading and a lie. In the following paragraph—you mentioned something about a conspiracy. Now, I have not said that there is any kind of conspiracy. I have simply said that I found Mr. Williams inadequate and endangering me, not representing me appropriately, and I tell you it's my privilege under the Constitution to have an attorney of my choice.

Now, it's my privilege to dismiss him if I so like and I did. Now, I have also complained to you very briefly without going into any kind of detail that I felt the prosecution was smearing me with smears. Now, I did not say that both of them are a team, I did not say that there is a conspiracy. I simply felt there was some unfairness. . . .

In addition to this most of what is on Page three simply is not so. It consists of falsehoods, it consists of lies. Someone has been providing you with misleading and false information strictly to ruin my reputation, to ruin my future, to cast doubt about me and to be destructive of me.

Now, I hope that you will reconsider such falsehoods and such lies which have been presented to you, and I also hope that you will change your mind about me.

So Murray had given a denial, forfeiting in the process his chance to cross-examine.

The art of digging into a resisting mind, to compel admissions in order to salvage credibility, requires unique psychological skills. The witness' personality indicates the best way to pierce his armor. If he is belligerent, he should be goaded gently to expose his nastiness; if he is friendly, and attempts to give an impression of candor, he may be provoked to reveal his pretense and thus expose a hypocritical stance.

Murray Gold, whose own competency was at issue, was hardly the one to exercise such skills. To make the scene even more bizarre, sitting behind him was his attorney, barred by him from using a lifetime of experienced training in the required arts, a defender silenced by his client.

Psychiatry is not an area of scientific certainty, and so is especially a subject for skillful cross-examination. Mental sciences more than any other are judgmental. Dr. Merikangas had at one time reported that Gold was competent to stand trial. His written report less than three months later offered an opportunity for a cross-examiner to point out the uncertainties of the psychiatric science and then raise doubt about the validity of his latest report of non-competency. Dr. Merikangas might have been able to demonstrate that intervening events, such as the necessity to increase Murray's antipsychotic drugs fivefold and the pressure of the third trial, accounted for the variance in his reports. But a first opening was there in the attack on the reliability of his conclusion. Medical inconsistencies give rise to jests, sometimes unkind—for example: neurotics build castles in the air, psychotics live in them, and psychiatrists collect the rent.

A cross-examiner must fish for contradictions while avoiding the embarrassment of being pulled into the water by his catch.

After Gold's fruitless "cross-examination" of Dr. Merikangas, the prosecutor, understandably, had nothing further to say. Judge Gill began to wind up the hearing:

COURT: . . . I'm going to declare that the testimonial part of the hearing has been concluded, that is the closed portion of the hearing and you may notify anyone outside who wishes to come in that the rest of our proceeding will take place in public and on the record.

There was a rush of people into the courtroom. Gold spoke up:

GOLD: Your Honor, may I ask something?
COURT: Wait just a moment, sir . . .
GOLD: What are you proposing to do from here on in?
COURT: I have to make a finding in the case.
GOLD: I see.
COURT: I have to do that publicly so I have to have the public in here. I can't exclude them. The court has been presented with a report pursuant to the statute which the court has read. The court has listened to testimony of the doctor who prepared the report and the court has listened to Mr. Gold's response both in argument and cross-examination on that subject. Based upon all the foregoing, the court makes the findings in this case which are as follows:

The defendant Murray R. Gold is found not to be competent because he is unable to understand the proceedings against him and because he is unable to assist in his own defense.

It's further found that there is a substantial probability that the defendant, if provided with the course of treatment, will regain competency within a placement period of eighteen months.

It is also found that [the] place of commission with the Commissioner of Mental Health for in-patient treatment is the least restrictive and appropriate place available to restore competency. Accordingly the defendant is placed in the custody of the Commissioner of Mental Health for a period of eighteen months at the Whiting Forensic Institute. A *mittimus* to that effect shall issue. [A *mittimus* is a special judicial order before the conclusion of a trial.]

A hearing is set to reconsider the defendant's competency on March 1st, 1985, at 10:00 A.M. My wish [is] that Mr. Gold be taken with whatever transportation vehicle there is from inside the building with the doors closed downstairs and that he not be held out for public view when he is leaving this building.

Gold's penchant for firing his lawyers had landed him in a mental institution.

As instructed by Judge Gill, the Court convened again on March 1, 1985, three weeks later.

> COURT: I have received a report from Whiting Forensic Institute pursuant to the statute concerning Mr. Gold . . . [I] again note that Mr. Williams is present in court and is able to advise him and consult with Mr. Gold if need be and also I'm going to take the added precautionary step of appointing in addition to Mr. Williams as guardian *ad litum* . . .

Murray attempted once again to put his grievances against Williams into the record:

> GOLD: May I say something?
> COURT: No, Mr. Gold.
> GOLD: It's extremely important that I say something.
> COURT: Would you address it to Mr. Williams; then, sir, perhaps he can approach the bench with the subject matter of your request.
> MR. WILLIAMS: Should we approach the bench?

A discussion was then held at the bench.

> COURT: Mr. Gold indicated that Mr. Williams is no longer his attorney, which of course is part of the record in the case, and he has another attorney.
> GOLD: I do not, and I do not have anyone else . . .
> COURT: We'll proceed then.

GOLD: And it's also the wish of Mrs. Gold [Murray Gold's
    mother] that Mr. Williams do not represent me. I dis-
    missed this man.
COURT: I understand that.

The prosecutor called to the stand Dr. Timothy Schumacher, a
clinical psychologist at the Whiting Forensic Institute, part of a
team assigned to evaluate Murray Gold. Schumacher told the
court that the evaluation team had met with Gold on three occasions since his admission on February 5th (the date of the last
court hearing).
    The prosecutor, Scanlon, asked Dr. Schumacher:

SCANLON: Doctor, did the team make a determination as to
    whether Mr. Gold is competent to stand trial?
DR. SCHUMACHER: The team's determination was that Mr.
    Gold is not competent at this time to stand trial.

The team's written report was offered into evidence, when Mr.
Williams interjected:

WILLIAMS: I'm not sure whether it's Mr. Gold or I or someone
    else who should announce the position of the defendant
    in this respect, your Honor.
COURT: Well, it is a problem. I think what we'll do, why
    don't you show Mr. Gold the report and we'll see what
    happens from that point on.

Gold was supplied with a copy of the team report, and the
prosecutor continued to question Dr. Shumacher on his findings.

DR. SCHUMACHER: . . . he lacks sufficient capacity essen-
    tially to deal effectively and neither fully and coherently
    with counsel and consequently is not capable of assisting
    properly in his own defense. . . . His ability to tolerate
    stress was minimal and likely to be unacceptable . . . Our
    team is of the opinion that provided with a sufficient

period of hospitalization and care that there is a substantial probability that his competency may be restored.

The doctor went on to suggest in-patient care at Whiting for eighteen months, with a new report on Gold's competency within ninety days. The judge then asked if there was anything further, and Mr. Williams responded:

WILLIAMS: Your Honor, I believe it's my understanding that Mr. Gold does not desire me to ask something of this witness.
GOLD: For technical reasons, he does not represent me.
COURT: All right, Mr. Gold, I'm going to presume that you object to the findings of the team.
GOLD: Yes, I do.

Murray could not appreciate it, but Judge Gill was protecting him from further disaster. The jury had seen and heard his outburst against his own lawyer. Added to this, the report that he was paranoid would probably translate in the jury's mind to a persuasive implication that he was sick enough to have committed a horrific crime.

So Gold faced an increased risk of an adverse finding by the jury if allowed to stand trial.

The judge's next declaration gave Murray another chance on another day, perhaps, finally, to vindicate himself.

The judge declared a mistrial.

22

IDENTIFICATION, COMPETENCY, DRUGS

So THE THIRD trial ended without a resolution and in disarray, yet some rather significant developments and issues came out of it.

The testimony that caused the first eruption was Perugini's "identification" of Gold near the Pasternak home three days before the murders. Even though Williams had extracted the admission from the witness that "he [Gold] looks very different" from the man she had seen in the car, that did not appease Gold. What greater neutralization of a witness' point could be achieved? Murray's hypersensitivity here was not only sadly unjustified but misdirected.

Identification of an alleged culprit is such a vital element in the solution of a crime, and the errors in making identifications so grievous, that the law has adopted rules to prevent improper or overzealous attempts by a prosecutor to "identify" the accused. Vulnerable defendants must be protected against a careless pointed finger. What are the precautions to eliminate mistaken identification, no matter how sincere, which would "do in" an innocent defendant?

Criminals, of course, fear identification. Sometimes they wear ski masks or wigs or other disguises to mask themselves, and the law needs to be especially alert to fraudulent identification. The risk is that a prosecutor may by subtle suggestion lead a witness to identify an alleged criminal when there is no certainty. The stakes are high. If a mistake is made, an innocent person may pay the price for another's crime. An error of identification results in a violation of civil rights.

The physical "lineup" of suspects or the submission of a series of photographs from which the witness designates the "criminal" he claims he saw must be so presented that selection is uninfluenced by anything which could mislead the witness. The courts have defined "suggestibility." Hints may not be provided to the identifier that lead him to a wrong choice.

The Gold case was like a number of decisions in which a witness who had described the criminal as wearing a beard was then shown a series of photographs of which only one suspect was wearing a beard. This was clearly suggestibility. There should have been a *series* of pictures of suspects, all of whom had beards.

Gold had shaved off his moustache before going to the Catskill resort. Later he ran into the rule of law that changing appearances might indicate consciousness of guilt. At the identification procedure Ms. Perugini-Kelly again looked at ten photographs shown to her by the police. One photograph had a moustache drawn in ink over the subject's lip. She picked that photograph. The appellate court held that the inked drawing of a moustache was impermissibly suggestive and set aside her identification.

I now plead a bit of self-indulgence. When I was a student at Columbia University Law School we were visited by a judge of the highest court of Canada. He contrasted the endless appeals of a convicted criminal in the United States and the dilatory procedure generally in our courts with the efficiency of Canadian justice. Perhaps he deliberately exaggerated. To make his point clearer he told us that in Canada when a murder occurs the

A line-up of mug shots—
eventually declared improper
because of a mustache *drawn in*
over Gold's lip (*bottom left, this
page*).

 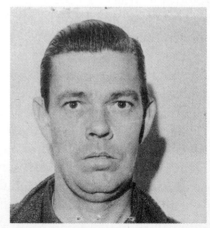

criminal is caught, tried, his appeal rejected and he is hung within four weeks.

After the laughter had died down, a student spoke up and asked how this speed could be achieved if the defendant pleaded insanity.

"Oh," said the judge, "if he's crazy he won't know that he is being hung, so it doesn't matter."

Followed by more laughter, but most of us felt uncomfortable with a concept that held a deranged defendant to a primitive standard. In Judaic and Anglo-Saxon law insanity is considered a disease. We don't punish people because they are sick. This does not mean that they are let loose in society to do injury. They are, if necessary, confined to an appropriate hospital until they are no longer a threat to society and, ideally, are cured.

So the rule is that insanity, if proved, constitutes a defense against imprisonment, in some states against execution, but it is not a door to freedom, only to a medical facility. The theory is that if the defendant is unaware of the proceedings going on around him he can't aid his counsel in his defense. The law is violated in the same way as if he were not in the courtroom.

Drugs intended to calm a psychotic defendant are frequently applied by prison authorities to preserve discipline. When psychotropic drugs dull the defendant so that he is abnormally quiet, and his reasoning faculties are affected, he may become incompetent in the process. He can cease to be obstreperous but—dulled by the "calming" medicines—insufficiently comprehensive to understand the proceedings.

Gold was to be confined in the Whiting Forensic Institute for eighteen months. At the end of six months he clamored for a trial. He retained James Kinsella as his attorney to relieve him of confinement in the hospital and to demonstrate that he had become competent in the legal sense of the word. Kinsella made an application to the court and submitted another report of Whiting's Evaluation Team declaring that Gold's condition had improved and that he was now competent. Judge Gill entered the order provided that "he [Gold] must maintain his present medication."

The court thus acknowledged the difficulty. In the event of a fourth trial, Gold must continue to be pacified by medicine so that there would be no new outburst. Even in the third trial he had been dosed so that he was nodding. The doctors had to increase his "medicine" fifteen times during that trial.

Dr. James Merikangas had first examined Gold on November 27, 1984. He reported to Judge Gill that:

> It is clear that Gold is paranoid and feels that the prosecution has some sort of plot against him.

Dr. Merikangas evaluated Gold a second time in January, 1985, and reported to Judge Gill. He repeated his prior conclusion that Gold was incompetent:

> He [Gold] has admitted in interview that he believes he is the victim of a plot and that his attorney is part of the conspiracy to convict him of a crime which he claims he did not commit. Clearly, one cannot consult intelligently with counsel if it is believed that the counsel is part of the conspiracy involving the Court, and other unnamed forces, to convict an innocent man. It is clear that such an accused person does not comprehend his position and we have in the case of Mr. Gold exactly such a circumstance.

The court agreed that the appropriate measure was to return Murray Gold to Connecticut's Whiting Forensic Institute until such time as he was competent to stand trial. To insure that the court was regularly advised, a special evaluation team was appointed to test Gold at certain intervals and report to the court on its findings.

At the time of their first report on February 21, 1985, Gold was medicated but despite this medication the evaluation team concluded:

It was in the area of his capacity to collaborate with counsel that the evaluation team found Mr. Gold to be unacceptably poor and incompetent to stand trial ... [his] ability to tolerate stress in Court and to refrain from irrational behavior in this connection was rated as unacceptably poor.

Four months later, in May of 1985, the evaluation team began to prescribe for Gold the powerful antipsychotic drug, Navane. They also rediagnosed Gold and concluded that his was an acute paranoid disorder. At this time the doctors at the Whiting Institute assumed that one milligram of Navane per day would be sufficient to keep Gold manageable:

Given the behavior exhibited by Mr. Gold during the examination, it was again concluded that he is incapable of working in a proper manner with an attorney. . . . the patient produced digressions and tangential explanations similar to that witnessed during his previous examination, which lacked comprehensible meaning or plausible basis.

Apparently one milligram of Navane a day was not enough and one month later Gold's medication was increased to five milligrams of Navane a day. In spite of the increased daily doses the evaluation team in their August 8, 1985, report concluded that Gold had still not yet regained competency. By October 31, 1985, Gold's dosage of Navane had been increased to fifteen milligrams daily and the evaluation team now diagnosed Gold as suffering from schizophrenia as well as paranoia. So Gold's condition had worsened. His paranoia was characterized as delusions of persecution, including the fear that his lawyers were cooperating with the prosecutor to do him in—another reason why he kept firing his lawyers. And schizophrenia was a more severe psychotic state—a withdrawal from reality, resulting in bizarre behavior.

In spite of all this, on the basis of the pacification promised by the increased drugs, the evaluation team declared: "The patient is competent to stand trial." By the time this last report was issued Gold's daily doses of Navane had been *tripled*.

Gold's cries for a speedy trial had, unfortunately, won the day.

Is a prisoner protected by the administering of psychotropic drugs, or is it a violation of the prisoner's rights? In a very recent case the Supreme Court of the United States by a 6 to 3 decision upheld the right of prison officials to impose drugs on psychotic and dangerous prisoners.

Inmates who need a fix are virtually uncontrollable. Because of this, prison authorities often close an eye to the importation of drugs into prisons. So we have a tolerance in favor of evil in order to preserve discipline.

Navane is the most proficient of these drugs; it can be administered in capsule form or by hypodermic injection. It can produce a barbituratelike stupor in a patient, a torpor. Muscles become heavy. It induces "quiet" without unconsciousness. A patient who is experiencing an adverse reaction to Navane might appear to be restless or agitated, unable to sleep. The drug, and lack of sleep, often make the patient drowsy. Which explains why Gold was caught napping in the courtroom during the fourth trial. He was full of drugs.

Navane also affects a patient's muscle control. Side effects may include involuntary movements of the jaw, mouth, face or tongue. To an unsuspecting observer such a patient may appear to be talking to himself. Indeed, a sheriff reported Gold's muttering to himself in court.

There were other visible indications from the drug. I had noticed that Gold's skin turned darker as he became upset and called it, in my ignorance at the time, the "sunburn of anger." Also his eyes bulged and seemed to shine with an unnatural brightness. Navane may well have been responsible for these changes. The effect was doubly unfortunate because the heightened coloring frightened people who did not know that these were chemically induced phenomena. They might even have contributed to the false conclusion that this distortion of his personality indicated a dangerous propensity for violence.

23

ON IDENTIFICATION AND SATANISM

As I READ over the trial transcripts years later it was clear to me that there was other evidence that diminished the likelihood of Gold's guilt and strengthened the case for Sanford's commission of the crimes.

There was the matter of the missing fingerprints.

The Pasternaks' home was carefully searched for fingerprints that might have identified the murderer. Of forty-two prints found, all but eight were identified as those of the Pasternaks, their family and the police who swarmed into the house.

These eight unidentified prints were found on the fire extinguisher that squirted the liquid into Pasternak's face; on the brown paper bag in which it was carried; on the brown button claimed to be found at the scene of the crime; on the Buck knife, the instrument used for the murders; and on the sewing kit. The brown paper bag that held the fire extinguisher was tested, dipped into a silver-nitrate solution that revealed a palm print.

Of the eight *unidentified* prints, none belonged to Murray Gold. Therefore, no *identified* print belonged to Murray Gold.

Is the test of fingerprint comparison valid, or subject to exceptions? It has been determined to be an infallible technique.

We have been educated to the fact that the fingerprints of each person are different from those of hundreds of millions—yes, billions—who have ever lived. What scientist, even with the aid of computers, could arrange so many varied identifications from the small number of flesh lines on the one-inch tip of a finger?

Due to his many encounters with the law and fingerprinting, Sanford might well have resorted to wearing gloves during his criminal acts, just as he used a wig to disguise his identity. So not even the murder knife, nor the fire extinguisher and the paper bag yielded any clues as to the hands that held them. But no one claims that Murray Gold had any such knowledge which cunning criminals possess as a result of their activities. Therefore, could Murray Gold have carried out such horrendous murders without leaving one fingerprint?

Oddly enough, of all recognition factors, the voice can also be very reliable. We make this test inadvertently dozens of times during a year. We hear a television drama or a comedy in the next room and identify the performer instantly. How often do we know who is greeting us before we look up, simply by the timbre of the voice? The resonance or lack of it is almost as reliable an identifying factor as a fingerprint—and much more commonly used.

This fact alone might have eliminated Gold from the murder charge.

For when Rhoda Pasternak became aware of the animallike, stifled screams that came from her husband as each knife thrust crushed the bone in her husband's body and severed the arteries, she cried out to her daughter on the telephone to call the police. As she hung up the phone she decided to make her own call to 911: "Please come to 53 Fern Street—a crazy man is here. Hurry . . ." She also told her daughter that "a crazy man is yelling at Daddy."

Since Murray Gold had been her son-in-law, would she not have referred to him as "Murray" or "Murray Gold" instead of "a crazy man"?

The killer had blinded Pasternak by squirting a fire extinguisher into his face. But Rhoda had more opportunity to see him, hear him, refer to him. Even his silhouetted figure might well have been enough for identification, given her long familiarity with Murray Gold.

Therefore, her reference to "a crazy man" had to mean a stranger, not her former son-in-law.

Then there is the question of the call on the night of the murders to Judge Milton Meyers.

Would such a threatening call in such vile anti-Semitic terms have been made by Murray Gold, himself a victim of oppression, who quietly celebrated religious holidays with his parents, whose sister had died at the hands of anti-Semitic criminals?

Whenever a horrifying crime is committed we tend to turn to psychiatrists to find a possible derangement of the criminal's mind as an explanation, often hoping to find a common underlying cause for such atrocities. In some cases, though, the cause may not just be a form of simple insanity but also the acceptance of a sick philosophy—Satanism. Thus Manson, Berkowitz ("Son of Sam"), Sirhan Sirhan (who killed Robert Kennedy), the modern Nazi and motorcycle gangs that kill strangers and the continuing display of the swastika, a symbol of Nazism (which can be traced according to Satanists to the "Devil's symbol"), all are seen to be in the service of Satan and his struggle with God. To such believers it is a war between good and evil. They are not interested in waiting for reward after death. They believe in and practice evil so as to obtain the immediate thrills and "advantages" from their defiance of the good.

Witchcraft, a form of Satanism, dates back to the Middle Ages. Much later it would surface in the United States. It was an anti-occult hysteria that triggered the Salem trials in Massachusetts in 1692. The Satanists even have their own "church" dedicated to evil—the Process Church of the Final Judgment, founded in England in 1963.

Charles Manson had insisted that Sharon Tate, though pregnant, be killed with a knife, and his disciples, who did not even know her or why she should be done away with, obeyed. Sirhan shot Robert Kennedy in the back of the head as he happened to pass through the kitchen on the way out of the hotel after a political rally. Hundreds of murders of strangers are committed in our country by cultists who believe they are serving the Devil. For example, a Satanist, Aleister Crowley, formulated a "set of laws" which he embodied in his "Hermetic Order of the Golden Dawn." One of its precepts was that "evil is good, and good is evil." Also, the Satanic bible exhorts: "To slash with grim delight this victim I hath chose."

If Murray Gold's prosecutor had had an understanding of what Satanism really is, would he not have been more suspicious of Sanford, the avowed Satanist? Would he not have seen him as a suspect to be pursued with the same thoroughness with which he pursued Gold?

BOOK
VII

24

Revelation Under Hypnosis

Surprises: as one disappeared, another occurred. Who would have expected, for example, informative revelations by a witness under an hypnotic spell?

Hypnosis is not harmful. It cannot make one do anything that is embarrassing to the subject; it cannot force one to abandon one's inherent standards or do something shocking to one's values or something that is irreversible.

Thorough preparation, as I have observed for a long time, gives a lawyer many rewards. What might elude him otherwise can strike with special force when he digs deeply into old files. So, while rummaging through the voluminous files in the Gold case I came across a transcript of a tape recording made of Glorianna Sanford's "testimony" while under hypnosis. I did not pass it by as an aberration. Could it throw additional light on this tragic murder mystery?

The transcript revealed that a private investigator, James Conway, who had been working with defense counsel Kunstler and Ferrante, had persuaded Glorianna to be hypnotized. Conway and his assistant had been present at the session, which had taken place before the first trial that ended in a hung jury. The hypnotist first put Glorianna Sanford at ease before putting her under with the following soothing instructions: ". . . sit back in the chair and put your feet up . . . slowly close your eyes . . . now take a deep breath [and] exhale; let your eyes relax, let your body float . . ." Actually, "putting her under" could be described as lifting her consciousness to reveal her real meanings and motivations underneath. Emotions are often hidden or repressed by protective instincts to hide embarrassment or guilt, and the removal of such restraints created by fear can sometimes help to unearth the truth. The subject has not so much been "put under" as freed from self-imposed, if unconscious, artifices as layers of "protective" insulation are removed.

So the hypnotist put Glorianna "under," and he and the investigators proceeded to prod her memory of the events on the day of the murders and of Sanford's suicide.

HYPNOTIST: . . . Do you feel if you had stayed with Bruce he wouldn't have died?

GLORIANNA: Yes, yes, I feel like I did this, I feel I could have stopped him . . . if I had stayed right with him he wouldn't have done this, he wanted me to go upstairs with him but I wouldn't. He scared me.

HYPNOTIST: . . . Do you feel guilty because of Bruce's death?

GLORIANNA: . . . yes . . . I'm a good nurse, I did help everybody, but I couldn't have helped him.

HYPNOTIST: Do you feel largely responsible for Bruce's death?

GLORIANNA: Yes, I do.

HYPNOTIST: . . . Do you feel you're concealing something now to help him in death when you didn't help him in life?

GLORIANNA: I think so . . .

INVESTIGATOR #1: On September 27, 1974, you left very hurriedly for Florida with Bruce—why?

GLORIANNA: . . . It took me about three days to get there, West Palm Beach, looking for his friends. (Even under hypnosis Glorianna, by dodging the investigator's question, was protecting Sanford, her "master" in their sexual enslavement relationship.)

HYPNOTIST: . . . did you stop on the way down there?

GLORIANNA: Once in Georgia or North Carolina someplace like that and we're having a very hard time up there, he threatens to jump out into the road and kill himself.

HYPNOTIST: Why did he want to jump out in the road and kill himself?

GLORIANNA: Because I was screaming all over him telling him that he's nuts, the first crazy house I come to he's going into, and he says, "Fine, right after you." And then I'm screaming at him. I'm going about ninety miles an hour and he's throwing the door open which scares me and I just keep quiet—I get very quiet and I take my rosary beads out.

HYPNOTIST: Why did he want to commit suicide on the way down there?

GLORIANNA: Because I was rejecting him . . . "You already know you're sick and you're crazy and you know I can't let you hurt anybody" . . .

INVESTIGATOR #2: . . . Why did you feel that it was so necessary to take Bruce out of the state right away?

GLORIANNA: . . . I didn't know I was going out of state. I didn't have any money, I had to call the bank and they sent money.

HYPNOTIST: Subsequently Bruce came back. What happens then when Bruce comes back from Florida, how can he get back?

GLORIANNA: He hitchhikes and his foot was all swollen and he goes back into the hospital about the time of my divorce. . . . His foot swelled up to about ten times its size . . . his feet are all swollen and dirty and he's lost maybe thirty pounds since I seen him and he's sick-looking.

HYPNOTIST: Do you take him into your home again?

GLORIANNA: No, he goes to his mother's house . . .

HYPNOTIST: . . . Can you project the picture now to the day he committed suicide? Do you recall that day?

GLORIANNA: Yes, I'm with him in his house in the kitchen
and it starts—turns on the water, I guess he's doing something, all of a sudden he cuts his hand, the forearm and
skin turns back three or four inches over his wrist and the
red blood is running into his arms and he's got a very wild
look in his eyes. [I'm] extremely frightened. I said, "Bruce,
please let's go to St. Mary's Hospital . . . I'll say we were
doing dishes and I put a knife in the dishpan." He says no.
No. "Now, bitch, you're going to watch me die." He gets
down on his knees and he's acting very theatrically, bows
his head and says, "Don't leave me, please don't leave me,
please don't leave me." I said, "I will if you don't stop cutting yourself to pieces like this, I'm not going to stand here
and watch you do this." He takes the palms of his hands
and pushes me clear into the other room and I'm up against
a couch now in the other room and I can't get out now . . . I
can't go anywhere and I'm very very frightened. He's very
irrational now and he gets down on his knees and I said
"devil." He said, "If you're a devil I'm a devil" and he looks
just like the crucified Christ on the cross, his eyes look so
pathetic . . . lifts two hands up with the pools of blood in the
palm of his hands. He says, "I'm not a devil. I'm a crucified
Jesus Christ." All of a sudden running . . . [I] just copped
out I just don't know what happened, but I come back again
and its daybreak—you know it's dark and it's light and I go
up to his room . . . I couldn't step in because it was all over
there, it looked like a movie or something. His teeth are on
the dresser, he took them out, he's laying backwards . . .
HYPNOTIST: Who was upstairs?
GLORIANNA: Lillian, his mother . . . when I come on back I
go right upstairs the door is open because Lillian is drunk
and she's out upstairs . . . I can walk right into the house
up the stairs . . . I could see him laying there very still and
. . . another part of my mind picks up the blood on the
floor . . . I look up the hall I see his mother with her arms
hanging off the bed . . .

INVESTIGATOR #2: Glorianna . . . did you know he was dead?

GLORIANNA: I did and I wouldn't admit it . . . I said he's sleeping to myself but I wouldn't admit he was dead.

HYPNOTIST: You walk back out of the house?

GLORIANNA: I was very much up in the air right now I even see his neck. I saw the pills come out of his neck . . . I felt numb . . . I just walked and walked and I had to be in court the next morning. I just didn't go in and touch him and make sure he was dead . . . everything was wrong in the room, he was laying too still.

HYPNOTIST: As a nurse you knew he was dead?

GLORIANNA: Yeah, really when I seen all the blood out of him, there was like four quarts of blood there, it was from the door right up to the bed.

HYPNOTIST: You did nothing to help him?

GLORIANNA: No . . .

INVESTIGATOR #1: . . . You know we have photos of fingerprints found at the murder scene, we have been waiting weeks to get the results of these prints from the F.B.I. Before they come back, would you tell me whose prints they might find there in order that we can clarify this without arresting anybody?

GLORIANNA: I can't tell you that . . .

HYPNOTIST: . . . Are you protecting anyone else besides Bruce in this?

GLORIANNA: No, I hope to God you know from what I hear that his prints aren't there . . . what's there is there, it's going to be a scientific fact.

INVESTIGATOR #1: If I find [Sanford's] prints [at the murder scene] you could be charged with perjury . . .

HYPNOTIST: . . . What if the fingerprints show that Bruce was there. How do you account for that?

GLORIANNA: I'm not going to account with it, it's between Bruce and his God. I was not there, I was home. I don't know what Bruce did . . . we're pretending that [the Investigator] is going to say Bruce did it. I'm going to be very

aghast. I'm going to be very shocked but if the fingerprints are there then he did it . . .

INVESTIGATOR #2: . . . You loved Bruce very much, didn't
you?

GLORIANNA: Right.

INVESTIGATOR #2: Do you feel you failed him in life and you
don't want to in death?

GLORIANNA: . . . I just don't want to see him persecuted in
death.

Her reluctance was an illustration . . . however frustrating . . .
of the failure of hypnotism to overcome her feelings about Sanford.

The bloody letters Sanford left on the mirror at his death—
CURSE YOU GLORY—had made it a matter of honor, by her
lights, for her at least to protect his name in death. She did, as she
said, feel responsible.

She was, of course, "Glory."

Whatever help the hypnotic session might have been to the
defense—and that is equivocal—it was not admissible. The law
requires testimony be given by witnesses who are fully conscious.

In the same file box where the transcript of the hypnosis session
was discovered I also found an interesting document that was an
affidavit.

Glorianna had married again. Her new husband, John Tuckus,
made the affidavit to the police:

March 30, 1978.

For a period of one year from June 6, 1977, I have been married to
Glorianna Sanford. . . . During our courtship we stayed one night
at the Holiday Inn, Waterbury. During the course of the evening we
were discussing the Murray Gold case and she said I have something to tell you that I never told anyone. I said I wasn't interested.
However, she persisted and stated that on the night of the murders

Bruce Sanford, her husband, had taken her car, a 1974 Volkswagen. Approximately one hour later he returned to his home at 53 Myrtle Avenue, Waterbury. An argument ensued over his taking of the car because he didn't have a driver's license at the time. Shortly after, he told Glorianna that he had done a terrible thing and she didn't question him relative to what he was referring to. Later that evening Bruce cut his throat and she called an ambulance and he was taken to the hospital.

The rather obvious significance of Tuckus's affidavit is that it again put Sanford in the murderer's seat. Sanford took Glorianna's 1974 Volkswagen to drive to the Pasternak home. He must have parked it a distance from the Pasternak house before picking up the fire extinguisher, which he squirted into the victim's face and then proceeded to murder both Pasternaks. When the bloody deed was done he must have run up Fern Street to the block where he parked the car and driven home to Glorianna.

25

THE FOURTH TRIAL

SOON AFTER GOLD began receiving antipsychotic drug treatments in the hospital he asked for a new trial. Since he had never agreed to the diagnosis that he was ill, his impatience grew dramatically when he began to feel better. His Navane dosage was now up to twenty milligrams a day.

In fact, his cries for a new trial were wiser than he knew. The passing of time endangered the availability of defense evidence. It was essential for Gold's new lawyers to bring the Sanford evidence into the case. With more delay, the risk was that witnesses Sanford had confessed to might disappear. So here, as in most cases, prosecutors stood to gain from delay.

The defendant is usually content to offer proof of his own innocence, but in the Gold case the best defense had been, consistently, that it was Sanford, and not Gold, who had perpetrated the crime. Yet this created a double burden for the prosecutor.

A year earlier than the eighteen months the court had directed, Gold's demand for trial was supported by a medical finding that he was, finally, competent. This finding, however, was accompanied by a warning that Gold had to undergo continued psychiatric treatments in order to prevent a relapse, and made it clear that the heavy increases of drugs administered to him did not accomplish a complete cure.

The date was set for June 24, 1986, and a new judge, William Lavery, presided. William Collins and Nicholas Serignese, East Hartford attorneys, defended Gold. McDonald had been promoted from district attorney to judge, and the prosecution was conducted by his assistant, the able Walter Scanlon.

Ten years after the murders, Murray Gold was being tried for the fourth time.

Did the fourth trial involve the rule of double jeopardy—or for that matter quadruple jeopardy—the condemned's right not to be tried twice for the same crime?

No. That rule applies only where there has been an acquittal or a verdict of guilty, which is unappealed. If, as in the Gold case, the guilty verdict is set aside by the highest court, and a new trial ordered, it is legal to try the defendant again.

I doubt, however, that in all the annals of criminal law there is another instance of so many trials stretching over so many years, with an appeal and a reversal interspersed.

Once again, jury selection was tortuous. And when empaneled, the parade of witnesses began.

The prosecutor called detectives, police officers and experts on the stand to describe the scene of the crime. Drawings of the various rooms in the house were marked as exhibits. This extensive evidence had nothing to do with guilt or innocence. It was like the building of a set in a theater against which the drama would be played. In the course of mere description the police testified precisely where they had found the bloodless, drained corpse of Irving Pasternak, and the body of Rhoda Pasternak, lying curved and motionless in death.

Even the special terminology of the police, who decline to refer to the victims by name, or even as a man and a woman, but rather as "male" and "female," could not diminish the rush of emotion that survived the prosaic, measured references to the scene of bloody pools in which the slain couple lay.

Having learned from three previous trials, the prosecutor attempted to build a rebuttal against a contention that had not yet
been made. It was intended to bring a scientific answer to the
earlier evidence that while the killer was attacking her husband,
Rhoda Pasternak told her daughter on the phone that a crazy man
was fighting with her father and that when her daughter had
asked whether she recognized the voice of the assailant, the
mother replied that she did not. How then could the assailant
have been Gold, whose voice she had known so well when he had
been her son-in-law for approximately a year?

Is there any subject on which one can't find an expert? Apparently not. So the prosecution presented their expert on speech
and voice.

The author must admit to a certain delight in pricking the
pretensions of any expert who, according to the ironic definition,
having lost sight of his objective, redoubles his efforts, and for
every expert who says yes there can be found two who say no.

However, Professor Oscar Tosi was impressive. A professor at
Michigan State University for twenty-two years, he taught
physics and speech science. He had performed experiments in
voice identification under a $300,000 grant from the Department
of Justice. He was the author of a book, *Voice Identification
Theory and Legal Applications*. He had written "80 or 90" articles for scientific journals, twenty-five of which were on voice
identification.

Professor Tosi on the stand described the method he used to
determine how loud a voice emanating from the Pasternak living
room downstairs would sound upstairs. His instrument, a "sound
level meter," registered the voice downstairs at 86 to 91 decibels.
The same voice upstairs, where Rhoda Pasternak was, he said,
measured only 64 decibels.

Professor Tosi had been told that the television set in Rhoda's
bedroom was playing at the time of the murders. He therefore
assumed that television's sound would interfere or, as he expressed it, would "mask" the sound that came from below. He had
asked a detective to turn on the set at a volume the detective had
heard when he first arrived at the murder scene. Obviously,

though, this had to be an uncertain "measurement," and was vulnerable on cross-examination.

Professor Tosi also made the point once more that the length of time in which the voice is not heard by a person affects recognition. He claimed that since ten years had elapsed since the divorce the recognition factor would be very low.

But this was an assumption that Rhoda had not spoken to Gold during the ten years after his divorce from her daughter, Barbara, and was far from a certainty.

The prosecutor then called a fingerprint expert to the witness stand, Trooper Ronald Luneau. He had been a member of the Connecticut State Police for seventeen years at the time of the murders. He was a latent fingerprint examiner for the state police.

Q: What does a latent fingerprint examiner do?
A: He processes items to find latent fingerprints and then tries to identify them with certain individuals.

Any such prints were compared with fingerprint cards of known persons. Luneau looked for points of identification. If he found a minimum of twelve points, the identification had been made.

As testified to in Gold's previous trials, Luneau recovered forty-seven latent prints at the Pasternak home. Of these, ten remained unidentified.

On cross-examination, defense counsel Collins asked:

Q: And, of course, again, repeating, certainly there were no fingerprints of Murray Gold?
A: I am sorry, I didn't hear you.
Q: There were no fingerprints of Murray Gold?
A: Definitely not, no sir.

Subdued and competent or not, Murray Gold's behavior at the fourth trial was nonetheless eccentric to the layman. Apparently, the drugs fed to Gold to prevent any outburst during the trial had created a sweet tooth. Mounds chocolate-coconut bars became a necessity to appease his need, and obligingly Serignese, one of his counsel, would buy a small mountain of Mounds. Gold would watch the courtroom doors hungrily for his lawyer, who brought in the day's supply and slipped them under the papers in front of Gold. During each day in court Gold chewed bar after bar. I mention all this not as a curio but for its effect on the jury, which surely saw this devouring of the candy bars and would have been only human to think such conduct outlandish and neurotic, thereby perhaps affecting their judgment about Gold and his stability. And recall, his history of mental instability had been from the first trial one of the grounds for making him a suspect.

Glorianna turned out to be a dominant figure in the twisting events of all four trials. In her relationship with Sanford she had fulfilled the roles of mother and mistress. By now she had been married five times, almost always to weaker men. She was no femme fatale. She was slim and of medium height. Her honey-colored skin was consistent with her Italian heritage, but it looked much whiter against her very dark hair. She dressed simply. She was proud of having been a nurse and exercised her prowess on Sanford's many illnesses and neuroses, all combined and confused by a fanatical sexual relationship that outlived their ten-month marriage. Now she was stepping on the witness stand to spit defiance at the defense's mere intimation that it was Sanford and not Gold who should have been charged with the annihilation of the Pasternaks:

CLERK: Please state your name . . .
WITNESS: Glorianna . . .
COURT: I'm sorry. Your full name.
WITNESS: Glorianna Theresa Maselli LaPointe Sanford Tuckus Brazis Welsch.
SCANLON: How would you like me to refer to you?
WITNESS: Glorianna.

When defense counsel Collins referred to Sanford's conduct as bizarre, she retorted: "I know lots of people as bizarre, including yourself." Collins said: "I may not continue calling you 'Glorianna,' " and she responded: "I might reciprocate." This hostility toward Gold's lawyer clearly indicated her new, or renewed, determination to protect the late Bruce Sanford from evidence that he was the murderer.

Sanford's parting inscription, "Curse you Glory," scribbled in blood on the mirror was, it would seem, his final and perverse way of saying that his love and need for her were so strong that he had killed himself because he could not have her. As she apparently saw it, the message evoked an enormous obligation on her part not to sully his name further as an uncontrollable murderer.

Psychiatrists had testified that Sanford was antisocial and out of control. They warned that rejection of him might trigger the final violence. Glorianna, in fact, testified to that rejection: ". . . I can't tolerate this behavior. I can't have you do this to me . . . I went upstairs and unlocked the door and put this ultimatum to him by saying 'you will have to leave.' "

She had become rebellious. Sanford apparently could not blame Glorianna, the object of his obsession, for her rejection of him. He had to blame an outside influence—the lawyer Pasternak, a Jew, who in Sanford's chaotic mind was responsible, through his advice to Glorianna, for breaking Sanford's spell over her and causing her desertion.

Glorianna's guilt and her belief that she was responsible for Sanford's death made her a perfect witness for the prosecution. Even when she was under hypnosis and could reconstruct past events with greater particularity, she claimed she could not remember where and what Sanford was doing during the hours of 9:00 to 9:30 P.M. when the murders were committed. She was determined to protect him from even the suspicion of murder.

On the stand during the fourth trial, her animosity toward the defense continued to show itself at every turn . . .

The morning after the murders, Sanford was back again, insisting that Glorianna accompany him in her automobile to Florida.

She did not hesitate to call her first husband, Eddie LaPointe: "I wonder if you could do me a favor and stay with the children for a couple of days because there is something I have to do." He accommodated her but told his lawyer that Glorianna "ran away with her lover and abandoned the children." She revealed her resentment of LaPointe's lawyer, adding: "That is how much I trust lawyers [pointing at Collins]—you included."

Glorianna had changed from a seemingly easygoing, warm personality to a bitter accuser. Glorianna, who could have been a key witness for the defense, now angrily had turned her venom toward Murray Gold.

Sanford could not dispose of his blood-soaked clothes, because if discovered that would constitute evidence of guilt. He resorted to a desperate device. He cut his neck so as to pierce the skin, but not his throat. Then a suicide alarm was sounded, and an ambulance rushed him to the emergency room of the Waterbury hospital.

In this way he hoped to explain the immense flow of blood that covered his body as coming from his neck. However, the ruse was exposed medically. First, the ambulance attendant, Philip Palladino, testified that he brought Sanford to the hospital and observed that the entire visible front of Sanford's shirt was soaked with blood when he picked him up.

Dr. Thomas Spicuzza, who had treated Sanford in the emergency room, testified:

A: The purpose of the treatment was to repair a laceration on the left side of his neck.

Q: Would you describe the laceration?

A: The laceration was allegedly self-inflicted. It was very superficial, very straight and linear. Was not bleeding. And the wound edges were in pretty good approximation.

Q: Now did you observe the clothes he was wearing?

A: Yes, I did.

Q: Would you describe what you observed?

A: His clothing at least on the front side was covered from

the shirt and over the pants down and over the shoes with a large amount of blood.

Q: Now did you suture the wound?

A: Yes, I did.

Q: How many sutures?

A: There were fifteen sutures placed on his neck.

Q: Was this for cosmetic purposes?

A: Yes, it was.

Q: Now what was the relationship, doctor, between the physical exam, what you observed, and the cut on Sanford's neck?

A: The physical examination otherwise including the vital signs were entirely normal.

Q: Based on this now, Doctor, based on what you took, and the history and the vital signs, and the physical exam you made, did you form an opinion as to whether or not the blood you observed on Bruce Sanford's clothing, shirt, pants and shoes came from the superficial cut that you treated on his neck?

A: Yes, I did.

Q: And what is your opinion?

A: My opinion was the blood, the amount of blood was excessive for the nature of the wound observed.

Q: When you first saw Bruce Sanford what was your reaction?

A: I remember that night very vividly. And I remember turning to the nurse when he was brought in by the police, seeing the superficial wound. And I turned to her and said, "I wonder what he did to the other guy?"

The witness who gave direct testimony of Sanford's motive was Patricia Morrison, his childhood sweetheart. Even at fourteen, he was constantly in trouble and in juvenile jails. They continued their friendship through the years. Patricia Morrison was now a grandmother at the age of forty-two. Sanford confided in her more than in anyone else, even Glorianna.

Morrison testified:

> A: He told me about how they used to do drugs, and how
> they used to ride down the street, groups of them, in a car
> and pull girls off the street and rape them and, you know,
> that is about all I can really remember as far as the
> motorcycle gang went.

Judge Lavery, understandably, wanted to be certain that there
was a nexus between such testimony and the Pasternak murders.
She repeated her testimony. Sanford had called her three nights
before the murders, threatening to "get" Pasternak; he had made
anti-Semitic remarks; he had called her on the night of the murders that he had "done something I am never going to get out of";
he had asked her to help him flee the state.

The gruesome murders committed with satanic intensity challenged imagination. But Mrs. Morrison described an incident that
in its way exceeded all of Sanford's drug-ridden criminality. Was
he also a vampire? Two weeks before Sanford died, she recalled:

> We were talking small talk. And he was playing with a
> straight razor, and out of the clear blue sky, he just
> grabbed my arm and he slit my arm with the straight
> razor, and immediately dropped the razor, held my arm
> with both hands, and put his head down and began to
> drink my blood.
> Q: Now, what did he say after that?
> A: Why, he came up from my arm, for a second, he didn't say
> anything. He just had a funny look in his eyes. But al-
> most immediately he began to cry and he jumped up and
> said, "Oh, my God, what have I done, what have I done?"
> and he ran and got a towel to wrap around my arm and
> everything.

Before Mrs. Morrison left the stand she was asked:

> Q: Did Bruce Sanford have a collection of knives?
> A: Yes, sir, he did.

Q: He had?

A: One particular that I know of.

Q: One particular what?

A: Knife.

Q: Would you describe that knife to the ladies and gentlemen of the jury and to his Honor?

A: It was about this long [indicating]. It was all silver. I
remember that. Not real silver, but it was steel. And it
had certain weights on the handle to make it perfectly
balanced in your hand.

She had virtually described the murder weapon.

Q: And did he have other knives in his collection?

A: I was always taking knives away from him.

Q: And what would you do with the knives when you took
them away from him?

A: Threw them in the Naugatuck River.

On recross-examination the prosecutor, Mr. Scanlon, asked:

Q: This was a silver knife that you spoke about?

A: Well, it looked silver. It doesn't necessarily mean it was
silver. It could have been steel or something. It had that
silver color to it, this particular one.

Even the most serious trial has its lighter moments. They may,
indeed, be necessary for balance. I remember once when A.L.
Alexander, who presided over arbitration hearings on radio to
solve matrimonial disputes, was sued by an unhappy victim of
his arbitration decision. As attorney for Alexander, I objected to a
certain question asked by my adversary. Alexander, forgetting
that he was a witness in a real trial and not a presiding judge in his
radio program, shouted "sustained!" A gale of laughter greeted
this assistance to his attorney, and only increased as Alexander
apologized to the judge for usurping his authority, role, title, etc.

In the Gold case, too, there was one incident that briefly

changed the heavy mood. A forensic expert was put on the stand
by the defense to demonstrate that the two small pieces of plastic, supposedly found at the murder scene, could not be determined as parts of the same broken thread; the two ends had to
match to prove they came from an original single piece. Therefore, they were not traceable to the plastic thread of the sewing
kit found in Gold's home.

The expert witness had just given his opinion that "there is no
way anyone could make any match with respect to the two twisting pieces of thread in the box," when the two tiny pieces of
plastic fell out of their container.

The witness yelled: "Oops, we may have lost it." Mr. Scanlon,
the prosecutor, asked:

Q: That is the second [time]?
WITNESS: This happened before?

Collins immediately joined in:

COLLINS: The State's case is destroyed.
SCANLON: You know which experts to get.

Before there could be a further retort, the witness spoke up
again:

WITNESS: Something *did* drop out of here!
COLLINS (*in a melodramatic voice*): Nobody leaves the
    room!
COURT: Is that the one with the little piece in it? Is that the
    little piece right there?
COLLINS: I think you just broke the chain of custody, your
    Honor.
COURT: Isn't there a little piece . . . Mr. Scanlon?
SCANLON: I don't want to get near it . . . Is that it right over
    there?
WITNESS: Let's see.
SCANLON: Have you given up the search?

COLLINS: I have given up the search. As long as it is not in his cuff.

SCANLON (*asks the witness*): You don't have cuffs on your trousers?

WITNESS: I don't.

COLLINS: Is it in his shoe? It is not there? . . . Let's assume that it is on the floor for the present.

COURT: Is this the one with the little thing?

CLERK: Yes.

SCANLON: It was in existence at one time. What is this?

WITNESS: That is a piece of plastic.

SHERIFF: Why don't you just get up and move the chair?

COURT: All right. Jury is excused until we find the little piece.

(*Jury is excused.*)

WITNESS: Here it is.

COURT: You got it? All right. Will the attorneys come forward.

SCANLON: That is not the piece.

COLLINS: What is that?

WITNESS: It is just junk on the floor here.

COLLINS: Where is it?

WITNESS: Right there.

COURT: All right. Bring the jury back out.

(*The jury returns to the jury box.*)

COURT: All right, ladies and gentlemen. We found the missing piece. You may continue.

WITNESS: Should I cap this up again before something untoward happens?

"Hand it to me," said the judge.

The saga of the exhibit lost by the expert witness had ended. It

Prosecutor Walter Scanlon used "the full panoply of persuasion, candor, mixed with inflammatory appeal" —and, ultimately, compassion.

was the only light moment in the otherwise deadly, sad business of the fourth murder trial of Murray Gold.

But back to the plastic "evidence":

Q: Exhibit one twenty-one. And that is the plastic that you examined along with Doctor Refner [the other plastics expert] approximately three months ago, is that correct?

A: Yes, appears to be.

Q: And your conclusion after examining that piece of plastic was that it could not match the other piece of plastic?

A: The question of matching could not be addressed at that point.

Q: Because?

A: Because there was no detail on the fractured surface.

Up to this point the prosecutor had followed the plan of the previous trials. The lack of any direct evidence was the weakness of his case. He sought to fill this gap by presenting a new witness to assert that there was scientific evidence that Gold was in the Pasternak home on the eve of the murders. The evidence would be footprints, this time not involving the Cat's Paw heel inscription in the blood.

Scanlon presented an anthropologist, Louise Robbins, who testified that the uneven pressure of the forefront of the shoe could be "lifted" like a fingerprint and was as unique and identifiable as a fingerprint.

Professor Robbins's theory was that she could measure the length of the foot from the tip of the toe to the farthest point in the center of the heel, and similarly across the width of various parts of the foot, and thus discover the unique pressure points used in the course of walking, as revealed by the front of the shoe, and discernible from the blood prints on the tile and the carpet. In brief, she claimed to have discovered a new technique that equated footprints with fingerprints.

In view of the novel and startling nature of this proposition, Judge Lavery excused the jury and heard the evidence himself to determine whether it was legally admissible. He ruled that it was, and the jury was recalled to hear and evaluate it.

Defense counsel, Collins, then conducted a long cross-examination.

In the battle of persuasion, it is not necessary to destroy the adversary's contention. It is enough to surround the attack with sufficient doubts to decrease his firepower. Although Professor Robbins was an estimable scholar, the bursts of doubt that assailed her unique theory filled the stenographic record.

For example:

COLLINS: And, of course, you are the only one, so far as you
    know, in your field that makes this claim about being able
    to identify footprints through shoe measurements and et
    cetera in the United States, is that correct?
A: As far as I know, sir.

She conceded that she had not even submitted her novel theory for review by other experts:

Q: Did you ever consider in the last ten years producing
some of your work to your peers for some critical analysis? Did you yourself ever do that?

A: No, sir, I have not done that.

Professor Robbins testified that:

I examined one pair of [Gold's] shoes, I believe that was suspected
of being worn that day. Three pairs were . . . simply a part of the
series of evidence that I had to examine.

In other words, it was suggested to her that one pair out of the
four pairs was actually worn by Gold on the night of the murders.
The witness merely had to identify one pair of the shoes. By this
means she was led to the conclusion that one particular pair of
Gold's shoes was used by him on the night of the murders. That
was fatally suggestive, as impermissible as saying that a potential
witness' recognition of a suspect in a lineup was based on an
assertion that one of these people being shown to the witness was
definitely the criminal. It is illegal suggestibility.

Furthermore, she conceded that her unique footprint identification was based on extremely limited study:

Q: . . . so in the past ten or twelve years that you have held
yourself out as an expert, aside from that one lecture you
attended for four hours at Quantico, you never attended
anything else, did you?

A: Not focusing on footprint analysis, or shoeprint analysis.

Even if any testimony by Professor Robbins had not been vulnerable, because improperly suggestible, it would have fallen
in any event. It was contradicted by another expert presented by
the defense. Collins put on the stand Dr. Peter Cavanagh, who
held a Ph.D. in human biomechanics; he was a professor of that
subject at Pennsylvania State University and was the organizer
and director of The Center for Locomotion Studies. He also was a
consultant for most of the major orthopedic support-shoe manu-

facturers in the world, as well as a designer of shoes. He had written a book on the subject.

Dr. Cavanagh had examined Murray Gold's feet on January 10, 1985, and found them to be average, not notable and exhibiting no distinguishable characteristics. "A very typical foot."

Dr. Cavanagh also analyzed the carpet and tile prints taken from the Pasternak home and found that some of those prints exhibited unusual patterns, and further concluded that the footprints made in the blood were "asymmetrical," while the prints he took of Murray Gold were "symmetrical."

Collins then questioned Dr. Cavanagh on this critical point:

Q: So, for whatever purpose, certainly those prints taken at the scene of the crime did not match any of the foot characteristics of Murray Gold.

A: I did not find any foot characteristics of Murray Gold that . . . would leave distinguishable characteristics . . . I found that there was nothing recognizable, no deformity . . . of his foot that would make [Gold's] shoe leave an unusual pattern or the prints . . . there is [no] feature of that footprint . . . Murray Gold's foot would have left.

Q: . . . no one could determine then that these prints left at the scene of the murder were of Murray Gold, is that correct?

A: Not in my opinion.

Q: . . . there is a broad group of people that do not have these characteristics (including Murray Gold). And if they do not have these characteristics, is it scientifically possible to . . . identify their footprint from a shoeprint?

A: In my opinion, there is absolutely no scientific basis for that.

Q: None whatever?

A: None whatever.

In her testimony at the fourth trial, Barbara Pasternak, Gold's former wife, described again her father's fairness in making the divorce a friendly one, dividing the property between herself and Murray equally. She had heard testimony that Murray Gold liked her father. Myrna, her sister, had so testified. Above all, Murray had sought a reconciliation and her parents were not averse as, indeed, they had persuaded her to marry Gold originally, because they were eager for Bubbles "to settle down." But she also testified, vividly, describing how Gold's conduct during their brief marriage had driven her to the verge of a "nervous breakdown." Scanlon questioned her.

A: It was a very strenuous marriage from the beginning . . . Murray was very jealous of any friends I tried to have. And he was also very critical of me . . . there were a lot of instances where I was waiting for a nervous breakdown living with him . . . I had a friend who died of cancer who was a platonic friend . . . I was very upset . . . Murray . . . forbid me to go to the funeral. And he wouldn't talk to me for almost two weeks after that. In fact, it got to the point where he forbid me to talk to my parents unless he was present.

Q: And did you seek help from his parents?

A: Yes, from his parents and from my parents, and in fact his mother used to advise me to handle him [Gold] with kid gloves.

Cross-examined by Collins, her time for retaliation had come:

Q: How soon after that [her parents' death] . . . did you talk to the police?

A: . . . I was in California and I came back the next day . . . I was a basket case. So I don't know exactly how soon.

Q: But, in any event, you did talk to some members of the police department?

A: Yes.

Q: And did they ask you if you knew of anyone that might have done this?

A: To tell you the truth, I knew that Murray had been in

touch . . . It went through my mind that it could have
been Murray, but I dreaded the thought that it might be,
because he had been my husband . . . And if he did it, then
I am the one who introduced him to my parents.

Barbara's retaliation continued and took on an even subtler
shade than before:

Q: Isn't it a fact, Miss Pasternak, that you did give to them
   [the police] another name?
A: Well, I hate to say it, but I named a lot of people, because I
   was frantic.
Q: So, you did mention your boyfriend's name as a possible
   suspect?
A: Yes.

She told the jury that she also gave the police the name of an
erstwhile "boyfriend" who was included on the list of suspects,
and was also wanted by the F.B.I.

Since her association with such a discredited character might
reflect negatively on her and even involve her in a moral sense
with the tragedy, was she trying to deflect such a possibility by
pointing a belated finger at Gold? There is an ironic parallel with
Glorianna trying to protect Sanford by aiding the prosecutor's
effort against Gold. This testimony hit home, despite Barbara's
concession on the stand that Gold had never struck her or committed any other act of violence. She knew his record was spotless
of even the most minor offense.

The bitterness which often envelopes divorce knows no
bounds. Apparently, when love turns to hate there remains poi-
sonous disillusionment. Even so, Barbara's revelation that in her
mind she thought that Gold might be the murderer of her parents
seemed particularly unwarranted; her unhappiness in the marriage could not fairly be equated with such a conclusion or even
speculation.

26

SUMMATION

THE PROSECUTOR WAS now to proceed with his summation first, then the defense counsel would present his and thereafter the prosecutor would make his rebuttal. So the prosecution is given the opportunity to speak twice. It is a very substantial advantage. It permits the prosecutor to comment on any error made by defense counsel. Also, it leaves the final impression with the jury of the prosecutor's refutation or even ridicule of the defense argument. So, for centuries the principle of speaking last was urged upon the courts as a privilege that should be granted to the defendant rather than to the prosecution. When Sir Walter Raleigh was being tried, Sir Edward Coke asked him: "Have you done? The King must have the last word." Raleigh replied: "Nay, Mr. Attorney, he who speaks for his life must speak last."

A pertinent illustration of the advantage the prosecutor enjoyed was his argument that the human hair found on the mat of Gold's car definitely belonged to Rhoda Pasternak:

> In comparing the hair found in Gold's car and the hair removed
> from Rhoda Pasternak's head, [F.B.I.] Agent Wallace concluded, and
> I quote: "In this case here, with the comparisons I looked at, the

microscopic characteristics, I would state most probably the hair
. . . I found on the floor mat came from the same source as the hairs
present in the packet reported to me to be from Rhoda Pasternak.
Most probably Rhoda Pasternak's hair."

The devastating conclusion the prosecutor drew from this
"fact" was in contradiction to the testimony of the defense witness, Dr. Peter DeForest, Professor of Criminalistics at the John
Jay College of Criminal Justice, and a seventeen-year veteran in
the field of forensic science. Upon direct examination by defense
counsel Collins, Dr. DeForest had testified:

Q: Doctor, . . . I am going to ask you one question. Is hair
   evidence a positive means of personal identification?
A: It is not.

Similarly, the prosecutor's claim that the pieces of plastic sup-
posed to have been found at the murder scene matched the plastic
on the button kit taken from Gold's home was totally unwarranted, and not just because the plastic could not be matched.

The claim was bizarre in the light of the fact that *Gold's kit was
stolen from the prosecutor's office* and the one marked in evidence was *not* his kit.

Early in the investigation a friend of Glorianna had accompanied her to the prosecutor's office and, according to the evidence given by Glorianna, had stolen the sewing kit from his
office. Glorianna testified during the first trial that "Peggy took
the kit."

Therefore, the jury was asked to believe that another of thousands of kits matched the plastic pieces allegedly found at the
murder scene!

The art of presenting a convincing argument involves, obviously, subtle analytical and psychological skill. For example, the
prosecutor had stressed the fact that Gold had changed his explanation for his cut finger several times. The first time he said he
inflicted the cut on himself while peeling a carrot. On another
occasion he said it was a turnip. In any case, the cut was severe

enough to have a doctor bandage his finger. Did not such confusion create the suspicion that he was lying, and that he had wounded himself while slashing the Pasternaks?

There was evidence in the record to refute this suspicion. Dr. Bertrand Bisson testified that an assailant slashing with a knife in his right hand could not cut the forefinger of his left hand, and even if he could, he would have severed his finger and not just wounded it. If Gold had been the murderer, and had invented a story to explain his cut finger, he would surely have fixed his mind on the specific vegetable he was peeling to explain his

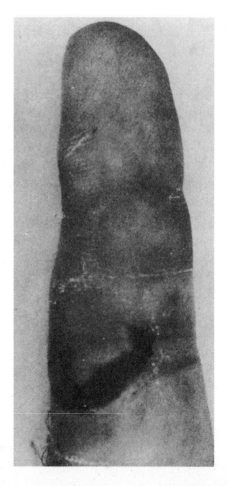

The "evidence" of Murray Gold's cut finger—supposedly gained in an encounter of multiple, slashing stab wounds to two people . . .

wound. Knowing the importance of such explanation, he would not have wavered and forgotten its details or varied them when questioned. Therefore, wasn't the fact that it was unimportant to him *what* vegetable he was peeling really proof of his innocence?

Such are the psychological subtleties that may erase from the jury's mind an otherwise damning assertion. Similarly, Gold's openness and cooperation with the police who came to his home with a warrant to seize his shoes was further psychological evidence of his innocence. He cooperated fully with the police and invited them to take whatever else they wanted, even though not specified in the warrant. Also, he submitted himself to questioning by the police for hours. He did not, as a guilty man would, refuse to answer questions through the night, before finally rebelling and saying that he thought he ought to consult an attorney in view of the persistent innuendoes that were assailing him. Was not his complete cooperation with the investigating police a significant sign of his innocence?

If the jury was fairly chosen to be unbiased, and in light of Gold's probable and actual conduct, how, in view of the overwhelming evidence of Sanford's guilt, could it reach a guilty verdict against Gold?

The skill of summation is, of course, as varied as the personalities of the advocates. Some lawyers even try to impress the jury with the clothes they wear. A number of lawyers have adopted a frock coat with silk lapels, adorned by a white carnation, winged collar and white bow tie. Others deliberately seek to achieve a humble impression, to "make the jury feel comfortable." Some advocates use flowing language, delivered in ringing tones. Others deliberately avoid such effects and speak in conversational intimate tones, striving to appeal to the jurors as one of them. Still others use shock treatment in their deliveries—from whispers to shattering bellows.

One thing is certain. Artifice is resented by the jury. A plain man must not put on airs and one who postures as an aristocrat must not resort to street language. Respect for the judge, courtesy to the opponent, and fairness to a hostile witness are persuasive with jurors. The attorney's attitude toward a witness is all-important. He or she must be treated with courtesy, unless and until lateral vision reveals that the jurors are disgusted with the witness. Only then may the lawyers attack frontally, knowing that the jury will be pleased at his or her discomfiture. Sincerity is essential, and an emotional deep concern for the client and his cause is persuasive.

The jury had heard two contrasting summations. Defense counsel Collins adopted the technique of reviewing the names of each witness and a brief statement of his or her testimony. It was a balance sheet just adding up the numbers of witnesses.

The prosecutor, Scanlon, had used the full panoply of persuasion, candor, mixed with inflammatory appeal. But experience testifies that eloquence and even brilliant coloration cannot substitute for the absence of hard fact. Which method of persuasion would succeed?

At one point in Scanlon's persuasive presentation he wandered away from the facts. That was when he argued that Bruce Sanford did not commit the murders:

> I . . . submit, ladies and gentlemen, that the attempt falls flat in that the evidence in this case shows clearly that Bruce Sanford was in custody first at the home of his former wife Glorianna and then by the police. . . . It is submitted, ladies and gentlemen, that Bruce Sanford was locked in the bedroom of his ex-wife's Glorianna's house after he came home drunk in the afternoon of September 26. She said that she kept the key in her apron and unlocked the door after she had fed her family and finished her other household chores . . .

In this way he was leaving the impression with the jury that Sanford could not have committed the murders because he was locked up during the time they occurred. This was untrue. Evidence was presented by Sanford's friends, Bourassa and Yashenko, that they came to visit him and found him missing. Glorianna had not locked him in the bedroom. There was evidence that there was no lock on the door with which to achieve this purpose had she even wished to do so. There was testimony that Glorianna had called Bourassa, greatly disturbed because Sanford was not in the house on the night of the murders. The jury was improperly left with the wrong impression.

Since Gold's chief defense was that Sanford and not he had committed the crimes, why did not defense counsel in his summation list—just list, if nothing more—the irresistible proof of Sanford's guilt:

First, the fact that he had an overwhelming motive. He believed, in his distorted mind, that Pasternak was advising Glorianna to leave him.

Second, a psychiatrist testified that if Sanford was rejected, it would set off an explosion in his disordered personality. Glorianna did, in fact, reject him on September 26, 1974. That night the Pasternaks were killed.

Third, Sanford was fascinated with knives and blood. He continually played with razors and even cut himself to see blood flow. His favorite knife was a balanced Buck knife, the same as the one used in the murders. The Pasternaks were destroyed by approximately fifty-six knife strokes.

Fourth, Patricia Morrison testified that on the evening of the murders Sanford had called her from a telephone booth stating that he was covered with blood, that he had done something he would never be able to get out of, and asking her help to get him out of the state.

Fifth, the next day he did indeed flee Connecticut to Florida. Wasn't his flight a physical confession of guilt?

Sixth, he did not return to Connecticut until *after* Gold had been indicted for the murders—three months later.

Seventh, two witnesses testified that they saw a man running from the murder scene with "long hair waving in the wind." When the prosecutor had Sanford exhumed years later, it was found that he was wearing a long-haired woman's wig he had apparently used while committing crimes. The exhumation photograph could have been shown to the jury.

Eighth, the extraordinary coincidence of the use of the fire extinguisher in the Woodbury murders, involving Sanford's cronies, was noted by Arthur Miller, the famous playwright. He wrote Dr. Elliot M. Gross, the Chief Medical Examiner of West-chester County:

> The question is whether "the white particles" you found in Kulosza's head wounds could have come from a fire extinguisher [as] was used in the Pasternak murders, apparently to blind the victim. I thought at the time that this was an extremely unusual wrinkle. And it seems to me now . . . that it might offer a possible link between both cases.
>
> Joseph Leblanc [one of the confessed killers in the Woodbury murders] was a very close friend of Bruce Sanford's, having partici-pated with him in a shootout with the police in 1970. From this distance, there also seems a resemblance in the way both murders were done, the vicious use of knives, for one thing. In any event, if in fact an extinguisher was used in the Kulosza killing, it would seem a very worthwhile line of questioning for the state's attorney—whether Leblanc did indeed have a connection with the murder of the Pasternaks.
>
> Very sincerely yours,
ARTHUR MILLER

Dr. Gross forwarded Miller's letter to Francis McDonald, the Connecticut State Prosecutor, who received it on May 3, 1979.

Weren't all these facts sufficient to have the jury find beyond a reasonable doubt that Sanford was the culprit rather than Gold? Yet not one word of these critical issues was mentioned in the defense's summation. Collins's failure to exploit these argu-ments, as we shall see, was commented upon by a subsequent judge.

Nothing reveals the genius of the American system of justice better than the judge's instructions to the jury at the end of the testimony—the "Judge's Charge." It explains the relationship be-tween the judge and the jury. Most important of all, the judge's instructions to the jury, designating their province and his exclu-sive domain, is an exquisite division of authority. The judge may not invade the jurors' exclusive right to determine the facts. However, each juror must be guided by the judge's instructions on the governing law that applies to the facts. How to maintain this equilibrium?

If the jury disagrees with the judge's charge on a legal point, may it disregard his statement of the applicable law and substitute its own common sense of what the legal rule ought to be? No. The reason is that even if the judge is wrong in his legal instruction, his error can be corrected by an appellate court. But if the jury disagrees with the judge's ruling, and particularly if it doesn't reveal its disobedience, the appellate court may not know that the correct rule of law stated by the judge was disregarded.

Sometimes the judge goes out of his way to tell the jury that even if they sense that he believes or disbelieves a witness' testimony, they should disregard his opinion. So, if a judge by grimace, or turning his chair, unwittingly displays his skepticism about a witness' recital of the facts, the jury, as the judge will instruct it, must not be influenced by the judge's gestures. It is its view that counts in deciding conflicts of *facts*, not the judge's.

The instructions of Judge Lavery in the fourth trial illustrate how sensitively the scales of justice are balanced by well-established rules created over the centuries. He began by instructing the jurors that their duty was to decide without bias or prejudice, nor were they to be "governed by sympathy . . . emotion or tears."

The judge described his role to the jurors, which was to decide whether oral evidence or exhibits were legally admissible. If he ruled them out and he was wrong on the law, the appellate court would correct him on appeal. The judge also explained to the jury the principles of law that applied to the case.

The second charge Judge Lavery gave the jurors dealt with the much talked about but not always understood principle of reasonable doubt. The defendant "is presumed to be innocent until he is proven guilty beyond a reasonable doubt of each and every element of the crime."

The judge stressed that it was the state's burden to prove that the defendant committed the crime and in doing so had to prove all essential elements of the offense beyond a reasonable doubt. The defendant, on the other hand, was not required to prove his innocence.

What does "beyond a reasonable doubt" mean? Judge Lavery explained that it was "not a surmise, a guess or a conjecture . . . not a hesitation springing from . . . feelings of sympathy or pity for the accused, [but] a doubt that is reasonable in light of the evidence and is honestly entertained by a juror after fair comparison and careful examination" of all evidence. Proof beyond a reasonable doubt, said the judge, was defined as "proof of such convincing character that a reasonable person would not hesitate to rely and act upon it in the most important of his or her own affairs." The jurors were then instructed to consider all testimony and exhibits received into evidence but were warned to be wary of the many statements made by the attorneys during the course of the trial because they were not witnesses, and their opening and closing statements were only intended to help the jury to interpret evidence from their contending points of view.

The jury was also instructed not to be influenced by the attorneys' objections. The court ruled on those, and if the evidence was let in, the jury was entitled to consider it. If not, it was not.

Following these charges, Judge Lavery explained to the jury the difference between direct and circumstantial evidence. "Direct evidence is testimony by a witness—what that witness personally saw or heard or did." Circumstantial evidence, the judge explained, was "indirect evidence" offered to prove a certain fact from which the jurors were asked to infer the existence of other facts. By way of example, the judge told them that if the streets are wet with water, the inference can be drawn that it has rained. If, however, a city sanitation truck was cleaning the streets, the inference would be just the opposite, that it did not rain. The judge concluded: "In deciding whether to draw an inference, you must look at and consider all the facts in the light of reason, common sense and experience."

The judge told the jury that the Gold case was based largely on circumstantial evidence. The jury was instructed that *intent* to commit a crime was a necessary element to constitute the crime with which the defendant was charged, and instructed the jury that it had to determine the existence of such intent from the facts involved in the case. This, too, had to be proved beyond a reasonable doubt.

The judge explained that the state was not required to prove a motive. However, if motive was introduced into evidence it too had to be established beyond a reasonable doubt, like any other fact: "Whatever motivates a man, however, rests only in his mind . . . whatever was in his mind must be inferred from his conduct in the light of the surrounding circumstances . . . If the existence of a motive can be reasonably inferred, that is evidence tending to prove his guilt. If no motive can be inferred or found, that may well tend to raise a reasonable doubt as to the guilt of the accused . . ."

Since many witnesses in the Gold case were police and law-enforcement officials, Judge Lavery emphasized that their testimony should not be given special privilege.

In many criminal cases the defendant, for a variety of reasons, decides not to testify. He or she is protected by the Fifth Amendment from doing so, since defendants may not make "good witnesses" and might therefore incriminate themselves. Judge Lavery instructed the jury that Gold's decision not to testify must not be held against him, nor should his failure to do so be taken as evidence of his guilt.

He emphasized that justice should be served always. He put it well: "Remember also that the question before you can never be, will the state win or lose the case? The state always wins when justice is done, regardless of whether the verdict be guilty or not guilty."

In this trial, the jury had to respond to the task of first proving that Gold killed the Pasternaks and that he intended to do so. If the state failed to prove any one of these two elements, then the jury had to conclude that the state failed to establish a case for murder. If this was the case, the jury's task was not finished. It still had to decide whether the defendant was guilty of manslaughter, an offense encompassed within the charge of murder. The basis for this charge was not in the intent to kill, but that

Gold intended to inflict serious physical injury that carried a substantial risk of death.

In concluding his charge, the judge stressed the need for a unanimous verdict.

In a final plea for justice that would not brook compromises, the judge said: "You must remember that it is your duty to reach your own conclusions by an independent determination of the facts. You should listen to your fellow jurors, but you should not merely follow their decisions. You should make up your own mind."

The whole story of Sanford's involvement had been admitted into evidence. The judge's charge was fair, and even though prosecutor Scanlon's brilliant summation had on several occasions overreached the facts, the requirement of finding guilt beyond a reasonable doubt seemed to be a firm barrier to a finding of "guilty."

At the end of every trial there is the tense atmosphere of guessing as to its outcome. When the fourth trial ended there was a general feeling that Gold would be acquitted. Even Judge Lavery had sensed a not-guilty verdict, if one is to draw an inference from his instruction to the court personnel to arrange for Gold's departure through a rear door so as to prevent any "scene" outside the courthouse.

This was greatly due to that severe basic test: a prosecutor must prove the defendant not only guilty, but guilty "beyond a reasonable doubt." In view of all the surrounding facts, including Sanford's confessions to his intimates, how could a jury find Gold, and not Sanford, guilty beyond a reasonable doubt?

Judge Lavery instructed the jury on July 21, 1986, and the jury began its deliberations. Gold was escorted to his prison cell beneath the courtroom to await the verdict. The visitors in the courtroom, who had increased its capacity by squeezing against each other, left the courtroom in a leisurely manner, many determined to walk the corridor to wait for the jury's decision. The lawyers on both sides of the dispute leaned back in their seats

while their assistants put their voluminous briefs and notes into
briefcases. Calm descended on the courtroom.

It was not until three days later, on July 24, that the jury sent
word it had reached a decision. Then suddenly the air stirred.
Somewhere in the distance a door had slammed shut. There were
hasty footsteps. A courtroom guard was seen hurrying toward the
judge's chambers. All moved toward the courtroom doors to re-
capture their seats. The judge had returned to the bench. The jury
soon filed in. The doors closed. Everyone scanned the jurors' faces
for a clue to their decision. Those initiated in court procedure had
anticipated the verdict by simply looking at the faces of the jurors
as they filed in. If any juror smiled toward the defense counsel,
they knew that victory was pending. If they looked sharply away
from the defense bench or table, with faces pinched from the
ordeal, defense counsel knew they had lost.

Criminal cases, particularly murder trials, develop a pro-
cedural mystique. It is almost as if the movements of the participants are paced by a musical tempo.

The dirge began when the court clerk asked the foreman: "Mr.
Foreman, have you agreed upon a verdict?" The foreman rose
slowly, responding: "Yes." The traditional, inevitable procedure
went on:

> CLERK: Mr. Gold, will you please stand and face the jury.
> Ladies and gentlemen of the jury, look upon the accused,
> you who are sworn.

The clerk continued to ask the jury, through its foreman, the
jury's verdict as to the first count, the murder of Irving Pasternak:
... "Is the defendant guilty or is he not guilty?"

The foreman responded: "Guilty."

An explosive sound interrupted the procedure for a moment.
The clerk asked the jury's verdict as to the second count, the
murder of Rhoda Pasternak. Again the foreman responded:
"Guilty."

Mr. Collins then requested that the jury be polled and the
procedure was recorded:

CLERK: Ladies and gentlemen, you may be seated. As I call
each of your numbers and names individually, would you
please stand, remain standing and respond to my questions.

Even though the jury verdict of guilty had been announced by
the foreman, its chosen spokesman, it could be that in the clashes
of jury discussion, one or two jurors had yielded their opinions to
the pressures of the majority among them. Such conclusion was
proper in the give-and-take of debate, but not in a verdict. A man's
liberty was at stake. If the juror's conscience won't be stilled, a
right is given him up to the last moment to announce his view
that he has not been convinced beyond a reasonable doubt. That
last moment is extended to a point beyond the announcement of
the foreman. The law, therefore, permits the defense lawyer to
request that the judge have each individual juror stand and announce whether he agrees with the verdict of guilty. If the individual juror has given in to other jurors for expediency only, he or
she has this last chance to assert the call of his conscience. It
rarely happens. But since a criminal case requires unanimity, not
a majority of the jury vote, this special privilege is the law's way
of protecting a defendant.

Each juror affirmed the guilty verdict. The repetition increased
the pain of the decision.

Even though the jury had condemned Murray Gold, the judge was
not ready to announce immediately what the punishment should
be. It is customary for the prosecutor to ask the probation department of the court to prepare a detailed report of the defendant's
background. Has he been convicted before? If so, how many
times? And for what offenses? Has he been a model citizen before
his present plight? What were his good deeds that might deserve
consideration of how extreme his punishment should be?

This is the reason why there is a considerable period of time
between a guilty verdict and the imposition of sentence. It allows
the probation department to gather its facts on the defendant so

that it can give the sentencing judge a full report on the defendant and guide the judge either to leniency or severity based on that report.

As the jury's verdict was announced, when Gold heard that he was found guilty, he was stunned. So was almost everyone else. His lawyers quickly tried to give him the comfort of an appeal. "I don't want an appeal," Gold said. Mr. Collins again urged him to protect his appellate rights. Gold was forlorn and adamant. "I don't want to appeal," he repeated.

As I've indicated, adverse reactions to Navane cause the patient to become weak or fatigued. Gold's refusal to appeal the guilty verdict was based on his assertion that he was "too tired."

The matter was then brought to the attention of Judge Lavery. Solicitous about protecting Gold's rights, he urged him to permit his lawyers to file an appeal on his behalf.

Gold again refused.

27

THE SENTENCE

A MONTH LATER, on August 29, 1986, prior to sentencing, prosecutor Scanlon addressed the court:

> ... We ... have a pre-sentence report. That lays out the factual situation, which is, briefly, Mr. Gold was convicted of the double murder of Irving and Rhoda Pasternak on September 26, 1974. And after a series of trials finally he was convicted in this Court on what was primarily circumstantial evidence ... the sentence report also indicated and the Court is aware of mental problems that the defendant suffered and that he was treated while he was the defendant in this Court a number of times at Whiting Forensic Institute at Middletown. And this is all documented in the file. And although it was never a part of the trial, the case against Mr. Gold, it may contain many of the answers of this brutal slaying ...
>
> It is my hope that if the Court would see fit to sentence the defendant to twenty-five years to life on both of these counts, and it is also my hope that Mr. Gold receives the treatment that I believe he needs. And maybe he could be transferred internally by the Commissioner of Corrections.

So, Scanlon did show his compassion, in the hope that Gold would receive psychiatric treatment for what was obvious by this time—Gold's deteriorating mental condition.

Murray Gold's ex-wife, Barbara Pasternak, who was present at the sentencing, addressed the court, asking that Gold never be released, and Judge Lavery responded:

> . . . I am bound by law by the prior sentence [referring to the 25 year sentence imposed at the second trial], and there is nothing that I can do to . . . enhance that sentence. My hands are completely tied by the United States Supreme Court case of *Perce.*

The climax of the courtroom drama had been reached. The awesome power of the judge to mete out punishment had arrived. As he had indicated, he was bound by the prior sentence and he might very well deprive the defendant of his liberty for the rest of his life, a punishment many think is prolonged slow death, even crueler than decapitation, poison, or electrical stoppage of the heart.

Such a solemn moment yielded again to formalism, as if it were choreographed for the occasion. The defense counsel was invited to make a statement in his losing cause.

William Collins then made an impassioned plea for mercy:

> . . . Throughout this long ordeal, there is one thing that I think we were always struck by. And that is that Mr. Gold has always maintained his innocence . . . in Murray Gold's own mind, he does believe he is innocent . . . it is a tragedy because there is nothing in his background ever to suggest violence of any sort. He has always maintained, always to the present day, right now, he said he is innocent.

Referring to the fact that the Supreme Court of Connecticut had freed Gold and directed a new trial, Collins said:

> . . . he was released from the custody of the Commissioner of Corrections for between five and six years on the promise to appear, when he remained all that time in Queens, New York. He

never had a traffic ticket. He never had anything charged against him. Surely, the fact that he spent all this time as a citizen maintaining his own, without breaking the law, even a spitting on the sidewalk, should, I think, go along with whatever sentence your Honor feels is just. I know Ms. Pasternak suffered a great deal. I know she believes, as the jury did, that Murray Gold committed these crimes. But I don't think that you can give up on an individual and throw the key away. Murray Gold was a very productive citizen early in life, a scientist, a stockbroker. I think all of these things should go into the measure of what his sentence ought to be. It has been a long time. And I don't think the suffering will end today. At least for Murray and his mother that will continue.

The Court then invited the defendant to make a statement:

COURT: Mr. Gold, you wish to say anything?
GOLD: No.

Murray Gold, who had been so voluble on prior occasions, even to the extent of interrupting the judge, lapsed into silence. It was the very time that an emotional assertion of his innocence, exceeded only by his suffering, would have been most appropriate. Perhaps Murray thought that silence would express his shock and outrage more than anything he could say. Perhaps he was just too defeated to respond. Whatever the reason, the opportunity for the defendant to cry out his innocence that provides the most dramatic and often traumatic moment of the trial was forfeited. Murray Gold had suddenly turned mute.

The formalities of sentencing now acquired the slow tempo of the funeral march.

Judge Lavery began:

. . . Mr. Gold, if you will rise. The Court wishes to make the record clear that a few weeks prior to the trial, the Court had Mr. Gold examined for competency and he was found to be competent. . . . Murder was wrong in 1974, and it is wrong in 1986. And the passage of time makes no difference . . . Therefore, I commit you to the Commissioner of Corrections on count one to a period of twenty-five years and no less than twenty-five years, nor more than life imprisonment. And on count two, I commit you to the Commissioner of Corrections for a period of no less than twenty-five years nor more than life imprisonment. If I had the power, I would make it consecutive, but I am limited and, therefore, it shall be concurrent. And that is the order of the Court.

Thus the doleful proceedings whose echoes of fury still quivered in the air eventually moved to tragic music, finally ending in silence.

As I thought of Murray Gold, the sad and solitary man, the Holocaust survivor who now seemed to seek his own punishment, I thought and thought ... and a sudden series of words descended. A compulsive march of *D's* ... He is being dragged away to doom, in deep despair, to the doleful drumbeat of draconian defeat, to a dark, dreary and dank dungeon, disillusioned and desperate, to demons of desolate, dull and dreadful destiny, to disgruntled demonstrations, deforming drugs, delusional and delirious deterioration, disobedience of dreadful duties, deceptive dreams of deserting, denied desires, to dusty disarray of drab domain, to double dementia and disgraced death.

Fate can be cruel even when deserved. But since I felt deeply that Gold was innocent, his departure to what could be his final years of torment worse than death shocked my lifelong feelings about our noble system of justice.

I was more resolved than ever to free him from the abyss into which he had fallen.

28

SURRENDER

THE PROSECUTOR WAS well aware of the risks to him of an appeal by Gold. He promptly took advantage of Gold's forfeiture of his rights and appeared in court on September 19, 1986. He pointed out to Judge Lavery that there had been a default:

> So the record is clear, that Mr. Gold's time for filing an appeal has run and has expired as of yesterday. And, that it's the State's understanding, your Honor gave Mr. Gold at the time of sentencing until today to be heard on his motion for judgment of acquittal.
>
> COURT: My understanding . . . was that the motion is only made for the purpose of Mr. Gold deciding whether he was going to do it by today. And, it hasn't been done, so, therefore, it's over.

The shock of the second verdict of guilty had affected Gold profoundly—he had fought every step of the way while spending years in jail over the span of the four trials. Now, after a new chance for an appeal was lost, he was not back at the beginning—he was at the end. It looked final. Something had snapped within him. Surrender.

Psychiatrists tell us that surrender is a common phenomenon

that motivates suicide. Gold's refusal to appeal and thereby con-
fining himself to jail for life seemed such an expression. He had
fought step by step for vindication. The possibility of a successful
appeal was very real. Yet he refused the opportunity for freedom.
He was choosing a living suicide—life in jail. Since an appeal
must be filed under the statute within twenty days after the
verdict or the right to appeal is forever lost, Gold closed the doors
to his relief. His mother had lost a son. The lawyers who had
helped him to keep the skein of life together to survive his ordeal
were again frustrated—by the apparent collapse of his will. However, psychic traumas are often clouded in mystery, and their
origin eludes the best specialists. A child severely embarrassed,
say, may carry its injury silently for years, like a festering wound
which never heals.

Gold's paranoia undoubtedly dated back to the days when a
whole nation pursued him and his family to inflict its verdict of
death. And never to be ignored was the trauma of his young sister
caught and reduced to ashes. His parents, hugging Murray protec-
tively, had barely escaped the Nazis. It was, as mentioned, a
remarkable achievement for Murray Gold just to have recovered
sufficiently to hold responsible jobs, to marry and to struggle to
reach some sort of permanent balance in his life.

Still, the impact of such tragic youthful experiences was lasting. The scar of yesterday is the paranoia of today. The jury's
likely inference was that, being paranoid, Gold was the killer, and
the wheel of injustice had turned full circle. The clucking confidence of such an assumption violated all standards of proof beyond reasonable doubt.

There was not one scintilla of new evidence to change the early
concession that Gold had no known motive to kill the Pasternaks.
Indeed, there was testimony which made that concession even
stronger. For example, Myrna Kahan, the Pasternaks' daughter,
when cross-examined by Collins in the fourth trial, testified in
connection with her last meeting with her ex-brother-in-law:

Q: Now, during that conversation, didn't Mr. Gold on two
occasions tell you how much he liked your father?

A: I don't remember.

Q: You don't remember. If I told you that you had said this in one of your statements [during the first trial], would that refresh your recollection?

A: Yes.

Q: That he did say that?

A: Yes.

There might have been a motivation in Myrna Kahan's wish to see Gold convicted. As mentioned, her son Mark had been on the police list of possible suspects for the murders of the Pasternaks. He had once attacked his uncle with a knife, and had spent time in Whiting Forensic Institute. Ten years later, in 1984, he had committed suicide. Could not Myrna have a personal motive to blame Gold in order to clear her son's reputation once and for all?

Both Glorianna and Myrna had motivations to clear the names of their beloved ones from suspicion, and therefore, it would seem, turned to the choice of Gold as the killer.

In vivid contrast to the prosecutor's admissions of the frailties of his case was the proof by the defense that there was a motive for the commission of the crime by Sanford. To his deranged mind, it was Pasternak who had broken his dominance over Glorianna.

The indestructible link which bound Glorianna and Sanford together—a link that survived their divorce, his constant sexual disloyalty with other women, sometimes by rape, his foul habit of being soaked in drugs or incoherent because of liquor, his frightening preoccupation with knives, his rambling jargon and frequent imprisonments—suggests a unique form of sexual enslavement.

Even if the evidence of Sanford's guilt was not in the record, it would still appear to be impossible to find Gold guilty beyond a reasonable doubt.

A more profound mystery than who the killer was is how the jury, under the circumstances, could have found Gold guilty.

The verdict was incomprehensible, and to find the answer we need to examine the selection of the jury in the fourth trial.

In a process so dripping with uncertainty as to whether a juror, because of his or her background, may tilt for or against a defendant, even the most experienced lawyer may make an error. It can come down to an imponderable guess. But often the choice is so clear that ninety-nine out of one hundred lawyers would have no difficulty in eliminating such a juror.

Yet a large number of jurors in the fourth trial were accepted by the defense, while the prosecutor must have been laughing inwardly. Of course, this was not Collins' or Serignese's fault. Once more, it was Murray Gold himself who, because of his distrust of his lawers, stubbornly interfered and insisted that the jurors not be challenged, and in the process got a jury that was seriously out of balance.

Presiding Judge Lavery himself had put some questions to the prospective jurors so that attorneys for the state and for Gold might be alerted to any prejudice. One of his questions drew immediate blood. He asked whether any of the jurors knew anything about the defendant. Prospective Juror #2 replied: "I know he killed two people." Then, suddenly, realizing that she had revealed her predisposition, she added, "or at least he's alleged to have killed two people." Although she had attempted to erase the unintended revelation of her belief that Gold was guilty, the inner prejudice had been clearly exposed. Could Gold's life be entrusted to a juror who tended to believe as the prosecutor did?

Even if defense counsel had been willing to overlook her answer as a "slip of the tongue," her succeeding answers strongly suggested that her background would incline her to believe the prosecution. Questioned about her occupation, she described herself as the "coordinator of services" at a women's emergency shelter. Her "contact with the police" as well as with the criminal justice system was extensive. When asked whether she had formed an opinion about the criminal justice system, she pointed out that sometimes she "wished a decision had been made another way," but that at other times "it goes the way you want it to go." Did she infer that her wish would be conviction? Clearly, she was *part* of the criminal justice system. She was eager to be chosen to sit on the jury. When asked whether jury

CATSPAW

duty would interfere with her work, she replied, "They will get over it."

But would Murray Gold?

All in all, here was a potential juror who by virtue of her service to a Connecticut state agency could be presumed to be naturally, even if subconsciously, inclined to favor the police. It was easy to predict that policemen or policewomen would be prosecution witnesses. One might as well have chosen one of McDonald's assistants to sit on the jury and expect a neutral approach to the evidence. This was so obvious that experienced lawyers like Collins and his partner Serignese would challenge such a juror, perhaps even for cause, but certainly peremptorily. Yet she was accepted as a juror. Of course, it was Murray Gold who insisted on choosing her, disregarding his lawyers' probable view in so clear a case for challenge, since he imagined that his lawyers were in league with the prosecutor.

Juror #3 offered that she had spent "23 years in government service" and that her last position was that of a "regional evaluation officer" of Community Services Administration, a "Great Society" program. Once more, a person serving the government had been chosen as a juror by the defense to sit in a case in which the government was making charges against an individual.

Juror #4 revealed that she had two first cousins on the police force. When asked a hypothetical question about which way she would lean if she heard of an arrest—would she be inclined to believe that the arrest was valid and that the arrested person was guilty, or would she be suspicious of a police overreaction— she said that she would take the "middle road." The question remained. Was her neutrality to avoid embarrassment and obvious exclusion from the jury? It is on such subtleties that a defense lawyer must play safe. Yet this juror, too, was accepted.

Another juror was seated even though she had given her occupation as a secretary for the State of Connecticut in Hartford. In addition she had also held a post in the office of the Attorney General of Connecticut. She had been employed in the *very de-*

partment which was responsible for bringing the charges against Gold. She should have been challenged for cause.

Another prospective juror revealed, under questioning, that he knew that there had been prior trials of Gold. He must, therefore, have suspected that Gold had been found guilty in one of the prior trials, which was prejudicial information sufficient to excuse such a juror. He was not challenged by Collins and he sat on the jury.

Still another juror was accepted who also knew that there were prior trials, and even more prejudicially, she too was employed by a state agency.

In every long trial alternate jurors are chosen in the event that if one or more of the jurors should become ill or, for any reason has to withdraw in the midst of trial. Then the alternates, who have been sitting in from the beginning, make it possible to conclude the trial and avoid a mistrial. Counsel on both sides must, therefore, be just as careful in choosing alternates, who may come into full authority as jurors.

Yet a juror chosen as an alternate by the defense had a son who was a corrections officer—another visceral link to the criminal justice system, and therefore very likely a biased alternate.

Another alternate juror was chosen even though he had blurted out that he believed in capital punishment. The question had not called for his view on this subject and in doing so he revealed a frame of mind toward guilt and severe punishment rather than openness toward the possible innocence of the defendant.

Still one further alternate juror stated that the reason the case had to be retried after twelve years was that she believed the defendant "was mentally incompetent." She might have been right, but she was not right as a juror.

An analysis of the jurors selected for the fourth trial reveals so many jurors who had a prejudicial history in their occupations that the risk was not that one or two were preconditioned in favor of the prosecution, but that only a few were *not* so biased. The result was almost inevitable.

This, then, was surely a "hanging jury." The scales of justice were out of balance. However, there was still a remedy—an appeal to point out the defects in this weighing.

But here again, Gold had intervened against his own interests.

In spite of this showing, I believe in the jury system. Two people who consult on a decision are likely to reduce the possibility of error that one might have made. Three reduces the potentiality of error even more, ten considerably more; and so I would rather trust the correctness and not the expediency of the decision made by millions of citizens than I would to that of one man, be he the very epitome of human wisdom.

There is a sort of instinct in mass judgment that reduces error to a minimum. You can observe it in the decisions of juries. They represent the average mass intelligence applied to individual rather than public disputes. A juror is usually chosen because he or she does not know the litigants, witnesses or anything about the dispute (a complete reversal of the old common-law doctrine that insisted that jurors be witnesses to the event and acquaintances of the litigants in order to qualify). Obviously, lawyers on both sides seek to obtain jurors favorably inclined toward their client (these checks and balances are the best method of excluding prejudice from the jury box). Any trial lawyer or judge would confirm that over time juries most often have an uncanny faculty of reaching just decisions. Several judges have kept records of jury verdicts and compared them with their own reactions and with subsequent appellate decisions. They have found that juries approximate justice in an extraordinarily high percentage of cases. The fact is, and my belief is, that the collective judgment of juries is usually sound.

Those who mock the jury process will talk about the seemingly trivial reasons on which verdicts are occasionally based. It is sometimes claimed that the real issue goes almost unnoticed while jurors resent the way a witness talked back, or the discourtesy of a lawyer to his assistant, or an unsatisfactory answer to a totally irrelevant question, or the conceit of the defendant, or the clothes of the plaintiff. Yet, curiously enough, the decisions are

still most often right, although the *reasons* for them be anoma-
lous, to put it mildly. This is no accident of justice. We are all
likely, even in our daily affairs, to reach conclusions and search
for supporting reasons later. Even if the reasons are inadequate,
the original conclusion may be sound. On hearing opposing contentions we feel we know which side is right. The rationaliza-
tions follow rather than precede.

Furthermore, a witness' manner may *rightly* shake confidence
in him. Credibility is the result of myriad impressions, each
finding its roots in our own previous experience. Is this not part of
the process of wisdom? So fundamental is all this that appellate
courts seldom reverse juries on questions of fact, because the
appellate judges have not had the opportunity to observe and hear
the witnesses. They must judge their veracity by simply reading
the printed record. So we see that the "absurd reasons" for the
jury's decision may often be founded in the wisdom of every
person's experience.

Justice Holmes once said: "The life of the law has not been
logic: it has been experience." Our history conditions us to react
to each new situation. It does not matter whether you call this, as
William James did, "the total push and pressure of the cosmos," or
as Cardozo unveiled it for judges, "the judicial process." It results
from all those mysterious forces within, sharpened by every moment of existence. It is the instinct of knowing what is right. The
lowliest citizen has it as much as the most exalted.

That is why I trust the mass judgment. It may err, and griev-
ously, but its chances of doing so are less and its resolve to correct
past mistakes are stronger than may be expected from any one or
any coterie of brilliant minds.

Lawyers cannot select judges who preside over our cases, but in
a jury trial they have the unique privilege of choosing the dozen
judges of facts—the jurors.

There are able counsel who believe that the extent of choice is
mostly limited and that they will make a favorable impression on
the jurors by merely asking a few formal questions and, with a
wave of the hand, announcing loudly that the jury is satisfactory.
They believe that the jurors will be favorably impressed with the

nonhaggling and quick selection as demonstrating confidence in their cause. I differ sharply with this theory. One cannot weed out all the prejudices by the few usual formal questions such as: "Do you know the counsel or litigant on either side?" or: "Is there any reason why you should not serve in this kind of an action?" etc. The genius of the adversarial system is that the *very partiality* of each advocate is most likely to result in a fair jury. Having disposed of the theory that a lawyer should aim for a fair jury rather than one disposed toward his client's cause, we can better analyze the techniques of jury selection.

It is necessary, by deft questioning, to have the juror reveal himself. Since the lawyer is not permitted to engage in general conversation but is limited to certain types of questions, there's a special subtlety in the limited banter allowed. Some signs are obvious. A juror who smiles readily because of some homey comment is probably kindly disposed. A juror who presents compressed thin lips and answers with a shake of his head may tend to favor the opponent. An important indication of a juror's affinity with a trial lawyer is not only his expression as he is questioned but whether he follows the attorney with his eyes as he goes to other jurors. This often indicates that he has invested some interest in the advocate, and his attention is riveted on him as he proceeds to question others. It is a good sign.

On the other hand, if after the lawyer has completed his questioning the juror looks straight ahead, it may very well mean that he is relieved to have ended the ordeal and is not very enamored of the lawyer who put him through it. In short, the best juror is the one who admires and attaches himself to the advocate.

A juror's candor must be wooed like a woman's love. It cannot be won by most formal questions. It is rare to find a juror who, when asked in a murder case: "Do you believe in capital punishment?" replied: "Generally, no—but in this case, yes!"

A defense counsel wants as many diverse jurors as possible. The prosecutor wants a leader, particularly if he appears not to be too sympathetic a person.

One has to admit to what may seem sexist, too. Lawyers agree that in cases involving sex questions, such as adultery in a divorce case, where a woman stands accused, it is best not to have women jurors. The theory is that they are usually ready to believe the worst of another woman, the possible psychological reason being an inner belief that under similar circumstances they too might be vulnerable. *But* the same principle applies to men accused of sexual crimes—it's best then not to have male jurors.

On the whole the jury system does work remarkably well. It is a microcosm of democracy, in practice as well as theory. There is a leavening process on moral and equitable questions that is best served by a multitude of judgments. For a scientific or mathematical question I would want one brilliant scientist or mathematician and not a common judgment. But in matters of morals, law, fairness, I prefer twelve men and women. The jury system truly is a jewel in the judicial diadem, and I like to think that justice served is the compromise between the wishes of the heart and the restraints of the brain.

29

DISINTEGRATION

IF IT WAS Sanford who believed in a descent into hell, it was Murray Gold who experienced its torment.

His medical history turned out to be grievous, gruesome, sad. Gold was returned to Somers Correctional Institute following the fourth trial, and he has remained there since August, 1986.

Shortly after his confinement there his physical as well as mental condition began to deteriorate to the point where he could no longer walk and was confined to a wheelchair. He spent long periods alone in his cell refusing to communicate with anybody; he was diagnosed as anorexic and steadily lost weight, complaining of chest pains, and had fainting spells. In spite of these ailments he absolutely refused medical assistance of any kind. Even though he had a history of hypertension, he would not allow his blood pressure to be monitored.

Even as early as August 29, 1986, the first day of his imprisonment after sentencing in the fourth trial, the medical record stated that he was "suicidal" and "somewhat incoherent." It was as if he began careening down steps with a fatal momentum. Soon his conduct became even more perverse so that the doctors increased his Navane dosage from fifteen milligrams to twenty milligrams daily. It is hardly surprising that for the most part Murray appeared to be incoherent.

Gold was kept in the prison hospital for several weeks, awaiting assignment to a cell. The admitting doctor ordered the staff to "observe him closely," which in prison talk meant a suicide-watch. During this time the prison doctors and nurses did keep a close eye on him and noted that he was totally uncommunicative. He stayed in bed much of the time, sleeping. They tried to interest him in games or light conversation but he continued to live in his own silent world, responding to no social stimulus. He even had to be persuaded to shower and shave.

On November 7, 1986, a doctor wrote on his discharge summary from prison hospital that Gold was "depressed, beaten down . . . a chronic mental patient." And then the ultimate warning: "possibility of . . . suicide is quite likely." I believe Gold's knowledge and conviction that he was *innocent* had apparently created a self-annihilating wish not only to escape the excruciating pain of injustice but also to prove to his tormentors the consequence of their awful error. It was of a piece with the rejected suitor who punishes his beloved by killing himself and thereby burdening her conscience. The doctor also diagnosed Gold as schizophrenic, but the astonishing recommendation of his report was—"no medication"! Gold had been, as mentioned, receiving massive doses of Navane. One can only imagine the torture of an addict cut off from his drugs. This sudden action caused every nerve in his body to scream for the relief of being "knocked out."

There is a gap in the prison medical records, but they again become active on December 10, 1988, when Gold fell in the prison dining hall and fractured his right hip. On December 14 the prison hospital progress report noted: "55 year old patient sustained direct injury to right hip . . . admitted to Johnson Memorial Hospital . . . films taken and evaluated by orthopedic consultant who advised that hip be pinned. Patient refused. Also declined body cast. Consultant was unable to dissuade patient from this decision. . . . Returned at this time for the only alternative remaining, bed rest."

On December 21, at the request of the medical staff, a "mental status examination" was given. A nurse reported Gold's response in refusing treatment of his hip: "G.[old]: I think you should do an exam on the doctor who wanted to operate, not on me. There's nothing wrong with my leg. It just hurts a little and then I need to stay in bed. The doctor said that the X-ray showed it is in alignment and healing well. . . . Patient seems to understand that the doctors are requesting to repair his fracture surgically and that he may have an impairment if he refuses this surgery . . ."

Interestingly, with only bed rest Gold's hip *did* in fact heal without medical interference, and on February 1, 1989, a progress report noted: "Inmate walking with no limp . . . patient's blood pressure is up—he, however, adamantly states that he does not have high blood pressure and nothing is wrong—he still refuses to take meds for this, claiming he does not need any." So medicine can learn from the most unlikely sources, as well as by accidents and by research. Not always is it necessary to peg a fracture with metal to assure its healing.

During this period of prison hospitalization Murray tended to disturb other patients by getting up at four or five in the morning and pacing the ward, talking to himself. An attendant noted that this was "normal for him but somewhat disruptive to other patients."

The next entries occur in April, 1989, that Murray was again suffering left-side chest pain which made him feel weak and he "half fainted." By December of 1989 he was refusing to eat and was again losing weight.

The latest reports, from January to March, 1990, state that Murray was refusing to walk and again had to use a wheelchair. He was in a very weakened state. His blood pressure was elevated. He did not leave his cell for prolonged periods of time.

The law of retribution, it seemed, was operating: Fear of retribution can be as motivating as retribution itself. Gold had become suicidal. No pain can equal that of an injury inflicted under the pretext of a just punishment.

30

STRUGGLE

WHILE GOLD'S STRUGGLE was going on I was experiencing another. Why, I had to ask myself, should I involve myself further with Murray Gold? He had offered me insult and resentment. The fact that he acted in the same way to Williams was no help. I had handled his offensiveness without retaliation. But I am human.

Our first reaction to the news that Gold had accepted complete defeat and refused to appeal was that he had brought the disaster on himself. We could only sigh and banish the thought that things might have been different. But he had made his own bed of disgrace and surrender, let him sleep in it, it was his doing—surely not mine.

Yet there could be no satisfaction in that. Something was gnawing in me. My sense of justice? I had to overcome the feeling deep inside that he was being repaid for his insults and ingratitude, not only to me but to the other lawyers, who had worked to save him. So he had rudely dismissed me when I brought him freedom. Could I stay silent when justice was bleeding? And, I wondered, how would the other lawyers feel about Gold's self-imposed internment?

I thought my emotion similar to that of a mother who dotes on

261

her infant, cleaning away its filth, coddling, cuddling and cooing to it, and who is rewarded by a slap in the face or a toy thrust into her eyes; she flushes with momentary anger but soon hugs the child and kisses it. She does not hate it. Such forbearance can sometimes be necessary with adults too. Murray Gold's slap in the face was the act of a neurotic, *not* an act of personal venom.

A man may, after all, be the victim of an injustice even though no hero in the storybook sense. Justice needs to rise above pique and emotional retaliation. Gold's slap had to yield to principle— better, to love.

But was I called on to try to save him again? Did I have to serve him and be repaid with rancor, however one rationalized it?

As I pondered this my mind went back to the day when I was deliberating whether I would enter law school or accept a career in business. During my college summer breaks I got jobs to aid my parents financially. Even in those days it was expensive to attend college and then law school.

One of my summer jobs was with a company that bottled a chemical called carbon tetrachloride, which was an excellent stain remover from clothing. When given the trade name of "Carbona" its effectiveness was rewarded with popularity and huge profits.

One day I noticed that a stenographer in Carbona's office was cleaning the black platen of her typewriter with a fluid. It was alcohol. "Why not Carbona?" I asked her. She tried it. "It's wonderful," she said. Thereafter I concentrated on selling the idea to large offices, and the president of Carbona, a Mr. Weinberg, soon learned about the increase in sales and a new use for his product. He perfected the idea by ordering larger bottles at special prices. Encouraged by this success, I informed Mr. Weinberg that I had tried out the idea of a wider use by visiting ferryboats and had found that Carbona was an efficient method of cleaning pistons. Perhaps even steamships might find it useful and economical if sold in huge containers at competitive prices.

A while later Mr. Weinberg sent for me, ushered me into his

office. Although his manner was usually curt he was benign: "How would you like to make your career with this company?"

I told him I was about to enter law school. "You will find business far more rewarding. Within two years I intend to retire. You can become president here with a contract that will guarantee you two hundred dollars a week with escalating clauses."

I stuttered: "I'll think about it . . . I mean, I'll talk it over with my parents."

Mr. Weinberg tempted me further: "I'll make a stock arrangement with you, too, so that you can become a part owner."

To hide my breathlessness I left his office as soon as I could.

The one thing I did not inherit from my father was his volatile temper. His moods were variable. At the drop of a hat, on happy occasions, he would jump on top of a table and dance. But on the subject of my career he was adamant. When I told my parents of Mr. Weinberg's offer my father exploded: "You are going to be a *lawyer*. You were cut out to be one. I don't want you going back into that office. No talk—this is final."

Money was not the issue. I am sure my father's stubbornness would have been the same regardless of salary. I was to be a lawyer and no other consideration mattered.

My mother, fearful of a dish-breaking tantrum, tried to calm him but he insisted that he wanted my promise immediately never to set foot into the Carbona office again. My mother's silence and pleading eyes won the day. I promised.

Of course. Weinberg was astonished at my hasty resignation. He wondered how he had offended me. I could only stammer that he had been generous and that I was grateful but that my parents, and I, were determined that I become a lawyer. He scratched his head. Who could blame him for his confusion?

When I graduated from Columbia Law School, I obtained a job in the office of Emily Janoer, one of the few women lawyers in the state at that time. My salary was seven dollars a week. Today, law associates in my office receive $75,000 annually. My limited duties were to serve summonses on delinquent tenants. There was not even a daily *Law Journal* in Emily Janoer's office to give me the illusion that I was practicing law.

But from the beginning I was imbued with the ideals of justice. There was no room for resentment at a client's lack of appreciation, or even his eccentric disloyalty. If he had suffered an injustice his lawyer had to correct it; if he was ungrateful, in spite of his lawyers' sacrifices for him, then those lawyers must overlook his behavior and make a greater effort to protect him; justice can't abide excuses for injustice. It is the closest sentiment to sincere religion, and is not subject to compromise.

A man once said that his adversary "was his own worst enemy." "Not while I'm around," came a voice from the rear of the courtroom.

As Gold's lawyer, I had no such privilege. He needed to be protected against himself. His "ingratitude" could not relieve his counsel of the duty to see that justice was done.

He had not slaughtered the Pasternaks. Sanford, I'm confident, had. Nothing else mattered.

I blocked out of my mind the protestations of Gold. I heard only the voices of Zola, Darrow, as well as those I had fought for—Quentin Reynolds, John Henry Faulk, John Garfield, Paul Crump.

So I pored over the trial transcripts of the four trials.

I owed my loyalty to our system of justice. The statue of Justice became articulate—I heard its approval. That was reward enough.

A unique remedy was still available—the great writ.

BOOK
VIII

31

THE GREAT WRIT

AMONG THE MOUNTAIN peaks of the development of justice is the writ of Habeas Corpus—"Bring me the Body."

It replaced the blood-feud theory, which was the early version of how to do justice among contestants—namely, revenge by the family of the victim. If a member of a clan was killed, it was expected that one of his relatives would revenge the murder by killing a member of the attacking family. Of course, this resulted in further retaliations, and so the wrong was almost never finally righted. Such a savage system of law was once claimed to be based upon the Bible's: "An eye for an eye, a tooth for a tooth." After centuries of reliance on that religious doctrine the church itself eliminated the literal meaning of that edict and interpreted it to mean that the punishment should fit the crime.

Societies have previously resorted to other methods. Isaac Asimov—a man of parts, including writer and historian—points out a novel device that the Athenians created after they drove out the tyrant Hippias in 510 B.C. to prevent the destruction of democracy in the future. They held an election to choose who was the most dangerous demagogue. He was exiled for ten years. His property was protected and he was honored for his sacrifice when he returned after his exile. What an extraordinary device—to elect a candidate for exile. But maybe not irrational. If when Hitler was ranting in beer halls he had been elected for exile, fifty million more people would be alive today and half the world's structures and treasures would not have been destroyed.

Still, the writ was used by Anglo-Saxon tyrants, and over-zealous lords, to order an offending citizen to be brought before them. On a peremptory hearing, the citizen could be dragged into a prison cell, and often disappeared from sight so that even his death went unnoticed. The writ was used as an arbitrary device to get rid of "protesting" or suspicious citizens. It was a typical violation of human rights.

Justice, like water, tends to seek its own level. The writ had become the instrument of a tyrant's unlimited power. The king or his magistrate could summon the "body" of anyone and throw him into a dungeon after a proceeding that had no resemblance to a fair trial.

The principle of physics that pressure in one direction often causes a concomitant pressure in the opposite direction (see the aborted Soviet coup of 1991) asserted its magic. In 1340 A.D. it was a prisoner, not the king, who had his attorney issue a writ of *habeas corpus* to have his body brought before a court to demand an explanation for his incarceration. The forces of social change caused the "king's prerogative" to be regarded as arbitrary and Cardinal Wolsey was dismissed from his office as chancellor of England for his excessive use of the writ.

That writ is the device which enables a prisoner to demand a hearing by a court to determine whether he is being legally deprived of his liberty.

My mind had now turned to the Great Writ. Was this remedy against extreme injustice still available to correct an injustice?

Of course, Gold, who had even rejected his right to appeal, was not likely to cooperate. Could we obtain a writ if he refused to it? Perhaps . . . and perhaps if the lawyers in the case together *it might substitute for his consent.*

One thing was certain, I could not rest.

I called William Kunstler: "Will you join me and other counsel in applying for a writ of habeas corpus or other relief in favor of Gold?" His assent was so prompt and enthusiastic that I knew he, too, had been troubled by Gold's plight.

I then called John Williams, the attorney at the third trial, who had been humiliated and discharged by Murray in the midst of the proceeding. He, too, responded quickly, as if relieved at my effort to right an injustice.

My next invitation was to William Collins, Gold's lawyer at the fourth trial. He was not available but suggested I call his partner, Mr. Serignese, who had tried the case with him. I did so. He, too, responded spiritedly. I was warmed by the readiness of other counsel to give their time and high reputations to this effort. Murray's lack of appreciation, for his own tragic reasons, did not matter.

Encouraged as I was by these responses, I decided to push the edge of the envelope, as they say. I called the prosecutor, William Scanlon.

To my delight, he not only accepted my invitation but told me how troubled he had felt about Gold's competency to stand trial. How exhilarating that even the prosecutor would want to join us.

I invited all the lawyers to a luncheon meeting in my office on March 16, 1989, where I promised that "courteous and efficient self-service would prevail." Also present were cocounsel, Timothy Moynahan, and four of my partners, Angelo Cometa, Sheila Riesel, Alan Mansfield and Paul Martinson.

Had there ever been such a gathering without benefit of client's approval that met to save him against his will?

The meeting was not without its humor. When I thanked all who attended for their sacrifice in a matter that was solely *pro bono*, Kunstler said: "That's all right—all my cases are *pro bono*."

The first and all-absorbing problem was whether we could make any application on behalf of Gold without his consent. The joining of so weighty a group as his counsel in four former trials, *including the state's prosecutor*, might be impressive enough for a move for action on Gold's behalf, even without his authorization.

However, the possibility of establishing such novel authority for relief against the defendant's wish was remote. We would try, but first we decided to test again Murray Gold's obstinacy.

Kunstler volunteered to drive out to the Connecticut Corrections Institution in Somers and find out whether Murray would change his mind and permit an effort to save him.

A week later Kunstler reported that Murray Gold had indeed changed his mind.

"Get me out of here," he had said.

Kunstler presented him with a document authorizing our committee to act on his behalf. Gold signed it.

Writs for habeas corpus are the last desperate resort. To be successful our application for a writ on behalf of Gold had to demonstrate that due process of law had been violated. We claimed it had been because he was not competent to stand trial. Again, competence is defined as being aware of what is going on around a person so that he can confer with and advise his lawyer and understand his lawyer's advice.

In our petition we referred to psychiatric reports that showed Murray Gold was suffering from paranoia and, even worse, from schizophrenia. He not only could not aid his attorneys but, indeed, he suspected them of conspiring with the prosecutor against him. What was irrational to us was in Gold's bruised, disordered mind self-protection. The law does not try incompetents any more than it does insane defendants. If we could prove Gold's incompetence, the verdict against him would have to be set aside.

The ancient rule held that an accused person must be present at the trial so that he can hear the accusations and be able to reply personally or through his counsel. If he was incompetent, that was considered equivalent to his being absent. An empty chair or an incoherent mind cannot fill the requirement of a defendant's presence in the courtroom.

Gold's health, as well as his mind, was deteriorating. We included in our application a detailed statement of his sinking health.

The risk of suicide meant it was a race against time. We took one more precaution and made a motion for an expedited hearing.

32

A COURTROOM IN JAIL

THE CONNECTICUT COURT that was to hear our application for a writ of habeas corpus set down a conference hearing before Judge Phillip Dunn on December 21, 1990, in the courtroom situated in the prison. The reason for this unusual site was the legal requirement that a defendant must be present at any legal procedure. Rather than bring the defendant to a courthouse, it was found more feasible in short applications to bring the courthouse to the defendant.

I picked up William Kunstler and then Victor Ferrante (John Williams and Walter Scanlon were engaged in cases and could not accompany us on this trip), and we headed for the jailhouse in Somers, Connecticut. After three and a half hours of driving, into which five hours of reminiscences were crowded, we arrived at the prison.

Upon identification, a gate built like a huge sieve rolled open sideways. We were then confronted with an identical gate. We did not know whether we were being kept in or kept out. The third time the gate swung open we faced two doors that opened onto a long corridor. At the end of the corridor we saw two courtroom doors. We opened them cautiously and stepped in to a new surprise. We had never seen such a room. There were seats in the rear for visitors, but the judge was seated at what looked like a mile away from the lawyers' table. The reason for this abnormal construction soon became apparent to us. In the ordinary courtroom violent defendants have in the past thrown heavy objects at the judge. Which is why pitchers of water or large books are forbidden on counsels' tables in many criminal cases where the judge sits only a few feet away from the defendant. In this Connecticut jailhouse courtroom a defendant would have to be a prize baseball player to reach the judge at the other end of the corridor. Even if he could smuggle in a pistol, the defendant would have to be a good shot to hit the judge down the long range.

Murray Gold, by forefeiting his right to appeal, had limited us to a narrow slit of relief. Rarely is a habeas corpus writ to reverse a jury verdict granted. Yet Murray had closed the door to any other relief. To make matters worse, he had at first refused to authorize us even to apply for the writ, thereby putting another obstacle in our path to pursue this unique remedy. At least he had now changed his mind about this and authorized our petition.

The judge set down the first available dates as February 25 and 26, 1991, for the trial. A psychiatrist I had retained, Dr. Walter Borden, was with us and had an opportunity to remain with Gold, who cooperated in a conversation of two hours.

We headed back to New York to prepare for the final test. .

The light banter on the way home only masked our serious thoughts. Legal friends assured us that no writ could be obtained where two juries had found the defendant guilty after long trials. These negative views, though, served mostly to increase my resolve to demonstrate that justice can overcome all handicaps. "You must believe in luck," a skeptic once said to me. "Certainly I do," I replied. "It sometimes visits me when I am in the law library at three in the morning. It has never come to me when I am on the golf course or in the theatre."

33

THE REMEDY

On February 25, 1991, almost seventeen years after the murders, what might be called the Gold Alumni Association of volunteer lawyers met in the stately building of the superior court, Tolland Judicial District, in Rockville, Connecticut, in a final effort to extricate Gold from jail for the rest of his life. Counsel for both sides were all assembled and the Honorable Howard Scheinblum presided over this habeas corpus proceeding and wielded the gavel that controlled Gold's fate. Like all able judges, he was authoritative without being arbitrary, precise without being technical.

Marcia Smith was the Assistant State's Attorney appearing for the warden (that is, for the state).

Gold was brought from his upstairs jail cell down to the courtroom by three guards. He was no longer in a wheelchair and looked contained and quiet. He greeted all of the lawyers with a silent nod that lacked enthusiasm but at least was not hostile. From Murray, it was a warm embrace.

His presence, compelled by law, created a dilemma. How could the defendant's counsel openly argue that his client was incompetent and psychiatrically too sick to be tried when such words infuriated his client, Gold, who constantly suspected that his lawyers were in league with the prosecutor. We knew that Murray would not understand or accept that to save him we had to prove him incompetent, whereas, ironically, the prosecutor, to prevent the writ, had to prove him competent during the fourth trial.

We had to worry that Gold would think his lawyers were betraying him when they asserted that he was paranoid and schizophrenic—were in league with his opponents.

We thought it would be awkward and perhaps cause an outburst by Gold if he heard a psychiatrist testify about his mental condition. However, as a defendant, he had a right to be present unless he voluntarily consented to leave. I asked the judge to excuse him. The judge suggested that I take Gold into another room and persuade him to leave voluntarily. I did so.

He had grown a broad white beard that covered the top of his chest, making him look more like a patriarch than a paranoiac.

"How is it," I asked, "that you have grown a beard?"

"What else is one to do in jail?" he replied.

Indeed, what else.

"I think it would be better," I told Murray, "if you didn't attend this court session. There will be talk of your suffering from paranoia and schizophrenia—why subject yourself to that kind of testimony?"

"Well, I know I am competent," he said calmly. (He had learned the legal word.) "But if you think it is better that I should leave, I'll do so, but I want to come back. After all, my life is at stake."

"Of course," I said, "you have a right to be present, and we'll advise you."

Gold then left the courthouse and the guards took him back to his cell. We were at last unshackled in speaking about his paranoia and schizophrenia—all to save him from an unjust conviction. Any irritation from his unreasonableness faded.

In law, too, absence makes the heart grow fonder.

The prosecutrix, Marcia Smith, announced that she had subpoenaed Judge Lavery to be a witness. Judge Lavery had presided over Gold's fourth trial (and later became an appellate judge).

Although we were not certain that the judge had indicated that he would voluntarily appear as a witness, we thought that subpoenaing the trial judge on a habeas corpus trial was improper. Overnight legal research revealed that we were right. The highest court in Connecticut disapproved of such tactics. This rule was followed throughout the nation. By nine in the morning of the next day we had faxed a brief on the subject. Judge Scheinblum agreed with us and vacated the subpoena. He quoted the leading Connecticut case of *Woodward* v. *Waterbury* (113 Conn. 457), which held that "the calling of judges of the superior court as witnesses should be avoided whenever it is reasonably possible to do so."

Another crisis had passed.

We called to the stand our first witness, Dr. Borden, a distinguished Connecticut psychiatrist. He spoke in a monotone, as if enthusiasm or emphasis might distort the soundness of his detached, scientific approach. I've observed this to be true of other scientists as well. For example, on a number of occasions I had introduced Albert Einstein to enthusiastic audiences who were thrilled to be in his presence. But their excitement quickly receded as his words were so subdued as to be near-soporific as they sifted through his moustache heavily tinted with accent. The audience, despite the greatness of the man, lost interest. (The only scientist I ever met whose delivery was as highly energetic as the molecules he described was Prof. Edward Teller, the "father of the atomic bomb.")

Dr. Borden, regardless of his delivery, came well-prepared. He stated that he interviewed Gold for two hours in December of 1990 and that he had reviewed the transcripts of the last two trials, the competency and hospital records as well as the transcripts of meetings in the judge's chambers.

I asked Dr. Borden to present his findings as to Gold's mental condition and whether in his opinion Gold had been competent to stand his fourth trial. In no uncertain terms the psychiatrist replied in the negative. He unequivocally stated that Gold had

Dr. Walter A. Borden, the psychiatrist whose expert testimony went to Murray Gold's defense.

been suffering for a long time from a very severe form of mental illness. He identified this illness as a "schizo-affective disorder" and presented its various aspects. He cited Gold's fear and resentment of doctors and lawyers, who in his mind represented authority. This, for instance, prevented him from working effectively with his lawyers. He pointed out that Gold's mental illness made him also deny physical maladies that would require medical attention since he did not trust doctors either. Dr. Borden stated that even Gold's father was, in Gold's mind, another authority figure to be feared and shunned. All of this tended to explain Gold's persecution complex.

Dr. Borden also took exceptions to the Whiting Forensic Institute evaluation team's findings, conclusions and method of testing of Gold.

It was as if Dr. Borden was painting with scientific brush strokes a mural of a psychological drama. He stated that Gold's transfer from Whiting Forensic Institute to the Correctional Center in New Haven (the Whalley Avenue jail) should not have been done since it was hardly the proper environment for a man with such serious mental problems as his and stressed that nine months passed during which Gold received no psychiatric treatment at all. Nor was he reassessed during that period. "That is mind-boggling to me," he concluded.

He criticized the unauthorized increase of the daily Navane dosages that were administered to Gold there. This increase, coupled with an additional medication called Inderal, administered to Gold against his hypertension, only exacerbated his condition. Dr. Borden explained that when Inderal is combined with Navane, each drug tends to magnify the effect of the other so that the tranquilizing effect of Navane in its increased dosage was further aggravated by Inderal. It was this chemical interaction, viewed in the courtroom by some as indifference, that resulted in Gold's lethargy and somnolence.

The scientific mural depicting Gold's tragedy was developing as Dr. Borden described Gold's condition at the time when he interviewed him, a condition that had remained unchanged since his third trial. Findings of schizophrenia and paranoia were made both times. But Dr. Borden also testified that there was an additional aspect to Gold's mental illness—his denial of the traumatic events in his life.

The psychiatrist reported that Gold experienced complete lapses of memory of his stay at a Montreal hospital as well as at Mount Sinai Hospital, where he received shock treatments as part of psychiatric care; that Gold maintained he was born in the Bronx, whereas he really was born in Germany; that Gold denied having been in concentration camps as a child and that he had a younger sister who died in one of those camps. He denied being Jewish and that his parents were Jewish (which was as credible as a claim that Hitler was born to an Hasidic Jewish family). The psychiatrist found that Gold's denial of his background was due to a devastating trauma experienced by Gold in his youth, caused by brutal and terrorizing forces that dominated his childhood.

He testified: "This is seen in concentration-camp survivors. In fact, many of the findings with Murray Gold [are] consistent with that syndrome—the Holocaust, the concentration-camp-survivor syndrome."

Dr. Borden again took especial exception to the performance—or lack of it—of the Whiting Forensic Institute. He said that the institute ought to have had Gold examined by a physician who was familiar with this psychosis found in concentration-camp victims and stressed that this had not been done.

He also called our attention to the Montreal Hospital records, which said that Gold had hallucinations of gas seeping out of his room. This was an olfactory hallucination found in severe schizophrenia cases such as Gold's, and was triggered by his memories of the gas chambers.

I asked Dr. Borden:

Q: Are you familiar with the phrase "survivor's guilt"?

Dr. Borden said he was and identified it. He stated that it was experienced by those who escaped the concentration camps, only to lose loved ones who were not as fortunate.

He elaborated:

"It's the mental condition which arises as a result of extreme terrorization . . . In the concentration camp that was the very condition . . . You put a child in that and you're going to get severe disturbances . . . chronic psychoses . . . morbid guilt."

So there it was. The tragic panorama of Gold's blighted life.

Dr. Borden was then cross-examined by the state. The state's objective was, of course, to minimize the seriousness of Gold's mental illness. Ms. Smith asked to have read the pertinent transcript section of the fourth trial in which Walter Scanlon called the court's attention to Gold's sleeping in the midst of the proceedings. She asked:

Q: . . . Isn't it true that people will often doze off . . . after a large lunch . . . other than just having Navane?

A: At their own murder trial would they doze off? I don't think so.

Then I asked Dr. Borden:

Q: I'm talking of a man in a courtroom on trial for his life. Would you say he'd doze off . . . [or] would you say that 20 mgs. of Navane would be more likely to be the cause of sleep?
A: Yes.

Ms. Smith reminded us that, after all, the death penalty was not asked for in Gold's fourth trial. I countered this by stating that the sentence imposed on him was imprisonment "for life." That was tantamount to death.

The prosecutrix next attempted to show that there was no conflict between Gold and William Collins, his lawyer in the fourth trial. However, the psychiatrist countered:

A: . . . He told me . . . it was nonsense; he [Gold] couldn't understand him [Collins]; they didn't understand each other . . .

If this was not quite the collision course caused by Gold with Williams, it was surely a showing that he was not able to work effectively with counsel.

When Ms. Smith suggested that the problem of providing adequate psychiatric services in state prisons might be due to lack of state funds, Dr. Borden replied:

A: . . . that may be exactly what happened . . . because there is a push to get people out and to find them competent. There is a push, and sometimes people fall between the gaps and it is a matter of public funds.

Dr. Borden had concluded his testimony. Then Judge Scheinblum asked:

THE COURT: Doctor, do you have an opinion as to the present status of Mr. Gold to understand the nature of the
legal proceedings?

A: . . . His condition does seem to have deteriorated . . . that
it substantially interferes with his capacity to . . . understand legal issues . . . Yes, he is incompetent to stand trial.
He's also incompetent to take care of his person.

The state presented its two psychiatric experts—Drs. Merikangas and Biassey. They both testified that before the fourth
trial began the court ordered an examination of Gold to determine whether he was competent. They found that he was. This
was the crucial test because it preceded the trial that resulted in
the guilty verdict by the jury. However, we carried the scalpel of
cross-examination, and in a few moments these particular doctors were in trouble.

Dr. Biassey admitted that there were four psychiatric reports
issued by Whiting Institute. I asked him:

Q: The first of those reports . . . was February 21st, 1985 . . .
and in that report you concluded . . . that Gold was
incompetent to stand trial, [because he was unable] to
cooperate and work with his lawyer [and] that he was
suffering from paranoia?

A: Yes.

Q: . . . in the second report . . . did you at that time make an
independent examination . . . as to his condition?

A: Yes.

Q: . . . and . . . you again decided for the second time that he
was incompetent?

A: Yes.

Q: I take you to the third report . . . what was your conclusion as to whether he was competent to stand trial?

A: In this report, we again concluded that he was not competent to stand trial.

Two months following the third report, Gold was examined by

the Whiting Team again, shortly before the fourth trial, and issued its report. I asked the expert:

Q: This fourth report differed from the other three in that in
    addition to paranoia you also found he was suffering from
    schizophrenia, didn't you?
A: Yes.
Q: Now, in the fourth report, despite what you have told us,
    you concluded what as to his competency?
A: We found that he was competent to stand trial.

I asked Dr. Biassey whether there were any concluding recommendations as a caution contained in the fourth report. Conscience can be a persistent nag. It was apparent, I felt, that the Whiting Forensic team was troubled by its own finding of competency. Dr. Biassey admitted that they wrote the following warning at the end of their final report:

We wish to emphasize that this should not be interpreted to mean that his [Gold's] mental condition has been completely ameliorated. He suffers from a mental condition, in our opinion, that will require some form of continued treatment in order to maintain his competency over the course of the extended future . . . and a continued program of psychiatric treatment is now advisable as a necessary adjunct to the maintenance of his competency.

By contradicting their own findings, they became vulnerable on cross-examination. They admitted that their own warning to continue a "program of psychiatric treatment" for Gold had not been honored. Only more Navane was prescribed.

Indeed, we called an unusual witness who confirmed Gold's stupor during the fourth trial. This witness was no less than the former prosecutor Walter Scanlon, who successfully prosecuted Gold in the third and fourth trials. Mindful of his duty to protect a defendant's rights as well as to prosecute him, he called this court's attention to Gold's condition he observed during the fourth trial by repeating his classic warning he gave at that time:

MR. SCANLON: I think his [Gold's] confrontation rights are being abandoned voluntarily by the defendant ... he seems to be sleeping.

William Collins took the stand, now being called as a witness for the state. When he was cross-examined by us, he testified that he did not recall having had discussions with Gold about the final report, which found him suddenly competent. He protested that Gold's mental condition was a medical matter that was not within the realm of his duty as his attorney. He did not see that it was his obligation to see to it that Gold should have received continued psychiatric treatment in order to achieve competency, nor that it was his duty to understand fully the type of medication Gold was receiving. He appeared annoyed and stated that he was already under time pressure to meet the obligations of his profession.

But Judge Scheinblum observed:

THE COURT: I think it is within the realm of defense counsel to know whether or not his client is on medication. It's within the realm of competent defense counsel to know what kind of medication. It's within the realm of competence and to be expected for defense counsel to know what the purpose of the medication is.

Judge Scheinblum turned to a more significant incident that occurred after the verdict of "guilty" at the end of the fourth trial. Gold, of course, had the right to appeal. He had succeeded on a previous appeal after the second trial, and won. Yet he told his lawyer, William Collins, that he refused to appeal! He resisted the judge's urging that he should protect his rights by appealing. Stubbornly, he refused, and thereby gave up that precious right. Judge Scheinblum asked the prosecutrix:

THE COURT: ... does Gold's refusal to allow his attorney to take an appeal constitute a showing of incompetence?
Ms. SMITH: No, not necessarily, your Honor. It's a rational

decision someone could make. I mean, just because one doesn't choose to appeal? ... This man has evidentiary [sic] taken his licks ... It's his fourth trial ... Mr. Collins says that his behavior wasn't any different, he wasn't incompetent with him at the time ...

THE COURT: How many murders have you tried?

Ms. SMITH: Very few.

THE COURT: The ones you've tried, has there been any one in which you obtained a conviction that the defendant has not appealed from?

Ms. SMITH: No, your Honor.

This exchange between the judge and the prosecutrix indicated more than Gold's incompetence. The other question was why Gold's attorney had not asked for a hearing to determine incompetence in view of his client's strange conduct. For that matter, why did not the presiding judge at the fourth trial do so? The prosecutor took the precaution of appearing in court and announcing, on the record, that the time had passed to appeal and so it had been forfeited. Here was an official termination of Gold's right to appeal and yet no action was taken to discover whether Gold was competent in light of his self-destructive behavior.

We called John Williams, Gold's attorney in the third trial, to the stand. I asked him in my direct examination to explain the issues involved and subsequent events that led up to the head-on collision caused by God in the third trial, which culminated in his being fired by Gold.

He stated that they occurred at a critical moment during the trial when the state presented testimony which claimed that Gold was parked near the Pasternak home early in the morning, three days before the murders. This claim by the prosecutor Gold had always vehemently denied. Williams cross-examined the witness, Kim Perugini-Kelly, who had identified Gold sitting in the car that early morning, and succeeded in obtaining her admission that the man she saw in the car early in the morning did not look like Gold at all. I asked Williams:

Q: And you obtained the admission of this lady witness that neither the physiognomy, the hair, the face, the color of his skin . . . looked anything like Mr. Gold?

A: . . . that's my recollection.

I told Judge Scheinblum that even if Gold had been in the car three days before the murders, there was no significance to that fact. There was no need for him to sit in a car, staking out the house, since he knew its layout quite well when he was the Pasternaks' son-in-law.

Mr. Williams then briefly repeated the dramatic episode of Gold's firing him in the midst of the third trial in open court, in the presence of judge and jury; this in spite of Williams' success in discrediting the state witness' testimony. Williams also rejected Gold's claim that he was discourteous to Gold by walking head of him during court recess on their way to lunch:

A: . . . That was part of his hallucination. I never walked ahead of him at lunch. I was very concerned that Murray had no trust in lawyers . . . [and] tried always to be solicitous . . . of him and that was not always an easy thing to be . . .

I asked Mr. Williams to give the court the background of Gold's complaint against him when Williams attempted to move the trial to another county and Gold's objection thereto, since Gold was claiming he was innocent and in his mind such procedure constituted a "second" proceeding, which he did not want. Mr. Williams testified:

A: Mr. Gold believed that the only motion that needed to be filed prior to his trial was a motion demanding dismissal of the charges on the ground that he was innocent and he felt that anything else constituted a betrayal of him . . . Mr. Gold simply could not [understand] . . . that's not the way the courts work . . .

A jurist who granted a
unique habeus corpus writ,
Judge Howard Scheinblum.

For obvious reasons, in highly emotional cases, especially in murder trials, it is customary for the defense lawyer to make a motion to remove the trial from the county in which the crime was committed—a change of venue. Gold objected to Williams' effort to do what was in his best interests. In Gold's mind this was just further evidence that his lawyer was cooperating and plotting with the prosecutor.

Williams concluded his testimony with the observation he made when he sometimes attended portions of the fourth trial proceedings. He said he "was struck in observing Mr. Gold by the fact that he seemed to . . . be in a trance. He was staring straight ahead . . . He was simply occupying the physical space."

At one point in the proceedings Judge Scheinblum asked Dr. Borden:

Suppose I set the verdict in the fourth trial aside and grant a
    new trial, would Gold be competent to proceed?

Dr. Borden said he did not think so, unless he received consider-able medical treatments first. This pointed out our dilemma. We needed the writ which would free him from a conviction forever and assign him to a civil hospital for cure. There was such a remedy! The writ could be granted for a far more conclusive reason than "incompetency." The other ground available for the issuance of the writ was "insufficient evidence"—namely that Gold was innocent and that Bruce Sanford was the murderer. Then it would not be necessary to restore Gold's right to appeal, which he had forfeited. Nor would it be necessary to try him a sixth time. He would be released to take more medical treatment. That was the least the law could do to make amends for an innocent man's confinement for a decade. As the Supreme Court of the United States had written in an historic opinion:

> [The] scope and flexibility of the writ—its capacity to reach all manner of illegal detention—its ability *to cut through barriers of form and procedural mazes* have always been emphasized and jealously guarded by courts and law makers. *The very nature of the writ demands that it be administered with the initiative and flexibility essential to insure that miscarriage of justice within its reach are surfaced and corrected* . . . There is no higher duty of a court, under our constitutional system, than the careful processing and adjudication of petitions for writs of habeas corpus, for it is in such proceedings that a person in custody charges that error, neglect, or evil purpose have resulted in his unlawful confinement and that he is deprived of his freedom contrary to law. (emphasis added)

When the proceedings were concluded Gold was returned to the courtroom. Judge Scheinblum said to Murray the sort of thing most lawyers love to hear:

"Mr. Nizer and his staff did an admirable job on your behalf."

Murray Gold then said, "I'm glad to hear it."

For some, this may have sounded curt, ungrateful. Not to me or my staff. It represented what was the best this tortured man could manage in the way of appreciation, which I believe, at this point, was far more heartfelt and went deeper than he was capable of expressing. Indeed, I was greatly moved. It was, after all, what we all were working for—his exoneration and his coming back to the real world.

34

DECISION

ON MARCH 11, 1991, the clerk of the court notified us that Judge Scheinblum had rendered an eighteen-page decision in the Gold Case. We immediately arranged to have it read to us. The words were filled with excitement. Our eagerness added exclamation points to the news.

Judge Scheinblum ruled:

> In the interests of justice, therefore, this Court finds that the petitioner is entitled to a new trial and that he should be retried once it has been determined that he is legally competent to stand trial.

The verdict of guilty and the two consecutive terms of twenty-five years to life were thereby set aside. The guilty verdict was wiped out. Gold had won.

The victory was enhanced in another way. There are two prongs to the finding of incompetence. One is the inability of the defendant to understand sufficiently what is going on around him. The second is the failure of his counsel (Collins) in the fourth trial to protect him adequately. Collins was the only lawyer who appeared as a prosecution witness. He conceded that he had not pursued the admonition of the Whiting Forensic Institute report that Gold be subjected to continued psychiatric treatments.

The judge concluded that "it was incumbent upon trial counsel to request a competency evaluation, at least for the purpose of determining whether or not the petitioner was legally capable of waiving his right to appeal."

The final order of the judge was as humane as it was legally sound. He directed the Commissioner of Mental Health

> to conduct a competency evaluation in accordance with the provisions . . . of General Statutes [and to] address the following questions:
>
> 1. Is Murray Gold presently legally competent to stand trial?
> 2. If he is not now legally competent to stand trial is there any reasonable likelihood that he will be restored to legal competency in the foreseeable future?
> 3. If he either currently is legally competent or if he can be restored to such competency in the foreseeable future, what specific treatments and/or procedures should be implemented to maintain competency and satisfy the trial court that he continues to be legally competent?
> 4. If not presently legally competent, what is the appropriate inpatient facility for treatment to restore competency?

Even if Gold had not defaulted on his appellate rights and had been permitted to appeal to the Supreme Court of Connecticut, the result would not have been any better than this victory in the habeas corpus proceeding. Actually, without resorting to the Supreme Court of Connecticut, the guilty verdict in the fourth trial had been set aside and Gold was in the same favorable position as if he had filed an appeal and had won in the highest court. In short, the result could not have been better than the victory in this unique habeas corpus proceeding.

There was only one ruling which we sought, and which the judge declined. That was our contention that he should find that the evidence demonstrated that Bruce Sanford was the murderer.

The judge refused on the ground that such a finding could only be made by the jury which heard the evidence.

Ordinarily, we would agree. But where the incompetent defendant interfered with his lawyer in selecting a jury, as occurred here, the jury's authority is vitiated. Even Judge Scheinblum had found that there had been interference with the selection of the jury. He wrote: "[Gold's] bizarre behavior . . . commenced during the third trial from jury selection *forward.*"

However, the matter may be moot in a practical sense. Would anyone seriously suggest that Gold be tried a *sixth* time? As Judge Scheinblum pointed out, Gold's ten-year incarceration might entitle him to apply immediately for parole, even if he were guilty. As we have seen, the prosecutor attempted to avoid a third trial. It was Gold who, because of his incompetence, refused to cooperate.

Sometimes the law falters. Its practitioners then owe it to justice to correct the situation. They have done so. And Murray Gold has a new chance in life.

Although freedom now was at hand, Gold's bad fortune was not over.

Dr. Jerry Neuwirth, an opthalmic surgeon, discovered that Gold's retinas were detached and unless eye surgery was immediately performed he would be blind for life. Gold resisted any treatment, saying that there was nothing wrong with his eyes and that he could see well.

When I was told of this new disaster I set out to try to do something about it.

Stephen O'Neil of the Connecticut Attorney General's Office called to express his concern and to cooperate. He told me that a patient's revolt was not uncommon, often leading to refusal to eat, but when the patient learned how painful forced feeding was he usually gave up resistance.

We needed something to convince Murray.

I sent Dr. Neuwirth a copy of Judge Scheinblum's opinion, which had assigned Gold to the Commissioner of Health of Connecticut for treatment. In the meantime, based on Dr. Neuwirth's opinion, an application was made to the Probate Department of the State of Connecticut to give authority for him to overcome Murray's resistance and perform the surgery.

Good news followed. Apparently, Murray's stubbornness had been overcome. Detail's weren't given, but it seemed injections in the arm gave the surgeon the necessary freedom to operate on both eyes on two consecutive days.

We waited to be sure that the blindfolded Statue of Justice would not be joined by a blindfolded victim of injustice.

35

THE INNER MYSTERY

THERE IS ANOTHER mystery in this case that lies inside Murray Gold. It has nothing to do with the murders. It is common to us all.

We know that violence can break a bone or cause damage to an internal organ of the body; but how is it that mere words may cause the most serious injury to a person's ability to function? How can insulting words or fear, which give no physical injury or bruise, create severe illness?

Obviously it is the brain that responds with dislocation of its functions. Then we are confronted with disease, even though there has not been a flicker of violence on the brain itself. Yes, there may be a hastened blood pressure, but this too is created by the brain's reaction.

This is the inner mystery of the Gold case. Fear during his escape from Auschwitz; survivor's-guilt complex; again a mere concept without the bruise of a fly bite set in motion his paranoia and schizophrenia.

We are familiar with the prizefighter who takes so many blows to his head that he is later unable to speak clearly—punch-drunk is a familiar diagnosis—but it is not only a blow to the head that sets off serious mental disease. What provokes the brain to record its vehement reactions to insult or fear?

To approach this enigma we ought to know much more than we do about this extraordinary governing organ of the human body. It is the least explored yet most important continent.

At birth it weighs between eleven and thirteen ounces, at maturity only forty-five ounces, but it represents amazing information—and sensation-processing equipment.

It is estimated that there are one hundred billion nerve endings in the brain. Some scientists calculate that during the fetal period brain cells grow at the rate of 250,000 each minute. As life progresses there is no further growth of nerve cells. Nature has provided a rich supply sufficient to permit millions of cells to be destroyed without affecting the thinking process. But alcohol or other drugs can accelerate the destruction and at some unpredictable points debilitate the brain's miraculous functions.

The number of nerve-cell connections exceeds a trillion. Compare this with the number of components in the most advanced computer. The latter represents a drop in the vast ocean of the brain's power.

No two cells in the brain are alike. Although the brain constitutes only two percent of the total body weight, it, together with the nervous system, requires twenty percent of the body's total oxygen supply.

The mysteries of the "mind" have confounded scientists for centuries. When confronted with the situation they ask: Just what is derangement? The phrase "a screw is loose" exposes the fiction that the mind is a machine and at best performs like a computer. Another mechanistic concept is expressed in the phrase "he's out of his mind," as if a less reliable center has taken over the thinking process. Unable to substitute for the miracle of normal thought and remembrance, scientists turn to other devices to correct the distorted functions. These are drugs, which eliminate the old necessity of tying the sick man to a bed or completely "knocking him out" to prevent his howling or his aggressiveness. Navane, which was administered to Murray Gold in substantial amounts, is one of these drugs. There were visible indications from the drug. I had noticed that Gold's skin turned darker as he became upset. I called it the "sunburn of anger." Also, his eyes bulged and seemed to shine brightly. Navane may have been responsible for these changes. The heightened coloring frightened some observers who did not know this was a chemically-induced phenomenon. It might even have contributed to the false conclusion that this distortion of his personality indicated a dangerous propensity to violence.

Unable to fathom the mystery of the brain's activities, superstitions have substituted for knowledge. Even Einstein willed his brain to scientists for study, and it has recently been discovered that other men of genius have provided that their brains be given to laboratories for study. So far there has been no significant scientific revelation, for example, that might enable us to understand why some human beings are creative and others are not.

The true mystery remains, barely touched or understood.

36

BLINDFOLDED JUSTICE

In the thirteenth century an unknown sculptor created a statue that was intended to represent the Christian angels serving God. During the Reformation the symbol was changed to represent civil justice. The statue's austere beauty and serene message made it a symbol of justice throughout the world. In a sense it was like the later Statue of Liberty—a tribute to woman. Man was the warrior. Woman the healer.

As a symbol, it was eloquent and complete. Justice was depicted as a blindfolded woman—an illustration of impartiality. The scales she held were to represent the evidentiary weights placed on them by the contesting parties. Justice required that they be read with exactitude, so that no matter how the scales teetered, no matter how close the result, careful and deliberate observation would determine the truth.

Of course, the sword in the other hand of the statue represents the enforcement of its decision and at times the punishment of those who disregard or trifle with the scale.

The symbol adorns as well as reminds us of the nobility of the ideas behind it.

But is there a flaw in the symbol? How could we have overlooked it for centuries? How can Justice "read" the scales when she is blindfolded?

It must have been intended that some other agency be entrusted with the ultimate task of seeing the verdict shown by the scales. Surely the legal system—lawyers, jurors and judges—were to have that responsibility. This did not mean that the law required certainty in every instance. Lawyers and judges appeal to the brooding spirit of the law—and to the intelligence of the future.

The uncertain atmosphere that surrounds the system must be cleansed by those who care for justice and understand the potential nobility of the legal profession. The lawyers who had participated in Murray Gold's trials had to overcome the challenge of a defendant's unreasonable behavior, ingratitude, even insult. Never mind whether they understood all the reasons for his behavior. The lawyer's relationship with the client is not, after all, a mere social or economic one that permits termination at will.

Although a client always has the privilege of debating or discharging his lawyer, a right too often exercised by Murray Gold, the principles of justice cannot be waived by him. More than an individual's right is involved.

The edifice of equity and fairness should be defended and preserved for all.

"Let justice be done even if the heavens fall."

37

A LAWYER'S PRAYER

DOCTORS ARE GUIDED not only by the code of ethics created by medical associations but also by the Hippocratic Oath that derives from the writings of Hippocrates and was created over a period of five centuries.

The legal profession similarly has been guided by codes of ethics created by bar associations. But it never has had an oath or prayer that reflects its aspirations as an idealistic expression of devotion to justice.

I have written such a prayer to express professional gratitude to the attorneys who accepted my invitation to join me in *pro bono* effort to right an injustice. The mere fact that the object of our concern, Murray Gold, was not exactly appreciative and, indeed, at times hostile, only made the Lawyer's Prayer a better reminder of the transcendent obligations of the law. Justice has nothing to do with gratitude, or the lack of it.

So this prayer tries to set forth the duty of a lawyer, in spite of perverse circumstances:

Please, O God, give me good health with which to withstand the rigors of a most arduous profession—the law.

Please grant me equanimity which calms everyone around me and enable me to balance like a gyroscope in the storms of contest.

Give me peaceful sleep, for while I must keep my mind on my work, I must not keep my work on my mind.

Touch my words with eloquence, not in the sense of harangue, but in the true meaning of oratory—a flashing eye under a philosopher's brow.

Diminish my worries, particularly those anticipated worries which are like interest paid on a debt that never comes due.

Increase my capacity for work, so that I will not suffer the fatigue of thought and will plow deep while sluggards sleep.

Please see to it that I never become afraid of the violence of an original idea or of a stretched mind.

Above all, O Lord, do not diminish my intensity for a client's cause, for from it spring the flames which leap over the jury box and set fire to the convictions of the jurors.

I would pray that my efforts do not blind me to the uniqueness of love, the comfort of friendships, and the joys of a cultivated mind.

Please teach me horizontal as well as vertical faith—vertical in obeisance to you, horizontal in my obligations to the community.

We cannot control the length of our lives, but we can control the width and depth of our lives. And I know that when you finally touch us with your fingers to permanent sleep and examine us, you will look not for medals or honorary degrees, but for scars suffered to make the world a little better place to live in.

I thank you for casting me in the legal profession, dedicated to justice, imbued with the sanctity of reason.

The law has honored me. And I shall always honor the law.   Amen

EPILOGUE

It has been a long journey. In the Preface I had invited you, the reader, to enter the Pasternak home to see the slashing murders of Irving and Rhoda Pasternak.

That was seventeen years ago. Since then, you have sat through four trials in which Murray Gold was twice found guilty of the murderous deed and sentenced to life imprisonment, only to have the highest appellate courts reverse these legal condemnations, leaving Gold free from prison but not from illness requiring medical treatment.

You have drunk at the fountain of justice after spurning the poisoned wells of prejudice. We have suffered together from the bias engendered by Murray Gold's paranoid "insults" to his attorneys. We have seen Bruce Sanford commit a slow suicide fascinated by the flow of blood, even when it was his own. We wished him Godspeed, as a Satanist, to go to hell.

You have participated in legal procedures, including the remote habeas corpus remedy. You have seen lawyers motivated by a dedication to justice seek again and again—and finally succeed—to save a profoundly troubled Murray Gold.

As Rousseau wrote: "Reasoning may mislead; conscience never does."